CONTRIBUTORS:
Paul Abramson
John R. Andrisek, Ph.D.
Oliver S. Brown
C. William Brubaker, F.A.I.A.
John C. Cone
Terrence E. Deal, Ph.D.
Charles W. Fowler, Ed.D.
Robert O. Guth, Ed.D.
Frederick W. Hill, Ed.D.
Susan Kaye, Ed.D.
Kitty Chase Kirby
Stanton Leggett, Ph.D.
Jerold Panas
Arthur Shapiro, Ph.D.
Ronald Simcox, Ed.D.
Donn Wadley, Ph.D.
Martha Stone Wiske
Alan P. Woodruff, Ed.D.

MANAGING SCHOOLS IN HARD TIMES

Edited by Stanton Leggett

teach 'em inc.

CHICAGO
1981

Library of Congress Catalog Card Number:
81-52030

International Standard Book Number:
0-931028-18-3 (Paperbound)
0-931028-19-1 (Clothbound)

Cover Design by C. William Brubaker

Typography by Accent Graphics, Inc., Chicago, Ill.

Printed in the United States of America

teach 'em inc.

160 East Illinois Street
Chicago, Illinois 60611

CONTENTS

A QUICK TOUR THROUGH THE BOOK AND WHAT IT OFFERS TO YOU

This book is based on the assumption that the reader has some idea what the problems are. The book focuses on how to act and what to do to cope with the hard times syndrome.

The first three chapters are concerned with the strategies of dealing with hard times. The point is made pretty clearly that the strategies of affluence offer little guidance. New approaches are proposed. Then come two chapters concerned with a few hopeful projections.

The remainder of the book links long-range planning with specific case histories on how to deal with cost-critical areas — special education, vocational education, and the like. As you will read, the authors waste little time telling you how bad things are. You already know that. They concentrate on telling you what to do to get yourself out of the mess your district may be in.

As I first read the galleys of the book, I thought that some readers would feel they already knew all they cared to know about certain chapters. But after rereading the material, I think there is much to be learned even if you have been through it all.

In any case, I made some notes as I read the chapters, and I want to share them with you now with the hope they may help you pick and choose areas of special concern that you might want to read right away.

Terry Deal and Martha Wiske, from the point of view of educational researchers, start off the book with a provocative chapter that tests your understanding of what the appropriate courses of action are in hard times. At one level, the response is to attempt to do better that which is being done now only to do it with less. This is the rational-technical approach in the chapter's hierarchy, which I found roughly equivalent to Mark Twain's "Innocents Abroad." The political approach acknowledges that in doing with less, a number of people get hurt. To keep from being the target of the natural response of the wounded, the strategy draws sustenance from Machiavelli's "The Prince." The third level — deeper, more primal and more important — is the symbolic level. The strategy is more of theater and emotion. It was one matter to take pride in walking six miles through waist-deep snow to school and quite another to battle one's way down a corridor of violence. The search must be for new sagas and new symbols to replace the old and the strategy must respond to the change. Probably the really effective manager of schools must use all three approaches.

From a state-wide background John

Cone, in Chapter Two, describes the two-way information system that schools should perfect in keeping the various publics of the community as supporters of the schools. The long-term systematic effort to cultivate the various publics of the school system are illustrated. Cone expects you to analyze the public you would hope to influence and to develop your approach to influencing that public, using the models he describes as illustrations of how to do it. The role of teachers and other staff members in a setting where collective bargaining has become the main communication between school and staff is a particularly intriguing issue not often dealt with directly in today's world. As almost an aside, Cone also speculates on the effects of size on schools and school systems in the process of reweaving alliances with the publics of the schools.

While Cone touched on students as a public, Sue Kaye (Chapter Three) examined the effect of schools upon students who are growing up to join the publics that will help us or hurt us, or worse, ignore us. She argues for a much broader view of the educational world of young people and an increased willingness to involve students in significant aspects of school life. To do so has resulted in schools that can point to specific improvements in attendance, in relating school work to work and in improving the student's attitude or perception of the value of the school in his or her formative years. We have the future publics in our schools for a long time. Perhaps part of the problem is of our own making if too few of the students are supporters when they are mature citizens.

The next two chapters bring a message of hope. In Chapter Four Paul Abramson lets statistics show the way in which our demography keeps changing. He points to the certainty of increasing enrollments in the public schools in the mid-1980s. The "baby boomlet," as Abramson terms it, will bring back some familiar problems but will probably cast them in a far different setting.

Next, Jerry Panas, one of the nation's most successful fund raisers, does a feasibility study of raising private money for public schools. His conclusion — the potential is there and a few school systems have been remarkably successful. This is a lesson the independent schools have long since learned. Panas goes on, having established that private money can be secured, and outlines the concrete procedures that should be used. He cautions against "bake sale" expectations, suggesting that the effort should be made to secure significant and major gifts. Procedures that have been effective are outlined in detail. For public schools, he opens up a new area of involvement.

The book then considers the planning process for schools during hard times. To someone brought up in education in the Depression years, this period may be called a return to normal. To those whose professional careers were centered on the fifties to the seventies, the current difficult years must indeed be a trial.

In Chapter Six, Dick Andrisek, out of many years of carrying out successful complex long-term planning efforts for the Berea public school system, describes how he does it. The long-range planning process that is described is for a moderate size school system with a small central staff. The plan is described and the modifications to the process required in systems with little money available are carefully outlined. Andrisek's plan contains a careful process of monitoring results and, perhaps, it is here that the attention is focused. Too many plans are made that are not put to use and of those put to use few can tell what happened. This planning process can report on the changes that took place. In view of the large community, staff, and student participation and the open process, there are no surprises and the support of the total community has been impressive.

One aspect of the plan was the acknowledgement early of the extent of enrollment declines and the inclusion of anticipated staffing in the various categories in the years to come. Andrisek attributes important advantages to this open planning process in reducing tension among employees and in achieving a stable financial status in the community during decline.

Chapter Seven, by Leggett, examines ways the administrator and staff can have a cost-effective central headquarters staff that is defensible against demands for cuts when money is tight.

Fred Hill uses his rich background of experience in school business management, in Chapter Eight, to examine the role of the school business administrator in hard times. His lists of "checkpoints" and "yardsticks" to evaluate the effectiveness of the school business operations represent a fine starting point for a renewed effort to have the highest quality operation in this significant area. Hill presents his advice for a series of analyses that the school business administrator should be expected to carry out in evaluating the need for services, in suggesting alternative levels of performance, and the answering of "What if . . . ?" questions such as "What happens if ceilings are washed yearly instead of being painted every five years?" Taking part in careful analysis of alternative courses of action using readily available, clean and accurate cost data becomes a major service the school business official shares with management offices.

Paul Abramson, from long experience in the field, makes practical suggestions about reduction of energy use. He emphasizes the importance people make in reducing energy usage. His recommendations (Chapter Nine) for savings bypass physical change and talk about the human effort in savings. He suggests review of board policies, involvement and training of staff and a whole series of actions that cost only the human energy to put into practice in order to save real dollars.

In Chapter Ten Leggett deals with getting the best out of your staff. When things get tough, the cultivation of those people working with you becomes a major concern. Starting with the approach that there is only a limited amount of staff time available, the chapter works on how to define that time and how to budget its use wisely. Time is, in a school system, more important than money, yet few school systems consider systematically how time is used.

This argument then moves along to the cultivation of the quality of individual employees, recommending that the school management institute an individual career development program for each employee and spend time to develop more proficient, more self-directed and presumably more self-satisfied people in the system. The prescription is important for those employed as cleaners as well as the most highly qualified professional.

Practical approaches to learning on the job in education are offered by Shapiro and Kirby in Chapter Eleven. Specific suggestions are made for improving the effectiveness of the in-service education process. The authors contend that a thoughtfully worked out in-service education procedure will displace the usual staff cynicism about the process and will have real effects upon the improvement of skills used in the classroom.

In two chapters (Twelve and Thirteen), Woodruff and Wadley describe alternative models of vocational education programs. Woodruff compares in specific terms cost effective cluster programs with the traditional self-contained shop focused on a single occupation. The traditional approach costs four times that of a general education program and has been proven to be less than totally effective. Woodruff looks to programs that develop good work habits, and the ability to transfer skills, avoiding the high cost, highly specialized programs. He points to the significance of such changes to small schools, discounting the need for highly specialized vocational programs shared by many school districts. The role of trainers and simulators in teaching skills at a fraction of the traditional program cost is pointed out. Woodruff emphasizes increasingly useful partnership arrangements with industry.

Wadley describes a substantial effort by the Board of Education of the City of Chicago and a group of major industries to develop the partnership further. Starting with the industrial scene as a career education setting in the sophomore year, the program moves to direct on the job training in industry in the senior year. The costs are split between school and industry. The results have been "real world skill development at the least possible cost per student unit." The reactions of students to the program are interesting. A list of employers involved shows the wide diversity of occupational opportunities.

Special education for the handicapped has been a source of considerable concern to school administrators because of the added costs that have been assigned to the school districts. In Chapter Fourteen Charles Fowler and Robert Guth provide a series of approaches to limiting the impact of these changes in the educational world. The chapter emphasizes that there is no magic to the words "special education" preceeding the word "teacher." A teacher is still a teacher and when a good one is involved, the children will learn best. Fowler — Guth stress that the manager of the system have a keen awareness of the need for competent and experienced legal talent in the field of special education to counter the specialization of attorneys experienced as parent advocates. Resistance to the tendency to overclassify students is another prime area of administrative concern. If you follow the suggestions in this chapter, you will have a humane and carefully organized approach to the needs of handicapped children, but you will have kept from overloading the system with inflated loads and from providing non-educational services to children.

The education of gifted children is of increasing concern in the United States, perhaps because of the general public perception that all the attention was going to disadvantaged and handicapped. Education for the gifted has been seen in some quarters as the schools' answer to the middle class. In any event, Ronald Simcox, in dealing with the subject (Chapter Fifteen), warns of the problems inherent in identifying students as gifted. He urges that school systems provide a well thought out procedure using a range of acceptable testing instruments to identify students eligible for programs. The chapter then turns its attention to low cost ways to serve the educational needs of gifted children. In this connection, Simcox points to the use of microcomputers in the field. Case histories of successful programs for the gifted are provided.

In Chapters Sixteen and Seventeen, Leggett wrote on the ways that can be developed to organize data for decision-making. Most school systems have enormous amounts of information but lack any way to put the information together for use. This is one of the reasons so many educators spend so much time preparing reports for school board members or school trustees. One of the ways to get at this problem is by developing more sophisticated analytic tools to help school administrators understand what is happening to them and to provide simpler ways to examine a wide range of alternative courses of action. One of the important outcomes would be an increased understanding of the consequences of an action.

In this process, the microcomputer is becoming an inexpensive and highly useful management tool. It does not require the staff or the intricate and costly programming characteristic of most of the dinosaurs of the computer trade. The ability to answer the question, "What if . . . ?" applied to many aspects of the school system will become critical.

In Chapter Eighteen, Architect C. W. Brubaker relies on his sketching pad to illustrate some approaches and options that districts may want to explore as they seek ways to cut costs and reduce classrooms in the most painless ways they can find.

An unusually helpful list of specific areas that the school administrator can check for cost savings in his school or system is provided in the concluding chapter by Oliver Brown entitled "How to Cut School Costs — Wisely." This chapter appeared originally in *The American School Board Journal* and has been revised and updated on experience with the list. This is down-to-earth material that can be used to see if all opportunities have been examined and also as a kind of checklist to evaluate the financial and business side of the organization.

Stanton Leggett
June 1981

Managing Schools in Hard Times

HOW TO USE RESEARCH TO WIN BATTLES — AND MAYBE WARS

Terrence E. Deal , Ph.D.
and
Martha Stone Wiske

Because research can't do everything to solve the problems confronting the school administrator, it does not follow that it can do nothing. Here are some routes to take that can help you enlist research on your side in these difficult times.

Martha Stone Wiske is an educational administrator, policy analyst, and a doctoral candidate at the Harvard University Graduate School of Education, Cambridge. Terry Deal is an associate professor in Harvard's Graduate School of Education with a special interest and involvement in the decision-making process.

In the next decade, administrative tasks of growth — building, adding, and hiring — are bound to give way to the onerous chores of decline — closing, cutting, terminating, and consolidating. Done wisely, decisions of decline may prune educational organizations to survive a lean decade. Done capriciously, or haphazardly, the decisions may leave schools misshapen and incapable of adapting to the conditions that lie ahead. How can research inform sound decisions or caution against the ill-advised?

Addressing this important question is the primary aim of this chapter. To answer this question, we need to ask two others: 1) in what ways are the times hard for schools these days? and 2) what specific problems do hard times present for educational administrators? Answers to these subsidiary questions sketch the context in which research is being asked to provide assistance.

The label hard times emerges from a period in which schools face a formidable troika: resources are tight and shrinking, public confidence in education has waned, and in many places, the morale of teachers and administrators is dropping below levels required for professional and personal stability or growth. These three conditions are related even though they do not originate from the same source. Each provides its own set of issues and problems. Together, they produce difficult choices for administrators.

Tight resources result from three developments. Over recent years, the population of elementary and secondary school age children has declined. At the same time, the economy is being crippled by inflation, reducing the value of the dollar. Finally, school systems in many states are facing a reduction in revenues because citizens have voted to cap public spending statewide or have refused outright to approve additional expenditures at the local level. Taken together, these three developments make for very tight school budgets.

But the financial crisis cannot be separated from what David Tyack describes as a society-wide "crisis of authority".

Future historians may regard the last 20 years as one of those great turning points in educa-

tional history comparable to the common school crusade of the mid-19th century or the campaign for centralization and social efficiency at the turn of the century. Recent complex changes have called into question some of the legacies of earlier reforms: that education was the most potent means of creating equality; that schools should be "kept out of politics"; that the professionals could discover "the one best system" through specialized knowledge; and that public schools could create one society from many people — *e pluribus unum.* (Tyack, p. 18)

In a nutshell, confidence in public schools has hit rock bottom. The public doubts whether schools can serve as instruments of social reform; the public even doubts whether schools can handle the more limited task of teaching basic academic skills. Many states have recently passed competency testing programs, in an attempt to force schools to focus more attention on basic skills.

These twin crises — finances and authority — wreak havoc on staff morale. Educators face myriad blows to their professional confidence. Reductions put jobs in jeopardy as schools are forced to cut staff. Declining faith in schools makes administrators and teachers feel unappreciated and unsuccessful. Their insecurity and feelings of bewilderment or defeat are compounded further by the inherent uncertainties of educational practice.

If teaching or managing schools were certain, clear, and straight-forward tasks, then educators could find a haven in a professional culture or technology. But education is an indeterminate enterprise. Its purposes and technologies are unclear. Its goals are diverse, diffuse, and disputed among various stakeholders. Why and how students learn — or whether they do at all — is hard to define, difficult to measure and unlikely to be disentangled from multiple events which contribute to student growth and development. For all these reasons, educational teachers and administrators have a hard time knowing, demonstrating, or proving their effectiveness. As doubts and accusations mount from a public that has lost faith in schools, educators are strapped for responses. Their ambiguous answers reflect the reality of what they do; their self-doubts increase as the public presses for more certainty in a process which is inherently ambiguous.

The combined effects of dwindling financial resources, waning public faith and confidence and ebbing professional morale creates an unfavorable environment for schools. Within this context, administrators are being asked to do the impossible: cut the school budget — eliminating people, programs and schools — without disaffecting influential segments of the community whose continued support is essential and without further undermining staff morale. Nested within this basic dilemma are a number of specific problems.

What schools should be closed? Each neighborhood has a string of sensible reasons why its own school should not be the one to go. Cutting programs or closing schools inevitably involve staff transfers and dismissals. How can these personnel decisions be made without creating divisive squabbles and saddling survivors with guilt and grief? For school administrators, a typical day or week is now filled with such questions.

Stationed at the front line under the rapid-fire barrage of such problems, most administrators want answers to two questions: 1) What should I do? and 2) How should I do it?

RESEARCH AND ANSWERS

As administrators look to the research community for help, they often seek a scientific basis for deciding what to do. But, in the past, researchers have usually either dodged important questions or provided general answers which never seem to work under local conditions. These irrelevant or non-specific results have shaped the perception administrators often hold of researchers: (1) They have theories which stimulate research but are of little practical use; (2) They have answers which are true under artificial experimental conditions but do not apply in the complex every-day world of schools.

A more contemporary response of researchers to administrators seeking assistance is: "it all depends". This answer leads administrators to dismiss researchers as fuzzy-minded, wishy-washy, and incapable of providing answers to the pressing questions confronting schools. But, behind the phrase — "it all depends", lies some knowledge that administrators may find liberating and directly related to the onerous task of deciding what to do as resources decline. Research can never provide answers that apply directly and unconditionally except for mundane questions whose answers administrators already know. For this reason, administrators — not researchers — must play the role of expert as solutions are developed at the local level. The search for specific answers in research results in a futile one. Practitioners are the rightful owners of real wisdom about what to do in schools.

RESEARCH AND NEW SCHOOL IMAGES

Research may not have answers but those researchers who study organizational phenomena have clarified new images of how schools work, and have begun to explore how images affect administrative practice. Decisions about solutions and strategies under conditions of decline are heavily influenced by one's vision of schools as organizations.

Many administrators, at least those who paid attention in administrative training courses, tend to view their role in decisions as one who gathers information, weighs alternatives, and arrives at a sound, just, and acceptable decision through professional judgment and expertise. Problems are seen as having solutions. Administrators are seen as having a central role in finding both problems and solutions. Research is seen as providing sensible alternatives based on logical reasoning and empirical evidence. This perception of schools, decision-making, and the role of research is based on a more general image of organizations as rational-technical systems. (see figure 1). From this perspective, purposes can be reduced to performance criteria for both students and staff and outcomes can be pre-specified and measured. Schools should be managed so as to achieve the highest output per unit costs where outputs are usually measured by student achievement test scores and costs are measured in dollars. The administrator's role in this view of schools is not unlike that of a chief executive officer or factory manager. The administrator attempts to plan ahead, to define performance or output criteria and to make decisions which maximize efficent use of resources and achieve desired outputs. In making decisions, a process is envisioned in which problems are identified and defined on the basis of objective information, alternatives are sought through logical analysis, and strategies are selected on the basis of tangible merits.

But there are other images which have begun to emerge from studies of schools as organizations. A second view emphasizes the political aspects of schools. This view focuses less on the goals and outcomes of schools and more on the process of contending with competing interests, agenda, and preferences that are important in attempting to administer schools. Policies and decisions must be able to win the support of a sufficiently powerful combination of constituencies. One of the administrator's chief concerns is to maintain enough power to stay in office. Longevity on the job may require the administrator to intimidate, collaborate, manipulate, bargain, bluff, and bully. Another concern is to form coalitions which will support desired directions. In trying to manage a school the administrator may feel more like a lion tamer or a power broker than a factory manager or chief executive officer. The process of deciding what to cut will involve the activation of a variety of interest groups, who will form coalitions and bargain around specific interests. The outcome will be decided more on the basis of power than merits of a specific proposal.

A third vision of schools emphasizes the importance of symbolic rather than technological or political aspects of school administration. The focus here is less on the functions of schools or on the political forces which make them work. Rather, the symbolic view emphasizes the meaning that schools and activities have for various participants. From this perspective, achievement test scores or political clout are not so important by themselves. What matters are the beliefs students, teachers, administrators, parents and citizens hold about the scores, political trade-off, or the effectiveness of schools. When schools are viewed symbolically, the administrator's role is to run the schools so that the vari-

---

FIGURE 1

Three Images of Schools as Organizations

	Rational/Technical	Political	Symbolic
Metaphor	Factory	Jungle	Temple
Emphasis	Goals	Power	Myth, ritual and ceremony
Basis of Effectiveness	Quality of Output	Satisfaction of Constituencies	Faith and meaning
Key Administrative Task	Planning, decision-making, and evaluation	Balancing interest groups and contending with conflict	Convening rituals, and ceremonies; mastering myths and maintaining faith
Administrators Role	Manager or chief executive officer	Lion-tamer or power broker	Guru or High Priest(ess)
Main Concern in Hard Times	Maintaining quality of people, programs, and schools	Maintaining support of key constituencies	Maintaining faith, belief, and meaning among internal and external groups

---

ous stakeholders experience schools as meaningful institutions worthy of their faith and support. This perception of schools as meaningful, effective, or worthy of support is influenced less by concrete evidence of effectiveness and efficiency than by public myths, values, and expectations. In the symbolic view, schools are institutions both based on and expressive of faith and shared community values. They are more like churches, temples, or community theaters than like factories or political jungles. The role of the administrator in such settings is more like a guru or high priest than a factory manager or lion-tamer. In this view, decisions about what to cut will be reached through a complex interplay of irrational forces. The process of this interplay is as important as the decisions it produces. In making decisions about what is to be cut in hard times, it is important that people have faith in the decisions, grieve about their losses, develop stories which explain why decisions have been made, and hammer out shared myths for future operations.

As administrators approach the difficult decisions of how to get along with less, they need to reflect on their own image of schools. How administrators view schools and their role will be a major factor in how they act in the face of hard times. Each view — rational, technical, political or symbolic — illuminates different features of the complex organizations within which difficult decisions have to be made. Administrators who are able to view problems from several perspectives will probably avoid obvious pitfalls and see more opportunities than those who are locked into one view. Research is helpful to administrators in hard times by offering some alternative images of school organizations and by illuminating alternative pathways that might be followed in defining and solving problems within a particular district or school.

RESEARCH AND WHAT TO DO

How can research help administrators actually decide which groups, programs, or schools to trim during hard times? The role research might play looks different from each of the three views of schools as organizations (see figure 2).

In the rational-technical view of

FIGURE 2

Image of Organizations and the Role of Research in Deciding What to do in Hard Times

	Rational-Technical View	Political View	Symbolic View
Key Problem	Quality	Interest Groups v. General Welfare	Faith, Meaning, Belief
Use of Research	Provide criteria for making cuts without sacrificing quality	Provide external power base in advocating decisions for general welfare and contesting positions of interest groups	Provide shared justification for cuts which reinforces, reinterprets or replaces old myths, beliefs, and meanings
Desired Outcome	Quality is maintained or improved	General interests prevail	Belief and faith in schools are renewed, new myths are developed
Metaphor for Research	Answers or Information	Shield or ammunition	Scripture

schools, the chief role of research is to provide information for making decisions about which programs to cut, which personnel to dismiss, which schools to close, or how to reorganize. Answers based on "hard" research data should provide a sound basis for terminating or cutting back without undermining the efficiency and effectiveness of a school.

The main problem is that the ability of research to provide such definitive answers is limited. In determining which programs to cut, research studies suggest that priorities be given to maintaining classroom teachers and line administrators — the backbone of a system. Specialists and special administrators have little impact on classroom activities. What teachers and principals expect and do probably bears more relationship to how much students learn than anything else. Research studies would also suggest that increasing class size, reducing the budget for instructional materials, or de-emphasizing individualized instruction would not make much of a difference. The link between these variables and student learning are not that strong or consistent.

In trying to decide which personnel should be cut, some research studies emphasize the importance of evaluation systems with clear criteria, regular observations, clear explicit oral and written evaluations, and an objective basis for ranking personnel according to their competence. But other studies caution against the use of formal evaluations in making decisions about personnel. They suggest that relying on formal evaluations as a basis for such decisions may further undermine internal morale and create conflicts which jeopardize the bond of faith and confidence between schools and local communities. Competence is exceedingly difficult to pinpoint among professionals who work in schools. Using competence as a factor in dismissals usually creates tension with schools and produces conflicts among constituencies outside.

Similarly, the usefulness of research in deciding which schools to close or how to re-organize falls considerably short of providing the specific answers that administrators need. The relationship between physical facilities or instructional characteristics and student outcomes is tenuous at best. So is the relationship between organizational arrangements and their effects. Research provides very little evidence that various patterns of decision making, grade organization, or administrative structures will make a significant difference in how much students learn.

From a rational-technical view of schools, research is of limited use in telling administrators what to do in hard times.

Because research does not provide general or specific answers about what to do, administrators need to consider locally-developed practices and standards of quality in making decisions. But, often, shared criteria are not available to guide systematic problem-solving. Various interest groups will have their own positions to support or defend.

In such circumstances, research results can become political ammunition in debates about which programs are cut, which teachers or administrators are let go, or which schools are closed.

As interest groups struggle to gain a political toehold, they look for backing from external sources. Research findings are often cited as a source of external expertise. Isolated research studies can be found to support almost any position if one ignores methodological limitations or flawed analyses of results. Many interest groups will attempt to bolster their ideological positions by linking their claims to research findings.

There are two ways that administrators can use research politically as decisions are made about cutbacks. Administrators can cite research results in advocating their own position or that of groups or coalitions favoring the general interests. By conveying an appearance of rational analysis, research can add clout to an argument. As administrators reach closure about what needs to be cut — through intuition, political expediency or divine revelation — they can use research to support or buttress their arguments.

Administrators can also use research to combat the claims made by interest groups opposing general interests. When the claims of interest groups are supported by research evidence, contradictory findings can be used as a shield to protect the position which the administrator considers in the best interest of the general welfare. From a political view, decisions get made on the basis of which group has the most power. Research studies can be used as a source of power in political contexts. Research does not provide definitive answers. But it can provide a basis of authority that tips the balance of political influence.

From a symbolic perspective, the primary role of research is to cloak decisions with an aura of legitimacy, to provide a justification for decisions which promotes (or maintains) faith and confidence, and to cushion individuals and organizations from the anguish of loss. Like the political perspective, the symbolic view portrays research as providing little help in determining what should be cut. The political view sees research as power which can be used to increase the willingness of interest groups to support a particular decision. From a symbolic perspective, research is more like scripture. A proposal supported by research invokes a higher, almost divine, authority which increases the likelihood that people will believe in its merits or utility. This authority or increased legitimacy helps people make sense out of new circumstances which result from a decision. In this way, research can smooth the disruption and can help generate new myths as old beliefs are challenged and undermined. For instance when the myth of neighborhood schools is undermined by closing a school, parents need new justifications for sending their children to a faraway school. When young effective teachers are dismissed, people may find new meaning in ideologies which support the wisdom of experience. When cherished programs in music and art are cut, people may find solace in extolling the importance of the basics. In taking away schools, programs, or people, old meanings and beliefs are often undermined or ruptured. Research results can play an important role in legitimizing decisions or helping people find new meaning in the changed circumstances which hard times create.

As administrators turn to the research community for answers to the tough decisions in times of retrenchment, they will find few answers. Research findings do not provide explicit guidelines for what to do. At best, research results can be used politically to advocate or contest specific decisions or symbolically to legitimize decisions or to provide a new foundation for beliefs which cutbacks damage or destroy. As administrators confront the decisions which hard times create, they will need to create their own answers. Research does, however, yield some suggestions about how administrators might approach the process of creating answers.

RESEARCH AND HOW TO DO IT

Although research is of relatively limited assistance in helping administrators decide what they ought to do, it can be helpful in determining how such decisions should be approached. Research suggests three main options that administrators might consider. These options cluster around the three images of organizations (Figure 3). A rational approach suggests that cutbacks may provide opportunities for school districts to cut programs, personnel, or facilities which are less effective than others. A political approach outlines a Machiavillian strategy in which an administrator plays a heavy-handed role in making cuts. A symbolic approach emphasizes the importance of negotiation and interaction among various constituencies as an avenue for building a shared justification for cuts and an opportunity for individuals to vent and to grieve. Each of these approaches is based on research. Each offers guidelines for the process of making decisions about which programs, individuals, and schools should be cut.

The rational approach to making decisions about what to trim as hard times hit schools is based on studies of innovation when resources were more plentiful. Berman and McLaughlin studied school districts using federal funds to implement a variety of innovations. According to this research, districts struggling to make new ideas work went through three stages: mobilizing (planning and getting support) implementing, (making plans operational) and institutionalizing, (making the change permanent).

In each stage of innovation districts experienced problems. The mobilization phase was marred by seeking funds for the wrong reasons and by poor planning. Many districts saw innovations as an opportunity to obtain money without addressing why the change was needed. In most districts, planning was short-term, crisis oriented, and dominated by administrators. Teachers and community representatives had little chance to make their views or concerns known. In the implementation phase, districts were swamped with conflict. The commitment of teachers and support of administrators was in short supply. The flow of information and the use of evaluation to pinpoint problems was absent. As a result, innovations rarely were implemented as intended and frequently left the districts basically the same as before the effort began. In the final phase — institutionalization — districts failed to make provisions for successful programs to continue after the external funding stopped. Programs were therefore allowed to "wither away" rather than being supported with funds from less successful efforts elsewhere in the districts. In sum, even under conditions of expanding resources schools often were unable to manage change effectively. As a result programs were added or dropped without developing a rationale or confronting the conflicts that they inevitably created.

Berman and McLaughlin argue that in times of plentiful resources, districts were able to manage change loosely and to add something for everyone without asking hard questions. The result was a patchwork quilt of people and programs with new ones added willy-nilly on top of the old. In a period of decline, however, many of the problems of managing change under conditions of growth will need to be confronted directly. Otherwise, schools and districts will tend to make cuts in people, programs, and schools, by retracing their steps. Those most recently added will be the first to be eliminated thereby missing an opportunity to select the most effective and eliminate those that are weaker.

To avoid these pitfalls Berman and McLaughlin suggest that administrators should approach cutbacks with the following guidelines in mind:

1. Decisions about cutbacks should be based on long-range educational concerns rather than on short-term political or bureaucratic needs. Administrators need to develop a clear vision of present and future needs and to keep this vision uppermost in

FIGURE 3

Three Images of How to Make Decisions in Hard Times

	Rational-Technical	Political	Symbolic
Metaphor	Think Tank	Coliseum	Theatre
Participants	Representatives from all constituencies	Administrator and interest groups	Key performers and audience
Process	Problem-solving	Game-playing	Role-playing
Key Ingredient	Information	Power	Script
Primary Focus	Exploring	Winning	Performing
Intended Outcome	The best decision	An acceptable decision	New meaning
Role of Administrator	Analyst	Politico	Conductor, Director or Choreographer

deciding what is to be cut. Renting schools temporarily to assure that facilities will be available for future growth needs or keeping talented teachers aboard to anticipate the needs of shifting population changes, or maintaining a special education program to deal with pressing issues three years away are examples of considerations that need to be taken into account in making decisions about cuts.

2. Base decisions about cutbacks on sound reliable information. Administrators need to gather information which provides a clear picture of the time costs, or tradeoffs of cutting particular staff, programs, or schools. This information needs to be put in a form which allows people to see clearly what is being sacrificed in one area to meet the needs in another. Modern budget techniques which permit comparisons across programs or units are examples of information systems that need to be used in making cuts.

3. Arrive at decisions about what personnel programs, or schools to cut through a comprehensive planning process which generates broad-based support from all constituencies in the community and provides an opportunity for individuals to observe directly the criteria, information, and considerations that go into a particular decision. Approach the problem of decline through a process which defines problems clearly, generates alternative solutions, and provide sound criteria for selecting and implementing the best and most workable alternative.

4. Involve the staff and community intensively in the planning process rather than keeping important decisions within the administrative realm. Carefully designed structures which invite the participation of staff and community and make their involvement important and influential rather than token window-dressing.

5. Ease the problems of transfer or reassignment by investing in in-service training which prepares individuals for new roles and new jobs. As programs are cut, jobs are eliminated, and schools are closed, individuals will often be asked to assume new responsibilities — many times in new and unfamiliar settings. Providing training gives people the skills and attitudes needed to meet these new challenges.

These recommendations exemplify a rational approach to decisions in times of decline. They emphasize the widespread participation of all important constituencies in a process which uses information, analytic tools, and a long range vision of educational needs to determine what is to be cut. For administrators, the key is effective management of this process.

A political analysis of decisions during decline has been developed from case studies of successful attempts to terminate policies and programs in the public sector. The specific cases involved closing public training schools in the Massachusetts Department of Youth Services (see Behn), and annulling the National Park Services commitment to a soil erosion project. (See Behn and Clark). This analysis is rooted in the assumption that public policies, programs, projects and organizations are rarely terminated and then only through a protracted and vicious political struggle. In these battles, the administrator is usually the loser or victim, witness the case of President Carter's 1977 decision to terminate several water resource projects or President Ford's 1975 decision to eliminate the office of Telecommunications policy. Cutbacks always take place in a political context and powerful groups can mobilize pressure to protect their special interests. As a result, the administrator must take the initiative operating from a position of power and employing Machiavillian tactics that enhance the power. Otherwise, decisions about what to cut, if anything, will be decided by groups that can marshall the most power. Such factors may not consider the overall welfare of the organization. The following guidelines are for the administrator who takes the political approach. The guidelines are adapted from Behn:

1. Don't float trial balloons. Trial balloons are traditionally a valuable strategy for testing the direction and strength of political winds. But when the trial balloon is something to be cut, its release will quickly galvanize the opposition, produce questions which cannot be answered, and reduce the chance that the decision will ever get off the ground.

2. Enlarge the constituency favoring the cut. Every position, program, or organization has loyal supporters who will be galvanized by a threat to their interests. Such supporters can marshal the forces to prevent a cut unless they are opposed by the larger and more ardent group who favor the cut. Parents of a school to be closed, for example, can carry the day unless their position is opposed by an equally vocal group of concerned taxpayers or parents who are concerned about the continuation of the special education program. Those directly affected by cuts are instantly activated. The administrator needs to develop a broader constituency whose interests are less directly affected by the cut or who favor an alternative program tied to supporting the decisions.

3. Focus attention on the negative aspects — or harm — of what is to be cut. Trying to eliminate anything on the basis of its inefficiency or ineffectiveness arouses only general concerns. General concerns provide little leverage in dealing with the specific issues which interest groups raise to kep a program alive. By calling attention to the harm done by an incompetent professional, an outmoded program, or time-worn facility adequate support for their termination may be obtained.

4. Inhibit compromise. Compromise is one of the most successful strategies for survival. Any candidate for termination — individuals, programs, policies, or organizations — will have a group of supporters who propose compromise in order to survive. Responding to demands for compromise can undermine a decision to cut something. In making cuts, the issue may need to be cast in "either/or" terms. Otherwise, interest groups may succeed in their strategies of defending their particular turf.

5. Recruit an outsider to terminate or make cuts. Insiders are often bound to past decisions and need to defend the status quo. Cutting successfully may require a change in administration or the retention of a special administrator or external consultant. Existing administrators may be so tied to special interest groups that they cannot represent the general sentiment of an organization. Retaining someone to do the unpleasant chores and then moving on may be the only way that necessary cuts can be made successfully.

6. Avoid votes. Votes by representative groups committees or governing boards are dangerous because they rob the administrator of discretion and create opportunities for compromise. Governing bodies are especially vulnerable to pressure groups since incumbents are concerned about political points and reelection.

7. Do not encroach upon the prerogatives of policy-setting groups. Votes should not be avoided at the expense of encroaching upon legitimate prerogatives of policy-setting groups such as school boards, parent associations, or faculty councils. The administrator must push for as much discretion as possible without stepping on toes and creating other issues which undermine the effort. If the issue becomes procedural, any termination effort can be derailed. Even its supporters may rally in defense of following procedure.

8. Accept short run cost increases. Often it may be more costly in the short-term to eliminate something than to continue it. Administrators may need to emphasize the long-range efficiencies of cuts in order to preserve their political viability in the more immediate political debate.

9. Pay off the beneficiaries. Short run costs may be incurred mainly to make certain that those directly affected are not able to use personal discomfort and dislocation to undermine the main decision. Severance pay to displaced teachers, attractive retirement benefits to older individuals, career counseling to locate new job opportunities, or promises of different or better, programs or facilities are short-term provisions which may protect needed long-term decisions.

10. Terminate only what is necessary. Making cuts can spawn a number of painful results. Reductions in programs may eliminate jobs. Closing schools may eliminate programs or positions. An effective administrator will focus on the cuts that are necessary, leaving others in the background. Every termination needs its justification. Scattering the rationale over many cuts will weaken the chances for the primary target.

The political approach to making cuts emphasizes the role of the administrator who must decide and protect needed decisions from the influence of groups that arise to protect specific interests. Behaving like Machiavelli may be necessary to carry off the tough decisions of cutting people, programs or organizations. The key for the administrator is to decide in the interests of the general welfare and to employ political tactics to assure that the decision is not undone by the actions of pressure groups.

The symbolic approach to making decisions about what stays and what goes in hard times is based on several strands of research: studies of change in rural school districts, studies of loss among grieving widows and individuals displaced by urban renewal projects, and studies of planning. The basic premise emerging from this research is that change inevitably results in disorientation and loss among both active participants and outsiders who have some stake in the enterprise. Particularly when programs are being cut, people are being dismissed, schools are being closed, and roles and relationships are being reorganized, the sense of disorientation and loss becomes acute and widespread. Disorientation and loss shake faith, belief, and meaning and create tension and conflict.

Typically, however, disorientation, loss, tension, and conflict are not confronted directly in organizations. Instead, issues are avoided and smoothed over until they become intolerable. At that time coercive strategies pit one group against another until a winner emerges and the issue is eventually decided by power. Administrators are often the victims of such power struggles, although the use of coercive power typically leave scars across groups within an organization or community. The scars take years to heal.

The symbolic view of organizations emphasizes the importance of shared values or beliefs as decisions are made. When resources shrink groups are pitted against one another in a struggle for a fair share. While these struggles can become political bloodbaths, they also provide opportunities for diverse viewpoints and interests to be welded into a shared perspective which bonds participants together in a common effort, reduces disorientation, and cushions loss.

Most organizations have sagas — shared stories or myths — which illuminate distinctive characteristics or practices and condense these into cherished symbols which bind participants together in a meaningful collective effort. Sagas or stories will affect cutbacks in two ways; they can buttress resistance or help marshall acceptance. In organizations with strong sagas, making cuts will prove almost impossible — unless the ongoing saga can be revised to fit the new circumstances. In organizations where things cannot get much worse, new sagas often arise to meet the challenge. Hard times may therefore provide an opportunity for schools to revise sagas that are strong but obsolete or to create new ones where none exist. In response to Pearl Harbor or the Great Depression, for example, America developed powerful sagas or myths which bonded the country together and provided inspiration, initiative and comfort. The saga also gave the President and Congress enormous power to respond to the emergency.

While it is not clear how organizations develop sagas, the concept has some intriguing possibilities for how decisions of hard times might be approached. In this view, the arena for making decisions about what to cut becomes a theatre. Various individuals and groups have parts to play. An audience watches as the drama unfolds. The interplay of the various roles and voices permits an expression of important issues and dilemmas. The ending may contribute to a shared outlook, new meaning, or justification for decisions that need to be made thereby uniting people and groups together. As individuals and groups watch, they have an opportunity to mourn and to grieve openly the loss of things that are important to them — much as an audience watching a funeral or wake. (Marris). Each individual actor has the opportunity to play the part well and to be acknowledged. A script (explicit or hidden) influences how the plot develops and how the drama ends.

The symbolic and rational-problem solving approaches resemble one another in that both emphasize the active involvement of all constituencies in an open process. But, the symbolic view focuses on the expression of beliefs and values, the playing out of scripts and roles rather than on rational analysis of information or cost-benefit calculation. The symbolic approach shares with the political approach the importance of interest groups and power. But rather than seeing interest groups as forces to be squelched, they become integral voices or parts — in a drama that ends with a justification or meaning that all can believe in and support.

The following guidelines provide administrators some direction in approaching difficult decisions in a novel and imaginative way:

1. Expect conflict as resources shrink. Decisions about what to cut will inevitably intrude on someone's turf. Both insiders and stakeholders will experience disorientation and loss as specific cuts are discussed and debated. Conflicts over decisions of what to cut creates dilemmas. These can be resolved only through myths, sagas, or stories which provide a justification which everyone shares and believes. In organizations with strong sagas, sagas will need to be refurbished, relabeled, and renegotiated. In organizations without sagas, new ones will need to be created.

2. Identify the players. Decisions of decline and cutbacks will attract individuals and groups with specific interests to protect. Administrators may have a role in casting the drama by trying to influence the selection of players in order to get the strongest actors involved. In addition, administrators may have to search actively for someone to play a part called for in the script which no one steps forward to fill. A student, representative from a parents group, or spokesperson for the "silent majority" are examples of parts that are often left unfilled.

3. Create the arena and set the stage. Before the drama can go on a stage is needed to create an appropriate backdrop. Individual actors need some idea of the script — even though in many districts the play will undoubtedly be more improvisational than planned. Administrators can play an important role in designing the set with appropriate props, communicating the mood, and assuring that each individual actor has a general idea of the plot and the other players.

4. Orchestrate the drama. For the decision-making drama to proceed, each player needs to attend and to play the part well. The upstaging of an undeveloped character, or a weak performance can impair the over-all impact of drama — for both actors and audience. Administrators can orchestrate the process through prompting, delivering their own lines strongly, and altering their lines to encourage a stronger response from a player with stagefright, to reduce the overacting of a "ham", or to solicit a dramatic performance from an actor with a key role to play.

5. Keep the audience involved and attentive. The drama of decisions in hard times needs an involved and attentive audience. Every attempt must be made to get as many people in the theatre as possible and to keep them engaged in the drama — even as participants if the plot seems to move naturally in their direction.

6. Call attention to the dramatic aspects of the performance and interpret its meaning. Following a performance, administrators can use the media and other sources to highlight the key features of the drama and to provide a coherent interpretation of what the drama meant. The interpretation, like the review of a play, may involve influencing the critics, responding to critics, or trying to get publicity for those who seem to pull from the performance the central meaning.

From the symbolic view of organizations, the dilemmas of hard times will produce disorientation, tensions, and conflicts. These are unavoidable and many are not resolveable through rational analysis or political exchange. The key issue is to encourage the development of a shared myth, or saga which bonds participants together and provides a shared justification for what needs to be done. One way to do this, is to approach hard decisions as if the process were a drama and to encourage the drama to play itself to as large an audience as possible. The administrator cannot control the drama but in subtle ways can orchestrate it.

Research provides administrators with three very different options for how decisions that hard times create might be approached and managed. The conditions of each setting and the images and preferences of individual administrators will dictate whether a rational, political, symbolic approach — or a distinct blend — will be used. Research suggests the alternatives; administrators must make the choices.

APPLYING PERSPECTIVES TO DECISIONS

There are two givens in the challenge of administering schools in the 1980's. First, decisions are going to be difficult and impossible to sidestep. Nearly all school administrators are going to preside over cutbacks in programs and personnel. Some may find creative ways to consolidate resources to reduce the number of cuts that are necessary. But eliminating programs, terminating staff and closing schools are tasks which most administrators will have to tackle and tolerate. Second, the unique characteristics of schools create a setting that is ambiguous, uncertain, and highly charged politically. Lofty, diffuse goals produce few clear criteria for decisions. Specific criteria that are set forth will be quickly and hotly contested. A weak technology makes competence an illusive factor in decisions about dismissals and obscures educational soundness as a basis for deciding which schools are closed. Political vulnerability makes any administrative decision a target for special interest groups to attack. These conditions are fixed, largely unalterable, and have frustrated nearly every effort of the past two decades to reform or to improve schools.

If administrators have any control at all, it is probably in how they respond to the challenge. Hard times breed inflexibility and encourage administrators to respond in ways they know best. If administrators search at all, the quest is for answers or fool-proof recipes that carry the backing of the research community. But either relying on old approaches or following verbatim a pathway that new knowledge dictates is bound to fail. As administrators confront the decisions of hard times, they can resist the temptation to tighten and rigidify. Instead, they will need to play creatively with difficult situations and be willing to view problems from novel perspectives, bouncing their experience against new images which the research community provides. Administrators must develop the capacity to learn, to invent under conditions of uncertainty, and to transform problems into opportunities on a continuing basis. They must be able to use wisdom from past experience as a starting point without expecting it to provide an end point in their deliberations. Donald Schon has described how knowledge from past experience can be applied to current conditions:

> The here-and-now provides the test, the source, and the limit of knowledge. No theory drawn from past experience may be taken as literally applicable to this situation, nor will a theory based on this experience be literally applicable to the next situation. But theories drawn from other situations may provide perspectives of "projective models" for this situation which help to shape and permit action within it.
>
> (Schon, p. 231)

"Projective models" are pictures, or theories, about the relationships among actions, conditions, and outcomes developed from experience. These models are projected onto new situations and shape the way that the situation is seen and the types of actions considered. As administrators confront the new situations of decline they will undoubtedly do so armed with projective models developed under conditions of growth. To succeed, however, administrators will need to develop new projective models. These will rise from experience and can be linked to the more general images which the research community has evolved from its wider vision of the past. While new images or projective models are not sufficient for administrators in dealing with the difficult problems of today, they are necessary, powerful, and one of the few aspects of the situation that administrators can control. As administrators resist the temptation to ridify and tighten their perspectives and instead embrace the opportunity to play and to learn, they can be guided by the imperatives

13

which Schon outlines:

• Learn to tolerate ambiguity and uncertainty

• Seek to develop convictions and commitment while recognizing that beliefs and values are ways of looking at the world rather than objective truths

• Engage with others

• Pay attention to the process of your efforts as much as to the products, while accepting the values of those products which survive the test of being applicable in the here-and-now

• Reject a literal view of the past, but accept the past as a projective model for present situations

• Recognize that often we must act *before* we know in order to learn.

CONCLUSIONS

Hard times frequently set off a frantic search for the quick fix. The danger is that research will be expected to yield solutions that can be broadly applied as panaceas. Dewey has warned against the waste and possible harm of trying to use research results in this way. Research findings must ripen before their implications and applications to real problems can be wisely recognized.

Others (Schon, McGowan, Wise, McDermott) have cautioned against trying to hyperrationalize educational systems. To the degree that education is an indeterminate process, attempts to tighten administrative control over schools or to force strict adherence to some research-based policy are likely to backfire. When school practitioners are required to comply with overly rigid administrative directives, they are likely to spend their time on irrelevant or misguided activities or to ignore the policies entirely.

Given these constraints on the utility of research findings, research cannot be made to provide recipes. Research results seldom, if ever, spell out exactly what must be done to produce a particular outcome. Their less specific, but nevertheless valuable, purpose is more like that of a metaphor. They offer a way of thinking about problems in schools which can help administrators reconsider the jobs they are trying to do. But these practitioners must look to their own wisdom and experience to find the particular implications of the metaphor within the priorities and resources of their particular settings. In hard times research can expand the options available to administrators by providing their context and their tasks.

BIBLIOGRAPHY

Abromowitz, Susan, and Stuart Rosenfield. *Declining Enrollments: The Challenges of the Coming Decade,* Washington, DC: The National Institute of Education, 1978.

Adler, Elaine. "School Effectiveness: The Relationship Between School Characteristics and Student Outcomes," Unpublished Qualifying Paper, Harvard Graduate School of Education, 1981.

Baldridge, J. Victor. *Power and Conflict in the University,* NY: Wiley & Sons, 1973.

Behn, Robert D. "Termination: How the Massachusetts Department of Youth Services Closed the Public Training Schools", Duke University: Working Paper 5752, 1975.

Behn, Robert and Martha Clark. "Termination II, How the National Bank Service Annulled Its Commitment to a Beach Erosion Control Policy at the Cape Hatteras National Seashore", Duke University, Institute of Policy Sciences Working Paper No. 1176, November 1976.

Behn, Robert, "Termination III: Some Hints for the Would-be Policy Termination", Duke University: Working Paper 577, 1977.

Berman, Paul and Milbrey Wallin McLaughlin. "The Management of Decline: Problems, Opportunities and Research Questions," in Susan Abromowitz and Stuart Rosenfield, *Declining Enrollments: The Challenge of the Coming Decade,* Washington, DC: The National Institute of Education, 1978.

Bolman, Lee. "Organization Development and the Limits of Growth: When Smaller is Better Can OD Help?" Unpublished Manuscript, Harvard Graduate School of Education, 1980.

Clark, Burton R. "The Organizational Saga in Higher Education" in J. Victor Baldridge and Terrence E. Deal, *Managing Change in Educational Organizations* Berkeley: McCutchan, 1975.

Cohen, David K. and Bella H. Rosenberg. "Functions and Fantasies: Understanding Schools and Capitalist America," in *History of Education Quarterly,* Vol. 17, No. 2 Summer 1977.

Cohen, Elizabeth G., Terrence E. Deal, John W. Meyer, and W. Richard Scott, "Technology and Structure in the Classroom: A Longitudinal Analysis of the Relation Between Institutional Methods and Teacher Collaboration".

Cohen, Michael and James March. *Leadership and Ambiguity,* NY: McGraw-Hill, 1974.

Coleman, James, et. al. *Equality of Educational Opportunity,* Washington, DC: U. S. Government Printing Office, 1966.

Deal, Terrence E. and C. Brooklyn Derr. "Toward a Contingency Theory of Change in Education: Organizational Structure, Processes, and Symbolism". This article is adapted from a paper prepared for the Stanford-Berkeley Symposium sponsored by the National Institute of Education, Finance and Productivity Division.

Deal, Terrence E., Barbara Neufeld, and Sharon Rallis. "Hard Choices in Hard Times: Evaluation in Schools", Unpublished Manuscript, Harvard Graduate School of Education, 1981.

Deal, Terrence E. and Samuel C. Nutt. *Promoting, Guiding and Surviving Change in Small School Districts,* Cambridge: Abt Associates, 1973.

Dewey, John. *The Sources of a Science of Education,* NY: Horace Liveright, 1929.

Dornbusch, Sanford R. and W. Richard Scott. *Evaluation and the Exercise of Authority,* Berkeley: Jossey-Bass, 1975.

Edelfson, Carla, Rudolph Johnson, and Nellie Stromquist. *Participatory Planning in a School District: A Study Using Three Theoretical Approaches,* Unpublished Manuscript, 1977.

House, Ernest. *School Evaluation: The Politics and Process,* Berkeley: McCutchan, 1973.

Johnson, Susan Moore. "Performance-Based Staff Lay-offs in the Public

Schools: Implementation and Outcomes", *Harvard Educational Review,* May 1980.

McDermott, John E. *Indeterminacy in Education,* Berkeley: McCutchan, 1976.

McGowan, Eleanor Farrar. "Rational Fantasies", *Policy Sciences,* Vol. 7, pp. 439-454, 1976.

Meyer, John W. and Brian Rowan. "The Structure of Educational Organizations", in Marshall Meyer, and Associates, *Environments and Organizations,* Berkeley: Jossey-Bass, 1978.

Morris, Peter. *Loss and Change,* NY: Penguin Books.

Schon, Donald. *Beyond the Stable State,* NY: Random House, Inc., 1971.

Tyack, David. "Historical Perspectives of Educational Reform", *The Final Report and Recommendations of the Summer Institute on the Improvement and Reform of American Education,* Washington, DC:U. S. Government Printing Office, 1974.

Weick, Karl E. "Education Organizations as Loosely-Coupled Systems", *Administrative Science Quarterly,* Vol. 21, 1976.

Weiss, Carol. "Measuring the Use of Evaluation" in *Utilizing Evaluation: Concepts and Measurement Techniques,* ed., James A. Ciarlo, CA: Sage Publishing, 1981.

Wise, Arthur. *Legislated Learning: The Bureaucratization of the American Classroom,* Berkeley: University of California Press, 1979.

2

HOW TO ENLIST AND KEEP SUPPORT
OF YOUR CONSTITUENCY

John C. Cone

Before you can serve your publics, you really should have a good idea who they are. Here is a list of publics that school officials should never forget — in part because they may require different approaches for support. Author Cone supplies a number of projects that are easy to do but not always implemented. They can start your district on the road to a better public relations effort.

Mr. Cone, a popular writer and speaker on educational affairs, is executive director of the South Carolina School Boards Association, 1706 Senate St., Columbia, SC 29201.

For this discussion it may be easier to refer to publics than to constituencies. Publics are those groups of people who can be identified as having some common traits. All parents might be considered as a public. All professional employees make up a public as do all voters or all taxpayers or all senior citizens.

Who, then, are our constituents or our publics and how have they changed in the last two decades?

The parents of public school children make up a public which has changed drastically in the last 20 years. At one time more than half of the adults in the typical community had children in public school. In fact, the annual Gallup poll on education indicates that, in 1969, 44 per cent of adults had children in public school. In 1978, that had dropped to 28 per cent. So a smaller proportion of the adult population has any direct interest in public education.

Add to this the increasing number of single parent families in which only one parent has primary interest in the child's education. Then add the increased interest in private schools and the number of parents whose children are enrolled in these institutions. The dilution of support from adults in the community is more than significant; it is staggering.

What about another public, the senior citizen? According to the U. S. Bureau of the Census one in every six Americans is 65 years old or older. The Bureau projects that by 1990 the number of people over 55 will be greater then the entire K-12 school population. These older citizens have, for the most part, been alienated from the public school scene. They have been ignored since the day their last child graduated from high school. And they often live on fixed incomes which are constantly worn away by increased school taxes. These grandparents don't even live in the same home with their grandchildren as they did once. So they are further removed from the daily interest of their own grandchildren.

Taxpayers can be classed as a public though a large one that includes most parents and grandparents. Taxpayers include businesses and industries who, in many communities, pay a larger share of the property tax than all the home-owners put together. These taxpayers represent a group whose support cannot be taken for granted. Of course, business and industry also have the role of putting our graduates to work when they finish school. The criticism coming from these employers is more than can be ignored. So perhaps employers should be considered as a special public.

Voters are constituents in the purest sense of the word. They may be taxpayers and parents as well but their expression comes only rarely — when elections take place. Voters show their support by passing referendums and by re-electing progressive trustees to the school board.

Of course, the students themselves are a most important public. They might be described as the clients of the school district, or even the patients, or as some have said dispassionately, the product of the schools. Since students are the primary communication link for all schools to the community, the role they play cannot be forgotten or taken lightly.

Employees of the school district certainly constitute a very important public. Their support is critical. Teachers in particular are a powerful constituency. In some ways teachers are considered the key to a good education system; they are where the "rubber meets the road", as the saying goes. Teachers are sometimes thought of as the labor force for the district while others view them as line management supervising the work efforts of their students.

It matters little how teachers are viewed. They, and other school employees, exert great influence on the health of the school system. In districts where collective bargaining takes place the importance for employee support of public education is easily verifiable.

Other publics might include vendors and deliverymen who are constantly in touch with what goes on in the schools. Governmental agencies such as the police, the mental health center, the recreation department, environmental protection groups, county and city councils, juvenile courts, and libraries all touch schools in their roles and can be supporters of or detractors from the public school effort.

Institutions such as churches, higher

education or technical schools, private schools, museums and research centers may be viewed as publics with special interest in public education. Certainly the role of the church has changed with more and more church-sponsored private schools. And with the reduced enrollments at many colleges one can see a gradual shift to a role of educating more youngsters who have not yet received a good high school education.

CONFIDENCE WANES

Now that we have discussed the kinds of publics that exist and some of the ways those relationships have changed let's look at the degree of confidence they have for public education. Public confidence in public education has declined in the past ten years since such polls began. Only 28 per cent of those currently surveyed said they had a great deal of confidence in the public schools.

That is not really as bad as it may seem. When asked about other institutions only the church rated higher than the schools. Big business, the courts, labor, government and all others rated lower than education. It's also worth noting that those who have children in the schools give the schools a much higher rating than those who have little or no contact with schools. To some extent the drop in confidence should be due to the drop in the percentage of people closely involved in the schools. It's also clear that confidence in all institutions and professions has been slipping over the years.

There are several other reasons for the decline in confidence. One has to do with the media explosion. A man can be shot in Boston or a plane bombed in Beirut and we know about it immediately. In fact we can usually see it in vivid color right in our homes. One reads about school violence thousands of miles away but the impact is instant and personal. Careless reading or viewing could lead one to believe the event took place right at home, or at least the impression is that it could have.

The instant replay of news worldwide has become so inflated it fills our horizons and blocks out our normal experience. When we watch the news we see thirty minutes of the most bizarre the day has to offer.

We don't see all the good, normal events of the day. We don't see millions of students working hard to learn their lessons, striving to be good citizens. We see one youngster who brought a gun to school and shot a teacher.

No wonder we think our world is changing for the worst. All we ever see of our world is the worst. And it is the nature of the media to make it seem so plausible, so much a reality, that we believe it could be happening anywhere, even in our own schools. Indeed the media has been blamed for generating epidemics of antisocial behavior such as airplane hijacking, pot smoking and streaking.

BIGGER MAY NOT BE BETTER

A second influence which has tended to drag down the perception of what our schools are like is the increase in the size of the school and the size of the school district. As more and more people have moved into the urban and suburban sprawl and away from the rural life, schools and school districts have grown large. Expectations of efficient operation have brought about consolidation of schools and districts.

Only recently have we begun to think that maybe bigger is not always better. Parents complain that they don't ever get to talk to the principal because he is running a $15 million plant with 200 employees. They say they don't even know the board members because they serve 20,000 constituents. The school is so big the kids don't know their classmates and what is worse the school authorities don't know all the students. Bigger may sometimes be more efficient but it is almost always less personal. That loss of the personal touch for the sensitive business of education has proven a thorn tearing away at public confidence.

Universal public education has been a dream in America for at least 200 years. We once claimed that we had it but the reality of universal public education is only a few years old. It began with serious efforts to bring into the system those who had been excluded for all of those 200 years. Blacks in the South were not a part of the universal picture until a decade ago. Hispanics in the Southwest and minorities in bulging cities all over the country were legally, systematically excluded from public schools. It might be accurate to say there was a universal public education system but there were two universes.

And right now we are just beginning to open the doors of that supposedly universal system to handicapped children.

What has it meant, this experiment in truly universal opportunity? In many parts of the country it has resulted in minority students and students from low income families achieving at academic levels much higher than ever before. It has even meant that students from diverse backgrounds have come together and learned that they have more in common than they ever believed. In many places it has been a social and educational phenomenon.

And yet this attempt at more universal education has had some negative results as well. Many students have been pulled from public education and placed in private schools thus diluting both the moral and financial support for public schools. Many believe that the decline in test scores and the increase in school violence and vandalism is due to the integration of the public schools. Some even believe that social promotion began with integration and teaching of the basics ended with it. (Whether there is merit in these assumptions is not the point. The point is many people believe they are valid perceptions.)

The increased mobility of our society has contributed to the general loss of confidence in the schools. The typical American today can expect to live in several different homes during his life time and probably several different cities. He can also expect to work for several different employers and most likely have several entirely different careers.

This lack of stability in the community has a devastating effect on the public school program. Most people tend to appreciate and support what they feel they own. But the mobility described above makes it hard for anyone to feel a sense of ownership with his public school system. Some

might say, "Why bother to become involved in the schools program when we might be moving again soon?"

It is human nature to compare what one has now with what was before. So when one moves into a new community and a new school system, common pride calls for comparisons which are almost always odious. It is standard practice to complain about the new school which is inevitably inferior to the school in the last community. Thus the level of ownership, pride and confidence declines as mobility of the constituency increases.

Finally among the dozens of perfectly obvious reasons for loss of confidence is the loss of ethnicity or cultural identity in our American society. Our public schools are deliberately void of cultural or ethnic identity. Rarely does one find a public school which is predominantly Jewish or predominantly Greek. Even those which are predominantly Black or Hispanic have been, to a large extent, broken up into ethnically balanced schools.

While this deliberate effort to integrate has had some very important positive results there have been some unfortunate drawbacks. To some extent the same loss has, in some cases, brought about loss of pride in and support of the school. Whereas the school was the community center for many groups just twenty years ago it has become, often, the center for no one. Other focal points and gathering spots have sprung up in the community and the school is viewed as a place for children to go for an education.

There is evidence that this is gradually changing: that school districts are trying hard to make the school building a center of community pride and activity. Clearly this is an effort to restore commitment and confidence in the school system.

There are many other reasons for the loss of public confidence in public schools. Those different causes should be examined. Once the causes for disinterest have been laid bare it is easier to move forward with a program for restoring confidence and enlisting support.

The process of enlisting support has been conveniently named public relations. Whenever a district is faced with a problem, be it a bond referendum, drug abuse or head lice the cry goes out for improved "p.r.". But public relations should not be seen as a cure-all for school systems. It is not a means of responding to problems as they arise but rather a "mind-set" which must permeate the entire system. It is an attitude of open communications even before the problem arises.

The generally accepted definition of school public relations is that it is "a planned, systematic, two-way process of communications between the educational institution and its internal and external publics". This brief definition centers on three key words. The effort must be planned. That is to say it doesn't happen randomly but is built around specific goals which can be measured and reset. The p.r. program must also be systematic. Rather like a payroll savings plan it should go forward with some regularity and with support and involvement throughout the system.

ARE YOU LISTENING?

Finally it must be a plan which involves two-way communications. It is not enough to simply tell the district's story. It is not enough to print fancy annual reports, hold press conferences, hit the lecture circuit and appear on talk shows. At least an equal amount of time and effort should go into listening; listening to what the various publics have to say about the school system. This can be done through question and answer sessions, advisory councils, surveys, and suggestion boxes. Feeling the pulse of the community is just as important as disseminating information about the schools.

With this definition in mind you are ready to begin planning your public relations program to enlist public support. Bring a few key people together and talk a little about your publics. Talk about what your communications problems are and how they might be solved. Here we will take senior citizens, for an example.

These citizens have been disenfranchised. We have told them by our actions that we are not interested in them any more since they no longer have children in school. They are not on the team and do not

support the schools primarily because we don't ask for their support. What can we do?

Project No. 1: Issue "Gold Card" memberships to all senior citizens. You can usually get a list of older citizens from your local Association of Retired People or a local agency working with senior citizens. Print a colorful membership card and send one to each senior citizen along with a letter. The letter should thank them for making the community a good place for today's children. Tell them that the district would like to offer them a special status and allow them to attend all school athletic events and drama productions free of charge. The gold card will be their ticket of admission. Ask if they know anyone else who would like to have a gold card. Then sit back and watch the smiles and expressions of gratitude.

Project No. 2: Go back to that same list of people and ask them to come into the school to act as volunteers. They may fit into two classes of volunteers. Some may want to help classroom teachers keep up with the non-instructional details of the daily routine while others will be eager and able to act as tutors for individual students. Remember, teachers retire too. Secondly, you will find a group of resource people who have skills and experiences you never dreamed of. One might come and tell you about his experiences in World War II and bring a history class to life with photos and relics. Another might bring an outstanding rock collection or show students how to develop photographs. There is no limit to the resources senior citizens have. You might consider providing transportation and a free meal to these volunteers as those are sometimes a problem.

Project No. 3: Many schools have Parents' Day with an open house and exert special efforts to bring parents into school. But how many have a Grandparents' Day?

This project is aimed at showing grandparents that they still have a vital interest in good public education. And it lets them see what a fine job the schools are doing contrary to all they have been hearing. Let the children invite their grandparents with personalized cards made with crayons and construction paper. Publicize it in the media. Allow the grandparents to go through the day with the children in their normal schedule. Provide a special lunch for the grandparents. After a few years this program will become so popular grandparents will fly in from distant cities so as not to disappoint their grandchildren.

Let's look at another important group, this time an "internal" public, one of the most important. The high school student today can be easily bored with school. He has so many attractive alternatives that studying and learning often take last place. So what can you do to enlist the support of your own students?

Project No. 1: Assume the principal meets regularly with student council representatives and reports of those meetings are made to the student body. Now he or she is going to try to form some means of communications with the informal or unrepresented leaders in the student body. Suppose the principal goes to the cafeteria two or three days a week and asks, at random, a group of four or five students to bring their trays to his/her office to have lunch with him/her. During this time the principal assumes the role of a listener. The students are encouraged to talk about whatever they want, be it rock music or pro football. The principal has broken the ice and created informal lines of communications.

Project No. 2: Schools with winning football teams are generally better schools in other ways. Just what role the winning team plays is unclear but it is undoubtedly true that student pride in the school leads to better discipline and an effort to maintain the school's good name. Unfortunately, not all schools can have winning teams and not all students can play on the first string. So the district may consider providing additional chances for each school to excel. Competition for a citizenship award among schools with the best citizenship project gives all schools another opportunity to be a winner. Competition for the "Sportsmanship" award scored by referees at the games can produce a new winner every week with a revolving trophy. Competition in events such as weight lifting, cheerleading, cooking, auto mechanics, singing, and a hundred other things gives

more students a chance to carry the school's colors, to be a winner for the school and to generate pride in the school. A setting for such events might be a county fair with individual trophies and cash prizes going to the schools from the fair promoters.

Project No. 3: The district might consider a project utilizing the finest high school speakers the district can identify. They can be selected competitively and recognized in various ways as the district's student speakers' bureau. These students can then be placed on the circuit of civic and service clubs talking about their schools to people who might not otherwise have any link with the school system. Adults in the community are always impressed with the poise and maturity of these students contrary to their preconceived notions about youth today. And the students appreciate being trusted by the district as a part of the team to promote better schools rather than just the product of the institution.

Clever p.r. projects are limited only by your own imagination. There are literally thousands of ideas already implemented and successful.

This has been a "how to" discussion of school public relations It is not intended as a list of formulae for enlisting support but a guide for your own exploration into the communications challenge.

Enlisting and keeping the support of your constituency should never be viewed as a one-time project to be geared up like a bond campaign and then forgotten. Like the hood-pounding used car salesman, that short-sighted approach will only work once.

No, enlisting support of your publics depends upon a communications program which includes all the players and is ongoing during times of tranquility as well as adversity. If you have laid the groundwork well you will have a virtual army of workers to support you when times are bad and what is more you will be returning the public schools to the public where they will grow stronger and better and more in tune with the needs of the people they serve.

3

KEEPING THE STUDENTS ON YOUR SIDE IS WORTH THE STRUGGLE

Susan Kaye, Ed.D.

The needs of the students can be over-looked during budgetary crunches and labor crises even though this is where the focus of education should be. While some student issues remain with us, several new ones have arisen. The school that can offer a positive response to these and enlist the participation of the students in the process is one that has greatly enhanced its chances for survival.

Susan Kaye, Ed.D. , is the director of student personnel services for the Bellmore-Merrick Central High School District on Long Island, New York.

Schools today are being asked to deal with decremental budgeting rather than incremental budgeting, staff reductions rather than staff recruitment, planning for fewer clients rather than more: we know why. High school enrollments are plunging for the 1980's — the decline is expected to bottom out in 1989, reaching a low of 12,300,000 students. Decline in secondary schools is reminiscent of what occurred in elementary schools during the 1970's where schools were closed, consolidated and reorganized to accommodate fewer students.

As schools attempt to work their way through a myriad of issues related to jobs, security and the financial crunch, we need to be sure that we do not overlook our true priority, reassessment and reorganization to meet the changing characteristics of our primary client, the student.

The alienated secondary school students of the 60's and 70's have generally disappeared from the scene. They have been replaced by "the working student", "the drop-out" and "the truant". Recent newspaper surveys of high school students point out that 20 years ago, fewer than 30 per cent of students between the ages of 16 and 19 were in the labor force. By 1978, their number had risen to 46 per cent. The 1980 report of the Carnegie Council on Policy Studies, *Giving Youth a Better Chance,* points out that nearly half of all students in the 16 to 21 age group are in the labor force or are seeking work (mostly on a part-time basis).

Informal local studies bear out this phenomenon. In Manchester, CT, 1,000 out of almost 1,500 high school students had part-time jobs after school. In West Hartford, CT, a concerned teacher surveyed 148 juniors and seniors in the Hartford area and found that 77 per cent reported holding jobs averaging twenty hours per week.

In addition to the natural struggle of an adolescent for financial independence, inflation is a major factor contributing to the growing number of working students. High youth unemployment, particularly among minority youth, continues since the 1960's to be a matter of national concern. The Carnegie Council reports that in "terms of numbers, most unemployed youths are white. Among those aged 16 to 21 and not enrolled in school in October, 1977, three-quarters of the unemployed youths or about 9,000,000 were white. But the unemployment rate was far higher for blacks than for whites — 36.1 per cent compared with 12.0 percent".

While employers continually have stressed that students who drop out of school or graduate without basic skills are the least likely to be employed, and available statistical data confirms this, the high school drop-out rate since 1965 has remained at about 25 per cent of our student population.

In a recent article on work habits, employers surveyed said that it is attitudes that count. When asked what traits they most frequently look for in a new employee, they cited "work habits", "dependability" and "concern for the job". Absenteeism and lack of interest in the job were the most frequently cited reasons for dismissal.

Absenteeism and truancy are problems that are pervasive to all schools — urban and suburban. Educators obviously must be more responsive and set as a priority the issues related to "the holding power" of our schools. Other factors, such as violence in the schools, the decline in test scores and student apathy and boredom, show few signs of diminishing.

In recent interviews of teachers, principals and students in schools across the country, interviewers found that a "good school" emphasized praise and higher expectations for students. These schools experienced fewer discipline problems, a lower drop-out rate and improved attendance.

However, opinions varied widely regarding student participation in decision-making in schools. One key issue in student involvement is accountability. Should student's opinions be considered as an integral part of the total evaluation procedure? How should the data be analyzed and by whom? Should teachers be required to ask for feedback?

As early as the 1920's, university students were involved in school and staff evaluation. Thus, for many years student evaluation of schools and their teachers has been an accepted practice in higher education institutions, but only recently has it come into practice in a few elementary and secondary schools.

If students are to be involved in the evaluation of staff, the value of student feedback should rest upon the changes that would result in school instruction. Results indicate that feedback from students is an effective means of influencing teacher behavior and sometimes can be more effective than supervisory feedback. However, as educators, we must be cautious that a student evaluation not be used as an opinion poll.

It is incumbent upon every school to address the changing and emerging needs as perceived by the students. We have all witnessed schools that have a mesh of staff, administration and curriculum, but student attitude determines the success or failure of these schools. If students feel that schools are not adequately meeting their needs, the best staff or most well-equipped school will find itself not meeting its full potential.

Students can be effectively involved. They bring to our schools a different prospective and, in addition, the students and community can acquire a broader prospective of their own school/community. Community members working jointly with students are able to avail themselves of an opportunity to get to know students' needs, attitudes and concerns on a first-hand basis.

Working with students in a productive mode can become an interesting and positive experience. Students in many communities not only participate effectively in the accreditation process but have been involved as participants in committees interviewing and selecting a school principal and/or superintendent.

Student involvement in the change process can effectively take place through a variety of techniques; i.e. participation in student government organizations, curriculum committees, school boards. Students need to help with developing recommendations that directly affect their welfare. Attendance policies and procedures have most effectively been implemented in schools where students have been part of the process of establishing the guidelines.

These strategies are often more stringent than the school administration had been able to implement, prior to student involvement in the decision-making process.

In a 1974 study, students rated characteristics of teachers that they valued most highly; these included: teachers should be knowledgeable, possess a sense of humor, be tolerant of students, be able to listen, be interested in the student as an individual, and maintain a warm and friendly attitude. It is interesting to note that the same characteristics have been listed as desirable by parents when asked to identify characteristics of the school superintendent and the school principal they most value.

Our schools are being asked by the youth of our nation to be more demanding and to encourage them to rise to expectations. Students are telling educators that they are more responsive to praise and success in school than to confrontation and failure.

We have an opportunity today to fundamentally restructure our schools to meet the changing needs of today's youth. A good example of this principle in practice is Public Law 94-142 for the Education of the Handicapped. Under this legislation, schools are mandated to identify and educate *every child* with a handicapping condition by developing individual education plans for each student in consultation with the parent and student; by providing alternative types of instruction and curriculums geared to best meet the educational needs of the individual child; and by being responsible for the education of a handicapped child up to the age of twenty-one. The issue addressed in this legislation is based on the premise that *every child* can and should be educated in our schools. As a result of Public Law 94-142, alternative educational programs have been developed across the country — physical education classes have developed new curriculums known as adaptive physical education; schools have expanded work-study programs to accommodate handicapped students; occupational and career education programs are emphasizing assessing the individual student's talents, abilities and interest; and small group instruction has been developed to meet these student's needs (particularly in the area of exploration of technological careers and training in the use of computers and word-processing machines). Individual educational plans have been instituted to assist students towards attaining a high school diploma, students, who prior to the legislation, were unable to meet the demands of the traditional high school curriculum.

Teenage pregnant students who traditionally have been forced by schools to terminate their education abruptly as a result of their condition, are being encouraged in many districts to return to alternative schools and programs developed to help them to further their education and graduate from high school. Motherhood should no longer be synonomous with drop-out.

Working to keep pregnant girls from dropping out of high school takes time, energy and the ability to seek out strong enough incentives for these students. Alternative programs that allow extended school day programs have been instituted in many urban high schools and have proved to be quite successful in preventing these young women from being school drop-outs. The administrators and counselors of one inner city school arranged special afternoon classes for these students to help them overcome the discomfort and the anxiety both the staff and students often experienced with pregnant teenagers.

ALTERNATIVE STRATEGIES

Many tradition-bound high schools across the country cling fiercely to their commitment to the 8th or 9th period day. They often continue to pressure students to attend pep rallies, varsity games and other extra-curricular secondary school activities. Students working part-time often find themselves open to criticism from staff for not being available for after school activities and as a result drop out of high school rather than risk further ridicule.

By contrast, other high schools have introduced *flexible scheduling* and *open campus* programs to increase the holding power of the school. By offering certain classes in alternate years or two or three

days a week (similar to colleges), these high schools have found that students are able to maintain full schedules and meet part-time work obligations.

Allowing senior high school students to select open 8th periods and/or eliminating a lunch period has eased the burden for many students who are then permitted to leave campus at the end of their classes rather than mandating that they remain in school for the full school day.

Rochester, NY, in an effort to reduce student absenteeism, surveyed employers in the city in order to assess how schools could be more responsive to the employers' priorities and concerns. Businesses overwhelmingly stressed attendance as a problem they experienced with their sixteen and over employees. By working closely with the business community, the school developed a procedure that has reduced absenteeism both in the school and on the job.

Students with annual 100 per cent school attendance receive a wallet-size card noting that they achieved excellence in attendance for the year. The students carrying these cards have reported that they have found it easier to both obtain an interview and a job as a result of having the 100 per cent attendance card. Employers reported that they gave preference to students who can show the card. In this instance, a strategy was developed based on recognition of the needs of the working student and the result has been reduced absenteeism by approximately 25 per cent both in the schools and business community.

Secondary school principals report a growing number of students choosing technical, business training and post-high school employment in the 1980's as an alternative to college. Our high schools are not adequately training students for these options. The traditional high school program for seniors leaves very little room for technical and career oriented subjects and exploration. At best, they either bus students two or three times a week to a vocational high school, or if the student attends a comprehensive high school, he/she will be receiving training on outmoded machines from a staff that often has not had the opportunity to update their own skills.

School districts working cooperatively with nearby two- and four-year community colleges, technical schools and businesses have enabled many schools across the country to institute a variety of alternative extended day programs. Representatives of agencies have often been brought to the schools and have provided so-called "turned off" students with alternative adult figures to model themselves after, while being introduced to new areas of career and job-oriented exploration.

In high schools where shrinking enrollment is reducing the student population for athletics, debating teams and other activities; inter-district sharing has been successfully employed as a solution. School districts that are ready to reach beyond their own boundaries and move beyond the traditional school and "school districts" have developed cooperative programs with neighboring school districts and found that both the participation and the performance of these programs have been enhanced. *Inter-district cooperation* is leading to greater diversity of curriculum and programs and, as a spin-off effect, has stimulated staff to upgrade their own skills as they relate to classroom performance.

Secondary school students today are often viewed as "apathetic and alienated" rather than unprepared for the transition of moving from programs composed of fixed periods, fixed requirements and hall passes to looser structures as represented by the world of work. Many high schools have introduced programs that create alternatives for students enabling them to adjust to the greater freedom and decision making they will face post-high school. These alternatives include internship programs for students in cooperation with community action agencies, manpower training programs, law enforcement and legal service agencies, municipal agencies, museums, libraries, and hospitals. In addition to internships, high schools have instituted on-site visits to private business and industrial sites as well as apprenticeship programs. These programs, which help the student develop realistic attitudes regarding future employment, also offer the student an opportunity to gain the skills and abilities needed to keep step with the changing priorities and skills of the working world. Programs such as apprenticeship programs, internship programs, and "shadowing" programs have been successful when the school has worked cooperatively with the community in developing these alternatives.

When the school districts began to develop viable systems of combined classroom learning and work experience, successful programs were mounted through cooperation with the local community. Issues such as lack of transportation, insurance and supervisory costs were readily resolved in order to implement effective programs aimed at training students to meet entry level skill specifications.

The message for our high schools today is that curriculum can be expanded beyond the classroom and beyond the immediate community. Developing options and restructuring school programs to enable students to develop decision making skills and work oriented skills is not something we should talk about for the future, but is an immediate priority for our high schools if we are to increase our "holding power".

CONCLUSION

The purpose of this chapter has been two-fold: first, to look at some of the possible causes for student unrest, and second, to offer viable alternatives. We are faced with an overriding demand by the public that schools do more and do it with less.

It is not always necessary that change and innovation be sudden and complete. Successful programs are often appended to the traditional school program.

In order to "hold on" to our students in the 80's, we need to recognize, understand, and be responsive to their needs. By introducing innovative programs within the structure of our schools, we can maintain the existing programs and at the same time begin anew.

Faced with declining enrollments, spiraling costs and pressure from students and parents to graduate "ready for work" adolescents, we need to assess our own school districts' innovative potential. Size and location of schools are not the determinants in developing exciting and promising new programs for students. Determining the success or failure of programs is based upon a careful assessment of student needs and the commitment and solid planning of the school staff and involved community members. The successful implementation of a program depends in large measure upon the individual leadership of the school and the commitment of the teaching staff. Programs such as we have described must have a commitment and process for evaluation and reevaluation if they are to be successful. Goals and objectives should be positive in nature and aimed at improving delivery of skills and service to students.

Education in the 80's for students can be both relevant and superior; basics can include a variety of strategies and programs. The Superintendent of Schools in Bismarck, ND, when talking about education commented, "Education is not expensive, it's priceless."

4

MORE CHILDREN ARE COMING;
MORE CHILDREN ARE COMING

Paul Abramson

Even though the short term outlook is forcing many districts to close schools, a look down the road just a few years ahead indicates a new baby boomlet. Consultant Abramson explores some of the reasons and consequences of increase in student population that he sees coming.

Mr. Abramson, president of Intelligence for Education, Inc., is also the author of Chapter Nine on energy cost containment. In addition to publishing School & College Construction Reports, his consulting firm specializes in communication projects to and within the education industry. The home base is 2 East Ave., Larchmont, NY 10538.

School officials may face a dearth of money and other resources in the eighties, but they won't face a dearth of students.

The baby boom children of the '50's are charging forward for a second run at the schools — this time as parents. And while they are not likely to produce the huge student population their parents did, the sheer number of women of prime child bearing years today guarantees an increase in births and — five years later — of students.

That's not a hunch; it's a certainty. To put it in a phrase, there can be little doubt that by the end of the 1980's, our elementary schools in particular are going to be experiencing a "Baby Boomlet." How that boomlet will affect your schools, what you can do to meet it and what resources will be available to you and must be obtained, may well be the overriding problem of education in the next decade.

Why a baby boomlet? Let's start with a few facts. The baby boom of the post-war era lasted essentially from 1946 through 1957. More children were born during that decade than at any other time during our history. Altogether, 43 million children were born during these years, and though births began to tail off in 1958, they remained high for another seven years through 1964.

Then patterns changed. Births fell off significantly for the next 9 years, reaching a low of 3,137,000 born in 1973. (This "low," it should be noted, is higher than the number of children born in any single year prior to 1946.) The reasons for the change are not complex. Three major and obvious changes took place in our nation resulting in fewer births. It's as simple as that. The changes:

1. There were fewer potential parents around. The children of the Depression and the War years had replaced the Veterans as "young marrieds" and there were fewer of them. Therefore, they produced fewer children.

2. At least as significant was the changing role of women that began to emerge in the 1960's. Not only did lifestyles change — with less emphasis on marriage and families and more on living together and relationships — but in addition women be-

gan to enter the job market in unprecedented numbers, and to find that they either wanted to work or needed to work, and therefore could not or would not drop out to have babies.

3. Finally technology (in terms of better and easier to use contraceptive devices) and mores came together to make it possible to plan families or to plan no families, far more easily than in the past. There was neither the desire to create families or the likelihood that "accidents" would occur. And if they did, changes in laws and thinking made it possible for those accidents to be corrected through legal, safe and available abortions.

WHY THE CHANGE NOW?

Two of those three factors remain in effect partially or wholly today. But the key one — the number of women of prime child bearing age — has shifted markedly. It is estimated today that there are 51 million women between the ages of 15 and 44, with most of them 20-34 years old. Even if birth rates (the number of children/fertile female) remain as low as they have been, this huge number of women of prime child bearing years should bring on increases in births. As a matter of fact, they already have.

Every year since 1976 there has been an increase in children born, as compared to the year before. The increases have not always been great but the trend has been steady. What this means in school terms, quite simply, is that starting in 1981 and continuing until five or six years after the new baby boomlet ends, there is going to be an increase in the number of children entering kindergarten and the first grade. By 1987, all of the small classes of the "baby dearth" years will have moved into middle schools and junior high schools and the new baby boomlet will have established itself in our elementary schools.

As things look now, 1987 will only be the beginning. If history repeats itself even in moderation, it will be about 1994 before entering kindergarten classes begin to level off and then decline, which means that the real space crunch in elementary schools is liable to hit towards the end of this decade and continue through the 1990's.

YOU AND THE NATION

These, of course, are national trends and national trends needn't mean much in terms of individual districts. Many school districts rode out the first baby boom without an increase in students or space. Others have had to build at breakneck speed during the last few years when student populations were declining on a national basis. How then does one know whether the baby boomlet will affect a specific district?

One touchstone in answering this question is awareness. It should come as no surprise to most school officials that babies do not suddenly appear out of nowhere. Nor, in general, do babies suddenly show up in your schools. It takes five or six years for that to happen, a very critical early warning period. The problem is, too many districts squander this valuable time.

Awareness need not consume a great deal of time and energy. It certainly involves setting up a system to check with local hospitals on births, preferably on a month-to-month basis, and keeping records for comparative purposes.

Awareness should certainly include a regular pre-school census of your district to find out how many students will enter your schools in the following years. It could even include questions designed to elicit parents' plans in terms of migration or the use of public vs. private school. In each case, year-by-year comparative records will help to outline a pattern that can help in your planning.

Beyond these relatively simple ways of keeping in touch with incoming youngsters, the district must obviously stay in tune with local real estate people to learn of new housing developments or companies that might be expanding or moving into the area, bringing new young families with them. Industrial plants, like babies, seldom arrive unexpectedly. If a major employer is moving into your area, it behooves you to take the time to find out how many people it will employ and how that will impact on your schools.

The measures mentioned above seem so obvious they hardly need mentioning and yet, facts are facts. Many school districts, involved as they are in the day-to-day necessities of program and finances, often let such niceties as long range planning fall by the wayside. They don't have time to look into the future, until the future has arrived.

You must keep track of population, real estate and employment trends in your district on a regular basis. But there are some other ways you can look ahead too. For one, you can analyze your district even today in terms of the *likelihood* that it will experience a student population boomlet.

The original baby boom hit the suburbs, particularly in the east and middle west, very hard. Again, in retrospect, the reasons were simple. The suburbs offered inexpensive housing, good schools, open space and relatively easy access to jobs in the center city. They were the ideal place for young couples to settle in and start their families.

Ask almost anyone to name the "great" school districts of the United States in the last 30 years and the answers will be largely the same: Newton, MA; Winnetka, IL; Beverly Hills, CA; Scarsdale and Great Neck, NY; Clayton, MO; Ridgewood, NJ. For better or for worse, the old suburbs of our great cities have taken their place as the leading edge school districts. They and their sometimes lesser known neighbors have led the way over the last two decades or more as the finest educational school districts in the nation.

So what? So try to buy a home today in any of these older, prestigious, education oriented suburbs. The price of housing in these built-up areas has skyrocketed. The people who are there (and who have watched their children go through the great school systems) often won't, or can't, depart. Land is scarce and new building has come to a standstill.

Many young couples are now living in the big cities. As they start families, they may well look for housing in areas where they "want to bring up children." But, except for the wealthy, housing is not going to be easily available in the great suburbs. Predictably, many of these new families are going to have to look beyond their own former homes in order to find the same advantages that their parents found when they settled into the great suburbs a generation ago.

A generation ago, a young couple moving beyond the old suburbs was pioneering in more ways than one. Not only was it moving into "the country," it was letting itself in for a long commute to the husband's job in the city — a commute that might be as much as an hour and a half in the east, an hour or so in the less densely populated parts of the nation.

But today, that problem has eased somewhat. Many large and small businesses have moved out of the cities to suburban locations. The young family today can choose among a wide range of living areas where husband and wife can both be closer to work than the commuters to the central city a generation ago. The result is a far greater number of choices in terms of housing — from remaining in the city to moving into the old suburbs or to the newer suburbs that were formed during the 1950's, to forming still newer suburbs further out on the fringes, in what has been called the exurbs.

There is good reason to believe that the latter areas may prove to be most attractive to the new families of the 1980's.

Consider: Land is still available. Homes are less expensive. Commuting is easy or tolerable. The older suburbs (and family) are close by. A young family looking for a place to put its roots today must be attracted to these opportunities.

It all fits except for one item: The greatest reason for moving into the suburbs has always been to find a good place to raise a family. And the key to that was the quality of the school system. What will make the new suburbs equally attractive?

The answer may be money. That may be a funny way to start a discussion on educational quality, but no one knows better than school officials the importance of money to a school system. Sure innovation, leadership, enthusiasm and energy can make a real difference but money always makes the job easier. And, as money becomes tighter and more difficult to raise, its availability becomes more and more of

an issue. This may well be an area where the exurbs will have a great advantage.

There can be little doubt that the forces unleashed by California's Serrano decision are going to prevail. There will continue to be court battles and appeals, but the outlines of the final decision are clear. Education is basically a state function and a child cannot be discriminated against because he happens to live in a poor school district. Equal educational opportunity means equal spending, or some form of equalization.

State legislators and state educational bureaucracies have failed to fully grapple with what equal educational opportunity really means but one obvious outcome of the current court cases is a court ordered leveling of expenditures. District A and District B will be spending approximately the same amount per child, no matter how much they are used to spending, no matter the willingness or the capability of their citizens to spend more or less. Nor should it be assumed any longer that the fine older suburbs are still willing to spend more on their schools. With a majority of their citizens no longer having school-age children, there has been a growing resistance in many of them to continued high expenditures for education.

So what does this have to do with the newer suburbs? Consider District A (old, suburban, fine educational system) and District B. District A has a program of specialists, of administrators, of small classes and has had them for a number of years. Because school population has fallen over the last few years, most of its staff is experienced and at the top of the pay scale.

District B doesn't have all that. Whether it was formerly rural or poor suburban (i.e. no industrial or commercial tax base) it had less to spend and therefore had to give up certain educational amenities. It has fewer specialists, fewer administrators, fewer teachers all around. And, because it lacks the reputation and the dollars, it probably has a somewhat younger staff.

Now equalize expenditures. District A has a huge salary budget and must cut back in order to make ends meet. District B, the new suburb, has new money available, money with which to hire specialists, administrators and even classroom teachers. Moreover, it will be hiring them at the beginning of the salary schedule, not at the top. With benefits, the difference could well amount to more than $12,000 per staff member.

Consider a school district with 250 teachers. District B might have as much as $3 million more than District A for hiring of new staff. District B, the newer suburb, may not end up with a superior educational system, but it will have the opportunity to do so.

One more factor fits into this equation. Many older suburbs have had a tradition of valuing education and teachers very highly. As a result, when educational unionism began to gather strength, these districts often were the first to negotiate contracts with their friends, the teachers. And the early contracts were often designed mainly to define and protect the role of the teachers.

On the other hand, the rural districts held back. They weren't smart enough or modern enough to rush out and negotiate with their teachers. They preferred the old paternalism as long as it could last, and it lasted long enough to let them see the true consequences of collective bargaining with teachers. As a result, they are now moving into negotiations but they are moving with an entirely different attitude and understanding.

Their contracts tend to be shorter, less restrictive and to cover far fewer areas of administration of education. Whether these districts will use this freedom wisely to build outstanding educational systems is yet to be seen. But at least the opportunity is there. The older suburbs may not have that chance.

Where does all this lead? The picture seems clear, though it could still be clouded by events not taken into account.

There is going to be a baby boomlet over the next decade.

The parents will be seeking "good places" to raise their families and may well find them in the less expensive circle of communities that surround the traditional suburbs, especially if they are within easy commuting distance of industries.

And these districts may well be able to respond to the new residents with more flexibility than their older, more tradition and contract-bound neighbors. Equalization of funds plus less restrictive labor contracts are the ingredients that make this possible.

This script may be flawed in a number of areas. Tradition dies hard and educational excellence does not come from available money alone.

The traditional suburbs are still very attractive. But in terms of planning, if I were working in an exurban school district today, I would plan now for a probable baby boomlet starting relatively soon. All the signs indicate that that's where the action will be.

5

MARGIN OF EXCELLENCE: PRIVATE MONEY FOR PUBLIC SCHOOLS

Jerold Panas

Don't say it can't be done. And don't think it is out of the question for your district. The fact is that private donations for public schools may well be an idea whose time has come. In this provocative chapter, Mr. Panas tells why.

Mr. Panas is president of Jerold Panas & Partners, Inc., a large national fund raising firm with a good deal of experience in both the private and public sectors. In addition to development planning and campaign management, Mr. Panas specializes in institutional public relations and focus cultivation. His office is at 2504 Pacific Ave., San Francisco, CA 94115.

When budget cuts and the infamous Proposition 13 forced the community of Woodside, CA, to consider dropping two teachers from its elementary school payroll, parents took action.

They organized WRITE — Woodside Residents Involved in Tomorrow's Education — and set out to raise $60,000, to pay the teachers' salaries and, while they were at it, to settle the school system's $10,000 deficit.

In mid-June 1980, they sent out letters to everyone in town, asking for cash donations and pledges. They held a "county fair," complete with cotton candy and speeches from the grandstand. The Lions Club put on a pancake breakfast. Everybody came. By the time school reopened in the fall, the community had reached its goal.

What happened in Woodside represents one way in which school systems in isolated pockets all around the country are starting to turn to private sources to supplement their public school funding.

Not too many years ago, such an idea was unthinkable. The separation of private and public money was as sacred as that of church and state. American public schools received their support from taxes — local, state, and federal — and the suggestions of any other source somehow smacked of subversion.

But the ravages of inflation, smaller taxpayer pocketbooks, new laws that equalize funding distribution, and declining school enrollments are now forcing communities to reconsider.

Not too many years ago, the general public was so eager to provide high quality education that tax funds were readily available. A good public school system in the community was a symbol of status. Then taxpayers began to revolt, and although the pendulum may once again swing back toward widespread support of bond issues and school referenda, it is not likely ever again to swing all the way.

From now on, school districts can expect a greater challenge from the public as to how much money goes into the schools, and a deeper inquiry as to how that money is spent. It only makes practical good sense for school districts to begin considering private sources for some selective funding. The new concept could secure the margin of excellence for our children's future.

And why shouldn't public school districts turn to private sources for funding? Private schools and universities have always relied on alumni, parents, grandparents, corporations, and foundations for assistance. Public colleges and universities have done the same. And with great and growing success.

Public schools at the elementary and secondary level have traditionally sought some private gifts, but they have always kept their sights low, and they have tended to fund only limited, extra-curricular activities in this way. "Booster" clubs raise money for football shoulder pads and locker room benches. The local PTAs hold bake sales and raffles, but, again, only for "extras," and only on a small scale.

But the potential for significant, major gifts is there, if schools will only take advantage of it. Today, when the need for private support is greater than ever, school districts have every reason to feel that they can be successful in this new and exciting venture. Most of the schools that are meeting with success in private solicitation are using techniques previously untried in public schools. But a few are reaching major goals through the most traditional methods. The PTA of the Punahou School in Honolulu, HI, raised $360,000 in 1980 through a familiar vehicle: the annual school carnival. And in 1979, the Punahou School Thrift Shop brought in $24,700. Punahou is a private school but this same type of activity could have been as easily sponsored in any public school anywhere in the nation. What is required is a dedicated sponsoring group, a base of community support, some creative thinking, and plenty of hard work. Cultivation is the key. Just as private schools and universities have always kept track of their alumni, and have always encouraged emotional ties, public school districts must begin building and cultivating resources for support.

The length and difficulty of this process depends in large measure on the existing makeup of the community. Some cities and towns have never lost their commitment to

public education. Beverly Hills, CA, for example, prides itself on the quality of its
public schools. According to Mrs. Mary
Courtney, President of the Beverly Hills
Education Foundation board, real estate
agents in town use the school district as a
selling point.

"My family came to Beverly Hills 17
years ago specifically because of the
schools," she says. And she has witnessed
the ease with which the town has organized its foundation and raised $500,000 in
fiscal 1980 alone.

Admittedly, the success of this program
has had a lot to do with the income level of
the community's residents. While Mrs.
Courtney maintains that Beverly Hills has
a surprisingly large population of middle
income working families, many with
single parents, no one is likely to argue
that a majority of the town's residents can
well afford to make sizeable donations to
the schools. Still, no one queues up to make
a donation — no matter how wealthy. It
takes proper interpretation, a good sound
plan, creative cultivation, and plenty of
tenacity and patience.

But what about Averagetown, USA?
And what about districts that are frankly
struggling? Are private fund raising programs only for the affluent areas? The evidence is not yet in. But, while private fund
raising may not work for every community
in America, chances are that more school
districts can succeed in this field than
have yet tried.

Especially in communities where a single industry dominates, opportunities for
funding undoubtedly exist in the form of
corporate support. And almost every town
has an "old guard," with its inherent pride
in town and its sense of social responsibility. In many cases, "old money" families
have set up philanthropic foundations of
their own, which the public schools can
tap. Even in areas where funds will always
be limited, a broader base of private support is possible. Cultivation is the key.

In school districts throughout North
Carolina, for example, corporate execu-
tives and factory workers alike are tutoring individual children in reading, under a
volunteer program called Adopt-A-School.
Similarly, in Seattle, WA, a program called

PIPE (Private Initiatives for Public Education) links the resources and personnel
of major corporations with local high
schools. Project HOST (Help Our Students
to Read) establishes the same kind of link-
age in Vancouver, WA. In Stamford, CT,
the Rogers School Community Center Organization broadens the use of school
buildings for after-school education for all
ages. While none of these programs has
started out as a means of garnering support for the school budget, each of them
has resulted in a stronger sense of "ownership" of the schools by members of the
community who have taken part. And the
eagerness with which even the largest corporations have gotten involved is a measure of the great interest which exists. Financial support and involvement is certain
to follow if school districts will seek it.

"In the past," says Ilene Adams, director
of the Rogers School program in Stamford,
"when we talked about a school bond issue,
it was mostly parents who responded. Now,
since we have everyone in town going to
school — from age 3 to 83 — we find that
we see a much stronger sense of identification with the school system and its needs."

Although none of these school systems
has tackled a private fund raising campaign yet, the likelihood of support for
such a venture is growing as the community involvement grows. Programs that increase community participation, then, are
an important first step toward private financial support as well.

And the need for such support is indeed
growing all over the country. "Our tax
base has never seemed burdensome, so we
haven't had the backlash," says Charles
Petty, executive director of the North
Carolina Governor's Office of Citizen Affairs, which sponsors the Adopt-A-School
program. "But," he adds, in a prophetic
vein, "next year, I think we're looking at
very different times."

The time, then, to start cultivating community support and acceptance of the idea
of private funding, is now. Waiting for a
funding crisis may be too late.

Volunteer programs such as the ones
mentioned here rely on private sources —
usually a foundation or corporation — for
seed money. School districts may also turn

to private sources to set up a fund raising organization. While volunteers may provide the manpower and the materials, some need money for a paid, professional fund raiser and for communications materials can make the difference between a marginal success and an inspiring one. Consider, then, seeking one major donation before you even start.

Now that a number of school systems have succeeded in raising large sums of private money, other districts can look to them for guidance. The experiences of these pioneer fund raisers is as varied as their demographics, but some patterns for success are emerging.

Most of the schools that have launched private fund raising programs have not tried to add anything to the existing program or curriculum. Organizers have acted simply to maintain the present standard of education. And they have been careful to interpret it that way to prospective donors. They make it clear that the school district is not looking to add frills. This seems to be an important consideration for supporters.

But there is no reason to believe that private funding cannot be used to develop exciting new programs as well. Many individual philanthropists, public-spirited corporations, and foundations have special interests that the schools should target. In one Chicago suburb, for example, a major foundation helped make certain that local high school students were introduced to the whole major field of Creative Thinking. Funds from the foundation allowed the high school administration to develop a program within the existing curriculum to encourage creative thinking. Thanks to organizers who dared to aim high, this school now provides its students with that special margin of excellence that can mean the difference between a good education and a great one.

Most of the school districts that are tackling private solicitation for the first time are relying on the techniques which other non-profit organizations have found most successful. Local hospitals, colleges, YMCAs, and others have been raising funds for years — why not public schools, using the same techniques. As a matter of fact, the "case" for raising funds for public education is as compelling and dramatic as any organization could hope for.

Most school districts have made their first contact with donors through a carefully drafted letter stating the needs of the district and the benefits to the donor. The letter often mentions the high cost of private education, and the "bargain" available through public schools. It usually reminds members of the chamber of commerce that industries are attracted to towns with good school systems. It often urges real estate agents to consider the benefits to them, and appeals to homeowners' concern for property values. Sometimes the letter mentions the link between poor schools and high crime rates. And, in all cases, the initial letter goes to everyone in the community, not just to parents. Good schools are for all of us, not just for families with children.

It is always good policy to remind prospective donors of the tax advantages of giving. And, especially in cases where the funds will be used for a specific, pre-determined project, the initial letter might suggest a suitable dollar amount. The WRITE committee in Woodside, for instance, told potential donors that if each family in town gave $350, the total would add up to the amount needed for two teachers' salaries and the district deficit. As it turned out, some gave more, some less, but 80 per cent gave something, and the committee reached its goal.

Standard fund raising practice recommends a follow-up phone call after the first letter, and perhaps a second letter later on, as a reminding nudge. Of course a thank you letter goes without saying.

Obviously, a letter will not suffice for major donors. If you are approaching the chief executive officer of a major business, or a wealthy individual philanthropist, set up a private meeting in a comfortable setting, and send your most articulate spokespersons to tell the school's story and outline the benefits to the donor. The larger the amount you are seeking, the more visits you will probably have to make. But, remember that you can expend just as much energy seeking a small donation as you can for a much larger one, so set your sights high, and never forget that your cause is as worthwhile as any in America today. Enthusiasm is infectious, and it can make all the difference in securing a major gift.

If you do use the mail for gathering support, try to find a local printer and a paper supplier to donate services and materials. If you are planning a long-range, full-scale effort, approach a local graphic artist to design a logo and letterhead. These services are tax-deductible for those who provide them.

The single most common difference among the fund raising programs that have taken place so far lies in the legal relationship between the program and the school district itself. In Ross, CA, the school board appointed a committee of local residents to compose a letter to donors and to make followup phone calls. The $89,000 raised in 1980 went into the general fund of the county education office and the school board retained the right to determine how the funds would be spent.

In Carmel, CA, on the other hand, concerned residents set up an independent charitable organization which works closely with the school administration and board, but earmarks the funds it raises for specific purposes.

"We felt that if we gave the money directly to the school district, it would mingle with the general fund and get lost," says Richard Falge, a Carmel businessman who helped form FOCUS (Friends of the Carmel Unified School District).

"This way," he explains, "we keep our individual donors happy because we can tell them exactly how their gift was spent."

A third possibility is something of a combination of the other two. The Beverly Hills Education Foundation is a separate legal foundation, but all funds are turned over to the district, and the board of education offers guidance in the spending. The foundation board does stipulate that donations will not go toward teacher salaries in this particular situation.

The size of the school district will influence the structure of the organization and its methods. Where all the funds will benefit one small elementary school, as in Woodside, it is easy to keep track of where money is going. Organizers in Beverly Hills were careful to stipulate that donations would be spread equitably among the elementary schools and the one high school.

The make-up of the program's governing body will also vary according to the size and personality of the community, and the complexity of the fund raising effort. The Beverly Hills foundation board includes five representatives from each of the schools, plus 10 at-large members, for a total of 30 members. In the smaller districts, such as Ross and Woodside, the number is much smaller.

Regardless of the number on the board or committee, each individual should be carefully selected, not only on the basis of commitment to the schools, but also for his or her influence in the community. A "blue-ribbon" committee, made up of people who are in a position to make and affect contributions themselves, can go a long way toward boosting the credibility of the program and toward encouraging others to give. An excellent general rule is to include people on the committee who can "give or get" money.

Money raised from private sources can go toward the basics — from textbooks to teachers' salaries — or it can make possible an otherwise unaffordable program, such as remedial reading. While state laws generally forbid the use of public funds for promoting a school bond issue or referendum, funds raised privately and which go into an independent foundation could buy advertising time or print flyers urging voters to support the measure.

Private funds could also be used to launch or augment a scholarship program. The experience of one lucky school district stands out so distinctly from all the others that its story deserves telling, if only for the inspiration it offers. In 1947, Joseph Emory Sirrine, a prominent textile engineer in Greenville, SC, died, leaving the bulk of his sizeable estate in trust to his brother and niece. But Mr. Sirrine had foresight to stipulate that, if both of his beneficiaries died childless, the trust would revert to a scholarship fund for deserving students of the local city schools.

When the last of Mr. Sirrine's beneficiaries died in 1971, a friendly court settlement allowed the funds to be used by all the county schools, which by now had consolidated with the city district. Since 1973, more than 1,200 graduating seniors have received a total of more than $2.5 million. The trust still holds a sizeable sum, and school officials say that declining enrollment has actually made it difficult to find enough qualified recipients. But nobody in Greenville is complaining.

The unfortunate part of this story is that it is apparently unique. Greenville residents say they have never known of another town in America where a single businessman had the insight to make such a generous bequest. And yet the possibility is there. Other school districts should encourage people of means to include the school in their wills.

A study conducted by one major university revealed that the majority of individuals who include a gift to the university in their will are not people who have any particular connection to the university. They are simply people who want to develop their estate planning in a way that will most influence the future. People leave money to colleges, to hospitals and to other similar institutions so that their money will have an impact on the world after they are gone. What a perfect selling point for public schools seeking funds! A bequest to the public schools will train young minds, mold personalities, develop character, and ensure a strong future for the community — for generations to come.

Gifts through private estate planning need not always come from the very wealthy. Significant gifts can also come from an unexpected but understandable source: teachers. School teachers are careful with their money; they save it. And they have a built in belief in public education. College professors often leave gifts in their wills to the schools where they have dedicated their lives. Public school teachers can be encouraged to do the same. And remember, too, that many school teachers marry into wealthy families with a strong potential for giving.

At times private foundations and the public can work together. In a San Diego,

CA suburb, for example, a private foundation provided sufficient funds to build an auditorium for the local high school. Funding for the addition had already been turned down three times in voter referenda. The new auditorium was designed for use not only by the high school but by the rest of the community as well. This major show of private support so inspired the community that residents responded by raising enough money among themselves to provide important missing equipment and to put the finishing touches on the building.

The opportunities for private support of public schools are limitless, but the process takes planning and commitment. A fund raising program is only as strong as its volunteers. A good lawyer and an accountant should be part of the team. And at least one person with a knowledge of public relations techniques should be in on the ground floor. Large districts with a wide range of needs should consider hiring a professional fund raiser to ensure that the job is done properly and effectively. At the very least, they should study the material available on fund raising practices. Tried and true tips do exist, and they work. Get a copy of the pamphlet *Fund Raising by Parent/Citizen Groups* published by the National Committee for Citizens in Education in Columbia, MD. It can get you started. Or write to the publisher of this book for a copy of "The Ten Vital Questions," a listing of questions which need to be answered before launching a fund raising program. Check the public library for other books or articles that can keep you from spinning your wheels or making irreparable mistakes.

It looks as if private fund raising is fast turning into a permanent fixture on the American educational landscape. Those schools which take advantage of the opportunities, and begin cultivating their donors now, will find it easier to cope when a real crisis in funding comes along, if it hasn't already.

"None of us wished that we would have to do this," says Mrs. Barbara Menta, one of the prime organizers of WRITE, the Woodside, CA committee.

"Personally," she adds, "I hate to see this as an on-going way to support the schools. Still, it is gratifying to see that when we have a problem, families will step forward to help."

Importantly, raising funds for public education should not be seen only as a method of alleviating a crisis or a problem situation. That would be reason enough. There are other circumstances, however, where the infusion of private funds — even though relatively small — could provide the necessary incentive to tackle a new program, to probe an exciting new concept, to expand an existing activity but with a new innovative twist and turn. Private funds put into these types of developmental projects could prove to be of consequential proportions to the public school. In some situations, this type of private funding could indeed provide the added margin of excellence.

6

HOW TO PUT TOGETHER A FIVE-YEAR PLAN

John R. Andrisek, Ph.D.

Don't be without one; that is the advice that Superintendent Andrisek offers his colleagues. In this chapter, he tells how to put a five-year plan together that links the things you need to accomplish in schools with the money you will have.

Dr. Andrisek is superintendent of Berea (Ohio) City Schools and a frequent lecturer and writer on school administration.

Articles, letters, and even editorials in the media increasingly question the managerial skills of school administrators. So do citizens. Unfortunately, there are enough examples of poor management to *foster* this concern. When a school system is cited for poor management practices, all other school systems and administrators in the immediate area tend to be painted with the same brush.

Emerging from these citizens' concerns is a demand for long-range planning. The public concern is justified. Too few school administrators prepare coordinated and comprehensive long-range plans because most of the planning models are very complex and require large staffs to carry out the process. In this chapter a simple planning process will be presented. It can be used in a small or large district by varying the number of people involved.

A long-range plan can be as comprehensive as the superintendent and his staff desire. But, all plans should include the following basic elements: (1) enrollment projections, (2) financial projections, (3) staffing levels, (4) new initiatives in programs, and (5) the foundation for all decisions, the philosophy of the school district. The planning period should be at least three but, preferably, five years. The Table of Contents of *Five-Year Plan 1980-1984* for the Berea City Schools at the end of this chapter illustrates the elements included in our plan.

Since planning is essentially a management function, the superintendent is the key individual in this process. He must initiate the effort and see that the plan is developed. He has to be sure that the objectives of the plan are accomplished. Without strong leadership from the "head man," no workable long-range plan can be developed.

OUTLINE OF PLANNING PROCESS

The first step in the process is to make some assumptions about the future. From the assumptions, the planning issues (or future problems), are identified. Specific goals are then established, based upon the priorities of the school system and its financial ability to support the objectives.

After a time schedule is set, the plan can be implemented. The plan may be modified at any time. Note that Figure 1 indicates both a semi-annual and an annual status report. This procedure generates a rolling plan, and each year a new plan is generated for the succeeding three, four or five years.

USE OF THE PROCESS

The critical first step in the preparation of a long-range plan begins with the development of a "future scenario." This statement contains the superintendent's best estimate of what will happen during the next few years in such areas as legislation, state aid for education, collective bargaining, court decisions, and community attitudes. Excerpts from the scenario of the Berea City School District "Five-Year Plan" illustrate estimates of the future:

> "The shortage of energy will be an even more difficult problem in the future. Prices will rise and there will be crises. . . ."
>
> "Citizens will expect the schools to improve, to innovate . . . while at the same time they will demand more strict discipline and rigid rules. . . ."
>
> "Minimum competency testing will be in general use in Ohio and the nation."
>
> "The demand of school leadership will require a continual upgrading of specific skills — in psychology, social psychology, human relations, management systems. . . ."
>
> "Schools will be expected to develop methods to control the quality of the learning experiences at every grade level. The emphasis will be on the quality of the product rather than the process."

No one can predict the future with complete accuracy, but intelligent estimates of what *may* happen enable the administrator to prepare and plan so that rational decision-making can replace crisis management.

From the future assumptions, the superintendent and his staff identify potential planning issues or problems. The problems are organized by relative priority.

The highest-priority planning issues are then translated into specific objectives, and a time schedule for accomplishing them is prepared if there are adequate human, material and financial resources available. At this stage the superintendent must assign specific responsibilities for accomplishing the various objectives. In a very small school system the superintendent will be responsible for achieving the stated objectives. In larger systems, the responsibility is usually delegated. Regardless of the size of the school system, the superintendent needs to constantly monitor the plan to insure that the objectives are still appropriate and that the tasks are being accomplished.

Once the process begins, developing the plan for the succeeding year is less difficult. It seems to flow naturally from what occurred during the previous year.

When a superintendent decides to plan systematically, he has to make one more decision: Who else should be involved? This is not an easy question to answer. One way to proceed is described below.

In the Berea City School District, at the onset of the planning process, I formed a working group called The Planning Team. The team was, and is, made up of individuals from all levels of the administration. Each member serves for three years, and the terms are staggered. The planning team meets regularly during each school year. This group reviews and criticizes my future scenarios before all of the administrative team, including the board of education, has the opportunity to make suggestions.

When the scenario was finished, approximately 60 administrators plus the board members were divided into small groups (6-8). Each group had a mix of job assignments. The groups identified future planning issues, or problems, using the scenario as the source document. They ranked these problems from the most to the least important. The small-group work was followed by a general reporting session. Surprisingly, there was substantial agree-

OUTLINE OF PLANNING PROCESS

The planning process is illustrated in Figure 1.

Figure 1

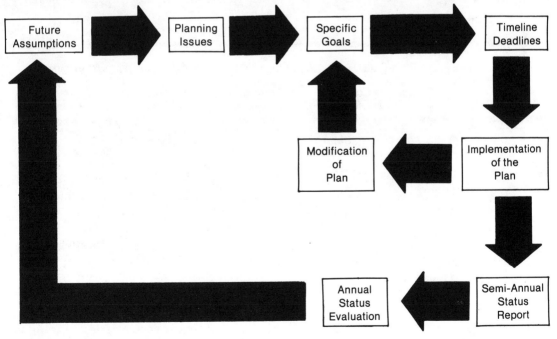

ment on the top 15 planning issues. In some of the subsequent years, there was less agreement on the top priority planning issues. On those occasions we had each administrator rank the identified issues. A composite ranking was prepared. This gave an organizational "sense" of the relative priorities. The planning team used this information to determine the critical problems on which to work.

The 15 problems were reviewed by the planning team, which determined that sufficient resources were available to attack 12 of the 15 problems. These 12 problems were translated into goal statements and a time schedule was set for accomplishing the tasks. Finally, the entire plan was submitted to the board of education for their consideration and approval.

The above process illustrates the importance of an on-going working group (planning team). The team gives a school system continuity and administrative skill when preparing a long-range plan.

DEVELOPING OF AN OBJECTIVE

An example of how one top-priority planning issue was handled in our school district will help clarify the process. The issue was related to concerns about the scope and sequence of the K-12 curriculum. This problem emerged from an analysis of the future scenario by the members of the administration. The problem evolved from the following assumptions:

> "Community expectations for their schools will become even more paradoxical. Citizens will expect schools to improve, to innovate and to individualize the learning experiences for students while, at the same time, they will demand stricter discipline and rigid rules. Furthermore, they will want both of these worlds without paying more taxes.
>
> "The community will continue to press for emphasis on the basic skills. . .
>
> "Reading will be even more important than it is today. There will be pressure to require a minimal reading level in order to graduate from high school.
>
> "Schools will be expected to develop methods to control the quality of the learning experiences at every grade level."

In addition to the assumptions above, there were concerns expressed by parents, teachers, and administrators that the K-12 curriculum needed to be clearly described and articulated. Also, a potential for unplanned duplication or omission of desired learning skills or concepts existed in some areas of the curriculum.

On the basis of the assumptions about the future and the existing concerns about

CURRICULUM REVIEW, IMPLEMENTATION EVALUATION AND MAINTENANCE VIEWPOINT

| Year | Estimated Cost | | Estimated Percent of Curriculum | To Be Reviewed |
	Review	Implement. /Maint.		
1976-1977	$120M	$30M	25	Mathematics; Written Communications
1977-1978	$100M	$75M	25	Reading; Literature
1978-1979	$ 80M	$60M	20	Citizenship; Social Studies
1979-1980	$ 70M	$50M	15	Music; Health and Physical Education; Driver Education; Science
1980-1981	$ 70M	$45M	15	Art; Foreign Language; Special Education; Career and Occupational Development (includes Business Education; Home Economics; Industrial Arts)

present K-12 curriculum, we decided that a comprehensive review of all areas of the curriculum, K-12, was a high-priority issue.

The specific objective developed by the planning team was:

> "Conduct a Program of Curriculum Review, Implementation, Evaluation and Maintenance in Accordance With the Following Schedule."

Not only did we prepare a schedule of curricular areas to be reviewed, but also we projected the estimated costs to do the job. This cost projection illustrates the importance of comprehensive programs and financial planning. Without the financial resources, we would have had to modify this objective.

The magnitude and significance of this curriculum review project can probably be better understood in the context of this school district. In the 1979-80 year, the Berea City Schools had 11,895 students enrolled, an operating budget of about $24,000,000, and a per-pupil expenditure of $2,200. Sufficient funds were available in each year of the review cycle to achieve the stated objective.

With the financial resources as well as the support of the Board of Education and the staff, it was possible to select and assign eight teachers to full-time curriculum writing during the 1976-77 school year as well as provide the best consultants in the country and necessary clerical and material resources. This team was under the supervision of an associate superintendent. It was anticipated that smaller teams and less time would be needed in succeeding years because of the areas of the curriculum to be reviewed and the knowledge gained the first year. This assumption proved to be correct. For similar reasons it was anticipated that the cost of implementation — instructional materials, supervision, printing — would decrease in subsequent years. Most of the in-service training was planned as part of our regular Staff Development Program.

One of the purposes of long-range planning is to allocate the available resources to accomplish the priority tasks. If there had been insufficient funds to accomplish the curriculum review objective, we would

have had to make some adjustments. For example, if only fifty percent of the needed dollars were projected to be available each year, the cycle could have been extended for more than five years, or certain "less critical" areas of the curriculum could have been excluded. The implementation schedule also could have been changed or extended. There are many options, and careful long-range planning allows school leaders time to select the best alternatives for their situation.

It is possible that a school system may have the desire and need to carry on a total curriculum review project, but have very little money or people available to do the job. In such a situation, a more limited objective which deals with the areas of greatest concern may be appropriate. Careful long-range planning is even more critical where funds were limited.

The objective also included a procedural outline:

> Comments with reference to *specific actions* and *assignments* required to implement *Objective Number Three — Curriculum Review, Implementation, Evaluation and Maintenance:*
>
> Generally, the following procedure will be followed for each area under review:
>
> 1. Conduct an extensive needs assessment to determine the present ("real") curriculum situation in the area under review.
>
> 2. Develop the "ideal" state for the areas under review based on research, study and assessed needs of students in the District.
>
> 3. Recommend alternatives for improvement of the curricular program K-12 based on an analysis of needs assessment data.
>
> 4. Develop a comprehensive K-12 scope and sequence continuum for the area under review.
>
> 5. Secure approval for specific changes in curriculum.
>
> 6. Recommend staff development needs in order to achieve the recommended changes in curriculum.
>
> 7. Recommend a specific program for implementing, evaluating, and maintaining the changes.
>
> 8. Develop a process for evaluating the changes.

I delegated the responsibility for this project to the associate superintendent for instruction. He and I determined the individuals who would be assigned to work on the mathematics and written communication phase of the project. We also set deadlines for various steps in the project:

The implementation of the Mathematics and Written Communication Curriculum began in the 1977-1978 school year under the supervision of the director of curriculum development. This process started with a large staff development program in August of 1977. In addition, during the school year there were many staff meetings in all of the schools as well as released-time training sessions for teachers. The director of curriculum development was required to report to me and the associate superintendent monthly on the progress being made. In addition, we asked principals to report on the use of the new programs in their classroom observation summaries. The following observation report illustrates how a principal reported that the metric system, which is an element of our math program, was being taught in a second-grade class:

BEREA CITY SCHOOL DISTRICT

Teacher Observation Report

Teacher   *Grade Two*   *May 25, 1978*
Mathematics   *1:45 — 2:15 p.m.*

"This lesson involves the entire class which consists of thirty-one students (fifteen boys and sixteen girls). The students are heterogeneously grouped and are involved in our primary team which includes extensive instruction aide assistance.

*   *   *

"Prior to this lesson students had completed a metric booklet dealing with metrics which included teacher directed activities and independent activities. Each student had also received a resource booklet for terminology dealing with metrics. A metric fold had been constructed to keep their papers on file. The objective for this lesson was organized as follows:

1. *Students were asked to match the prefix terms used with meters with their abbreviations and their value.*

2. *Each child received a pre-designed card of different size stickers that they attempted to estimate its dimension.*

3. *During this phase each student received an envelope containing precut colored cardboard. These pieces were then measured and the answers rewarded.*

4. *The final activity required the students to circle the most sensible answer.*

"The students were well behaved throughout the lesson. They appeared enthusiastic, cooperative and quite responsible. There wasn't any significant off-task behavior during the lesson.

"This lesson was extremely well organized and sequenced into a consistent format. The various teacher-made materials were quite well done and added significantly to the lesson. The extensive student involvement and the way the lesson was sequenced made it a model lesson.

"Some of the highlights of the lesson included: Prepared cards with each metric measurement, a packet of colored pieces of paper for estimation of size in metric measurement."

AN UNPLANNED OUTCOME

As we began using the new program in mathematics and written communication in the 1977-1978 school year, we recognized a need for a more systematic process of monitoring the effects of the program. With the help of Dr. Thomas Romberg, University of Wisconsin, we developed a procedure which we believe will make it possible to determine the degree to which the new curriculum is being used in the classrooms, the impact on the students and, finally, the student outcomes. The following diagram illustrates the design. This process is still in the trial stage, but I think it has great potential for providing more precise evaluation of any curricular program. Our major challenge is to make this tool useable by building principals. The initial trials have made us optimistic.

A PLANNED OUTCOME

Of course, there have been many results we have anticipated as a product of long-range planning. One of these is a clear systematic goal for achieving staffing levels as the enrollment declines. The goal includes all categories of employees, but the group most directly affected is the teaching staff.

SYSTEMATIC MONITORING PROGRAM

Design Overview

I. WHAT IS THE RELATED BACKGROUND INFORMATION AVAILABLE?

Related Information

1. Pupil Characteristics
2. Teacher Characteristics
3. Social Environment

II. HOW ARE THE PROGRAMS BEING USED?

Teacher Actions

Preliminary

1. Planning
   - Daily
   - Long-range
2. Knowledge of Program

Direct

3. Student Role in Learning
   - Structuring
   - Feedback
   - Motivation
   - Peer Relations

III. WHAT DATA DESCRIBES LEARNING?

Pupil Actions

1. Allocated Time
2. Engaged Time
3. Quality/Appropriateness of Instruction
   - Appropriateness of Activities
   - Effectivess of Activities

IV. HOW WELL ARE STUDENTS ACHIEVING?

Pupil Outcomes

1. Achievement: Knowledge and Skills
2. Attitudes

1. What changes and future goals are needed?

When we first included this goal in the plan, we anticipated a strong negative reaction from our staff. This did not happen. The people did not like what they saw, but they understood the reduced need for staff as the enrollment declined, and the fact that they could see what the future would probably bring allowed those vulnerable to make alternate plans. This reduced tension. In addition, we prepared a fair and equitable process for achieving the staff reduction which was understood and accepted by all employees.

The planning for staff reduction also resulted in a stable financial picture. By managing the expenditures prudently and keeping the work force at a level related to the enrollment, we have had the funds to undertake such major initiations as the curriculum review described in the previous section.

The following staffing level projections indicate how we view our future needs as well as what happened during the past five years.

COMMUNICATING THE PLAN

For each of the other objectives in the *Five-Year Plan,* a similar procedure as described above, was followed so that it was possible to make a precise progress report to the Board of Education and to the community.

The entire plan, including the objectives, the scenario and the various projections, should be printed in sufficient numbers for wide distribution in the school district. The ability to accomplish the goals of the plan depends upon support of the school community. Therefore, the people need to know about the plan.

INSTRUCTIONAL STAFFING LEVELS VIEWPOINT

					Special Certified Personnel				
Actual	ADM[1]	Regular[2] Certified Personnel	Rate/ 1,000	Title I DPP	Pupil[3] Pers.	Non-[4] Public	Sp. Ed.[5]	Sp. Ed. Students	No. of FTE[6] El. Lib. & Ed. Aids
1975	14,486	705	46.9	7	10		18	242	86
1976	13,495	667	49.4	7	10		19	225	82
1977	12,782	632.95	49.5	6	10	6	19	236	80.62
1978	11,932	584.3	48.97	9	10	7	22	316	77.22
1979	11,174	557.47	49.9	9	11	7	26	321	70.39
Plan									
1980	10,540	527-559	50-53	9	11	8	30	345	65-70
1981	10,000	500-530	50-53	9	11	8	30	350	60-65
1982	9,257	463-500	50-54	9	11	8	30	340	56-60
1983	8,701	435-470	50-54	9	11	8	30	330	52-60
1984	8,205	410-443	50-54	9	11	8	30	320	49-53

Notes

1. ADM — Average daily membership less children assigned to District special education classes.

2. Regular Certified Personnel — Includes classroom teachers, music, physical education teachers, secondary librarians, counselors, in-car driving teachers.

3. Pupil Personnel Staff — includes psychologists, speech and hearing therapists.

4. Non-Public Staff — Includes mobile van teachers and pupil personnel staff assigned to non-public schools.

5. Special Education Staff — includes EMR, LD, SBD, EH class teachers, TAG teachers

6. FTE — Full-time equivalents (7 hrs., 15 minutes equal to full time); excludes aides for non-public schools.

Involvement of people is the key to communication. Again, the superintendent is the critical catalyst in the process. His presentation of the plan to the board, to the PTA, to service clubs, to staff and to other community groups develops public confidence that there is sound management of their schools. In addition, he alerts the public to future needs and actions. The community is given an opportunity to react.

Along with personal contacts, the usual school-community publications should highlight the plan. Hopefully, local newspapers will find such an effort newsworthy. There is a never-ending need to let the citizens know the school system is managed in an exemplary way.

ADMINISTRATIVE, AND SECRETARIES AND CLERKS SUMMARY VIEWPOINT

Actual	Bldg. Admin.	Central* Admin.	All Admin.	Secretaries** Clerks
1975	40	21	61	76
1976	38	21	59	75
1977	34	21	55	73.8
1978	33	21	54	70.64
1979	33	21	54	71.4
Plan				
1980	30-35	19-23	49-58	62-70
1981	29-34	19-23	48-57	57-67
1982	28-33	18-22	46-55	53-64
1983	27-32	17-21	44-53	51-62
1984	26-31	16-20	42-51	50-61

*Includes Superintendent, Associate Superintendents, Directors, Administrative Assistant, Instructional Consultants, Treasurer, Athletic Director, Supervisors, Coordinator of Adult Education, Pupil Personnel Assistant (prior to 1979), Data Processing Manager.

**Includes all secretaries, bookkeepers, machines room operator, C. O. E. Students, and Data Processing Assistant.

SUPPORT SERVICES STAFFING LEVELS VIEWPOINT

(Full-Time Equivalents)*

Actual	Custodial Staff	Maintenance Staff	Transportation Staff	Food Service Staff
1975	106	20	38	61
1976	106	20	41	56
1977	96	20	41	54
1978	93.68	21	39.67	50.39
1979	93.13	21	39.86**	53.66
Plan				
1980	91-93	19-21	39-40	48-51
1981	90-92	19-21	38-39	47-50
1982	88-91	19-21	37-39	46-50
1983	87-90	19-21	37-39	45-49
1985	86-89	19-21	36-38	44-48

*Full-Time Equivalent is 8 Hours.

**Includes 14.5 full-time-equivalent drivers for special education and non-public school transportation in 1979-1980.

LONG-RANGE PLANNING AND THE BOARD OF EDUCATION

The understanding and participation of the board of education is critical to the entire planning process. They have to believe it is an important function of the superintendent, and they also have to be willing to spend time helping identify the planning problems and setting the priorities. However, the actual development of the plan is a management responsibility with the Board reviewing the final product.

Ideally, the initiative for long-range planning should come from the superintendent. But, if this does not happen, the board of education can initiate the process by asking their chief executive some very critical questions:

1. What is the financial picture for the next five years? — The best and the worst scenario?

2. What are the enrollment projections for the next five to ten years?

3. Has the administration projected the personnel needs for the next five years?

4. What are the five most critical problems facing this school district in the next five years?

5. What plans have been made to deal with these problems?

If the board asks the superintendent these questions, he or she will have to do some planning to provide the answers. Furthermore, the questions should alert the superintendent that the Board is interested in long-range planning.

Members of the board should be interested in evaluating the efficacy of a long-range plan, also. This can be done in a variety of ways. One test is whether the plan considers the problems the board and the community have identified (formally and informally). Another way to evaluate the plan is whether it plots a direction toward financial stability.

A plan should also reduce crisis management by making decisions early enough to have a real impact on the future direction of the school system. The check list below may be helpful to board members and superintendents who want to evaluate their planning procedure:

PLANNING CHECK LIST

	Yes	No	?
1. Does the administration make assumptions about what may happen in the future?	___	___	___
2. Does the administration make long-range financial projections (five or more years)?	___	___	___
3. Do the board, administration and citizens identify potential problems which may impact the schools in the future?	___	___	___
4. Does the administration make enrollment projections for five or more years?	___	___	___
5. Does the planning process include program, staffing, and students' needs as well as finance?	___	___	___
6. Does the planning process include a way to modify the plan if circumstances change?	___	___	___
7. Does the planning process include both semiannual and annual status reports?	___	___	___
8. Is the plan printed and distributed to all concerned and interested employees and citizens?	___	___	___

If the members of the board of education can answer these questions affirmatively, chances are they have a good planning process and the superintendent is carrying out one of his major responsibilities.

The board and the superintendent must also determine the degree to which the goals in the plan are being accomplished. To do this, the superintendent should receive periodic reports from his staff about progress. These reports should, to the degree possible, contain hard data so that more than subjective judgments can be made. From this information, the superintendent can make his semiannual and annual reports to the Board.

One way we have found to keep the board informed about progress is to have the people involved in the various projects report directly at public board meetings. This has several benefits: It gives the Board members opportunities to ask questions directly to the individual's working on tasks. It also provides deserved recognition to the staff, and it is a way of communicating to the public about the system's long-range plan and the progress being made.

CONCLUSION

I have described a relatively simple planning process which is adaptable to available human and material resources, and I related how it was and is used in our school system. The depth, breadth, and complexity of any plan is dependent on the amount of help the superintendent has. But, regardless of that help, it is critical that each chief school executive plan. A *simple* plan is better than *no* plan. No superintendent should allow himself to be open to criticism because he has no long-range plan!

BIBLIOGRAPHY

California State Department of Education *Planning Handbook,* Revised Edition. Berkeley: McCutchan, 1979.

Club of Rome *No Limits to Learning: Bridging the Human Gap.* Elmsford, NY: Pergamon Press, 1979.

Drucker, Peter F. *Management: Tasks, Responsibilities, Practices.* New York: Harper and Row, 1974.

Falconer, Merry "Long-Range Planning: Strategy That Works," *Leadership.* March, 1980.

Gross, Neal and Herriott, Robert E. *The Dynamics of Planned Educational Change.* Berkeley: McCutchan, 1979.

McNamara, James F. "Trend Impact Analysis and Scenario Writing: Strategies For the Specification of Decision Alternatives In Education Planning," *The Journal of Educational Administration,* XIV, 2:143-161. October, 1976.

HOW TO JUSTIFY CENTRAL OFFICE STAFF WHEN THE CRUNCH COMES

Stanton Leggett

Everyone knows that the Central Office is the first place to cut when money gets tight. Right? Well, maybe not. Author Leggett in this chapter tells much more than how to defend headquarters staff, he also offers examples of ways to get top performance from all members of the school team — from top to bottom.

Stanton Leggett, the general editor of this book, has long been recognized as one of the nation's outstanding school consultants. He has completed hundreds of assignments for public and private schools as well as community and four-year colleges. A leading writer on educational affairs, he has written several books and many articles in the popular and professional press. He now works out of his home-office in West Tisbury, Martha's Vineyard, MA 02575.

Much of this material is drawn, in part, from a study by Stanton Leggett entitled "Management of Educational Change," an analysis and proposal to change the management pattern of the Shaker Heights School System.

When money is tight the first place that negotiating teachers' groups, board members and the community in general look for cuts is in expenditures for jobs in the administrative categories. The thoughtful manager will have anticipated this phenomenon and will have in place a rational, cost-effective central headquarters staff for which the defenses have already been erected. It will be a flat central organization because the operating principles of the system place any hierarchy or levels of positions as close to the classroom as possible. It will be defensible because the central headquarters staff will have been perceived by teachers, board members, and community as helpful rather than a hindrance to progress. It will be cost-effective because it has been planned that way.

NECESSARY CONDITIONS

The first task of management is to help teachers work, not longer or harder, but "smarter": Peter Drucker's definition of increasing productivity of "knowledge workers."[1]

Under these conditions, the school system decides what is essential in order for teachers continuously to learn how to improve instruction and designs the administrative organization to support that task.

In this process, the odds are that the full-time permanent administrative organization found at headquarters will dwindle. The action will take place at the school and the provision of rewards for teachers to do better will be the major strategy.

EXHIBIT ONE

HOW TO ENCOURAGE TEACHERS TO LEARN TO WORK SMARTER

Find Out How Much Teacher Time is Available; Plan to Use It Well

Major Block of On-Task Time →	**Use of Time of Teachers**
	Teaching 62%
	Planning 10
Marginal Time →	Homeroom 6%
	Hall Supervision 8
What can be done to improve contribution of this time to improvement of instruction? →	Meetings — During and After School 14 * 28%

Data from Hinsdale, IL, District 181

*Some of this devoted to meetings with parents and students and help for students. Not clearly defined.

Most studies of teacher motivation state that intrinsic motivation — praise, recognition, admiration of peers and the like — is what moves teachers to improve. That is probably true since the financial reward system has been taken out of education by mechanical salary schedules that recognize only years of experience and training.

The school system would do well to expand the reward system, both in terms of money and in terms of increased respect.

Money rewards

Merit plan. This is a controversial system where it is relatively easy to discriminate superior from poor teachers but it is really hard

---

Exhibit One Cont'd.

- Develop a budget for faculty time, so that each school knows how much time is available for use for improving instruction, and has effective plans for its use.
- The fact that 14 per cent of the time covers a mixture of activities suggests that there is a certain amount of confusion and slippage of time in this area.
- Why does so much time seem to be taken up by hall supervision?
- On the other hand, much worthwhile happens in informal exchange among teachers. A school should not operate like a well-run railroad. There is need for room to vary and change as occasions arise, and to develop the friendly but demanding style of the school.

A budget of teacher disposable time and carefully developed plans to use the time may be the base point for a systematic effort to improve instruction.

Work Out a Cost-Benefit Analysis for Teachers Who Are Seriously Engaged in Learning How to Do Better What is Already Done

SLEVIN'S MODEL[2]

"An individual will try new things if the probability of success of the new thing (P_n) minus the probability of success of the current strategy (P_s) is greater than the ratio of cost (c) to rewards (R).

$$P_n - P_s > C/R"$$

Strategy

- After careful and objective appraisal, and only if it is justified, maximize the probability of success.
  - Sell the change
  - Provide great demonstrations

- Have convincing research available to support the change
  - Don't get caught supporting a fashion that does not produce useful results
- Be honest about the limitations of the present approach.
  - While few miracles occur, substantial but limited improvement is possible in extending present practice to include moderate changes.
  - Don't overkill.
- Reduce the cost of the change to the individual in financial, personal, psychological and physical terms.
  - When the school or the system wants change, it should pay for it.
  - Teach the new skills as effectively as is known how. Schools should be models of adult learning. *Do* provide:
    Demonstrations, models or simulations well done
    Internship and apprenticeship
    Explicit descriptions of roles of teacher
    Opportunities to practice
    Learn small pieces, with feedback to learner on results
    Encouragement and help in process of installation of change
    Have all supplies or materials on hand before launching instruction in the change
  Don't:
    Rely on lectures
    Start out without the supplies or materials
    Fail to plan the learning experience — college courses are not a useful model
    Fail to learn from previous experience with teacher learning.
- Increase the rewards
  - Extrinsic rewards — money
  - Intrinsic rewards — status

to make decisions in the middle. Some teacher organizations accept the principle but quarrel with the process.

Extra pay for achievement of stretch objectives. It may be most appropriate to offer opportunities to teachers on a voluntary basis to earn more by contributing significantly to the goals of the school or the school system. (See Chapter 10.) The precedent is extra pay for coaching, band director, drama coach, journalism teacher and the like. Establish a wide variety of "extra" rewards, offering a choice for teachers to participate or not.

Increase the hierarchy of teaching. One approach is to have the following hierarchy:

> Aides
> Apprentice Teachers
> Regular Teachers
> Teacher-Curriculum Workers
> Teacher-Teacher Trainers
> Teacher-Clinical Supervisors

Such a hierarchy could well involve a series of levels of pay until the schedule for regular teacher was reached. Levels beyond regular teacher would mean more pay for the assumption of extra tasks and more responsibility. A variety of higher level tasks could be developed in which many of the functions of full-time permanent supervisors could be undertaken by teachers who would be in temporary assignments to extra duty of their choice. The system obviously would determine who would be eligible for such appointments. The challenge to management is to truly be selective and not to distribute largesse to all who happen to have worked five years in the system.

The career ladder itself is recognition of growth and the advancement involved may be as important as the money.

Other Approaches to Increasing Pay. Contracting for services, awarding grants for specific purposes to improve instruction, providing of stipends for summer work related to improving productivity. The creative use of modest sums to reward staff may be much more important to proficiency in the learning setting than supervisory personnel.

INTANGIBLE REWARDS

Sydney Thompson's booklet,[3] "Motivation of Teachers," lists the following ways to enhance the motivation of teachers.

> Praising
> Encouraging
> Honoring
> Creating sense of accomplishment through goal setting, information feedback and evaluation
> Accomplishing individual teacher's personal goals. (See also Chapter 10 for discussion of a career plan.)
> Increasing teacher control over work
> Aiding teachers to teach more effectively with less strain (work "smarter")
> Fostering interaction with colleagues
> Gaining a sense of having reached or influenced young people

The astute building principal will mobilize the dominant teachers and groups to support the ceaseless search for improvement and to isolate or reduce the effectiveness of the cynics or skeptics on the staff.

HAVE CLEAR, SIMPLE GUIDELINES

If a principal knows without doubt the limits within which the school has freedom to make decisions, less time will be spent in asking questions at the school and the overall management level.

Develop policies and guidelines that have the following characteristics:

> Complete, in that all the possible routine questions are answered.
> Clear and unambiguous
> Written in simple English (or Spanish)
> Continuously shrinking in size

ESTABLISH SCHOOL SITE BUDGETING

The school system, in examining its process of placing responsibility for performance closest to the learning scene, or with the teachers, will do well to allocate as much of the money of the system as possible to the school. The school, then, can use the available resources to get the job done using the procedures that, in its judgment, are most effective. The responsibility for results implies control over the available resources within the usual constraints of the system.

INSTRUCTION AND LEARNING

The main division of the school system relates to the actual instruction and subsequent learning that takes place. The components include a management position and a series of principals, each responsible with their staffs for the operation of a school. If the system is concerned with providing many opportunities for rewards to teachers either in status or pay, and in stimulating improvement in instruction, there will be many temporary, part-time or added time opportunities for classroom teachers to participate in management. Examples would include rethinking of a social studies curriculum, evaluation of the effectiveness of operation of a special education program, planning a vocational experience, and the like. Matters of direct concern to teachers' organizations, such as salaries, would probably be handled separately, but teachers would have a series of choices of participating to varying degrees in the decision-making process. This offers opportunities for growth by teachers, offers rewards, keeps the teachers in classes, and by the use of groups of respected teachers to develop proposed changes, would authenticate the change in the eyes of other teachers.

A LEAN ADMINISTRATION MODEL

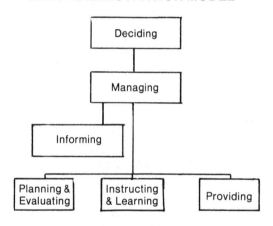

A LEAN AND HUNGRY ADMINISTRATION MODEL

The following major components (see Model) make up a superior educational management organization.

- Policy making board — The board of education, school committee, board of trustees, board of school commissioners, etc.
- Chief school administrator.
- Teaching and learning center or series of centers — schools, if you will.
- Logistics branch that provides staff and the things of education in order to make learning possible. It also accounts for the resources.
- Planning and evaluation branch that monitors what is going on and makes suggestions, some of which are eventually incorporated into plans, for the im-

provement of operation of the system.
- An information, public relations service — optional but desirable.

SOME CRITERIA FOR ADMINISTRATIVE MODELS

A Flat Organization Is More Effective and Less Costly

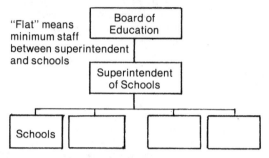

"Flat" means minimum staff between superintendent and schools

"Flat" means that there are the fewest possible number of levels above the school.

The fewer the number of levels above the school, the fewer administrative staff members. The fewer administrative staff members, the fewer secretaries, the fewer calls for assistants, the lower the demand on computer services, and so on. Besides, the principals can get to the highest level decision-maker readily.

But if the Organization is Too Flat, It May Become Unmanageable

(This is known as dealing with the concept of "span of control.")

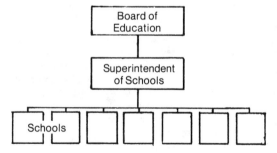

In a stretched out model like this, the superintendent may lose track of what is going on in left field. The administrative leader has much to do, within and outside the school system. You may have to compromise.

INTERMEDIATE MANAGEMENT POSITIONS

Every school system has had the experience of having a weakness disclosed in its instructional program as conditions change. The tendency has been to bring someone in to develop a program to meet the weakness; someone with experience, knowledge, and the ability to get things done. An example, presented to many school systems by the requirement of federal legislation concerning the education of handicapped children, has been the establishment or upgrading of a position of director of special education.

The importance of developing opportunities for teachers to participate in management should be weighed against the practice of providing full-time permament supervisors or directors of discrete educational activities, such as director of music or vocational education or supervisor or coordinator of social studies, for example.

THE ART OF COMPROMISE

The school system, if the continued professional growth of teachers is seen as a central problem, should opt for maximum teacher participation in management.

Still Fairly Flat, But Responding to Realities, Many School Systems Will Have a Second Line Manager Handling Each of the Major Areas of the School System

• Here the system submerges the principals as the management system gets more complicated.

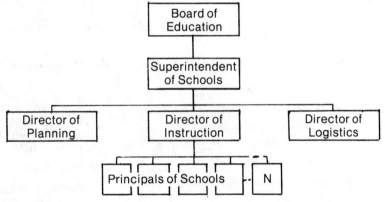

The uncertainty about number of schools in a reasonable span of control depends upon how good the principals are

• Here the system reaffirms the importance of the principals.

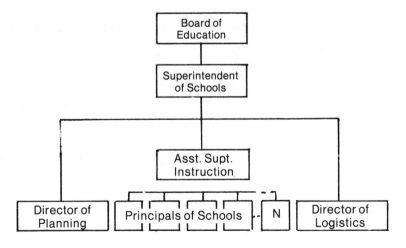

There may be times when this is not enough. There may be a need for special expertise, or the problems of meeting detailed regulations may demand more time than a group of teachers can provide, or some other reason may require the system to seek a full-time manager of a discrete educational function. With much of the system operating through systematic use of participating teachers and strengthened principals, an area of special concern may well be established in one of several ways.

- Hire a permanent full-time manager.
- Hire a permanent full-time manager with a sunset law restriction on the position. The job to be accomplished is specified. A period of time is provided for getting the service operating well and for training the principals to carry on in operating the system. At the end of the agreed upon time the position is abolished.
- Contract for the performance of the function by some agency outside the school system.
- Phase in faculty representatives and principals to manage the enterprise as you phase out the full-time special staff or outside staff.

EXHIBIT TWO

The Pros and Cons of Permanent Intermediate Level Management Staff Vs. Teacher Participation in Management

Permanent Intermediate Management Positions

Advantages	Disadvantages
1. Brings expertise.	1. Reduces role of principal by exacerbating the dual allegiance problems of knowledge workers who are responsible to their discipline or field *and* to the organization.
2. Provides continuity in time and across the system from kindergarten to twelfth grade.	2. The change model may become fixed.
3. Responsibility can be fixed.	3. Reduces the opportunity for teachers to participate significantly in management.
4. Leadership qualities can be emphasized in selection.	4. The principal, instead of being strengthened, tends to leave the area to the administrator from the central office.
	5. Costly to hire and provide support staff and services.

Temporary Part-Time Teacher Assignments

Advantages	Disadvantages
1. Provides significant opportunities for teacher participation, providing rewards and increasing opportunities to learn.	1. Loss of continuity.
2. Strengthens role of principal who must continue to learn as more areas are placed under the control of the principal.	2. The temporary assignment precludes fixing responsibility.
3. The fluid membership in management reduces the chance of fixing the change model.	3. Staff may not include people with the necessary expertise.
4. The cost can be controlled and limited support staff required.	4. The provision of opportunities for teacher participation reduces the opportunity to select for leadership qualities.

LOGISTICS

The logistics division of the school system supports the system by providing the people, space, materials and supplies without which the system could not operate. To do this the logistics branch receives money and spends money in salaries, payments, and purchases. It accounts for the receipts and expenditures, and the reporting of this accounting becomes an important part of the system of information that is necessary for improved decision-making.

With school site budgeting, the principals and staffs of schools control much of the use of resources within limits established by the system. The principals need a well organized management information system that helps them make better decisions. The management information system must show what is available for spending, including information as to expenses contracted for but not yet paid. It will be a long-term information system, showing forecast expenditures over the next five years, particularly staffing and needs to set aside funds for major repairs, for example. The school, with objectives to meet, needs to have a clear understanding over time of the forecast resources it will have and the major foreseeable demands that will be made upon those resources.

In this model, the recruitment, selection, and care and feeding of staff is included in the area of logistics.

PLANNING AND EVALUATING

The Second Law of Thermodynamics states that any spontaneous process results in an increase in net entropy, or disorder, of the system plus its surroundings. In my language, inexact as it may be, this can be paraphrased to say that any system, no matter how much energy is in it, will tend to run down if left to itself, or unless new energy is added to the system. The clock, the social organization, and the solar system, among others, are subject to the law.

A changed condition does not continue in force effectively year after year unless it is constantly watched, given injections of energy, or restated purpose to keep it going at the same or higher level of effec-

tiveness. The Eight Year Study was a formidable educational undertaking in the 1930s in which major innovations in 30 secondary schools were analyzed with respect to the later success in college of students who had attended those schools. The study showed that students who experienced widely different preparations for college had equal success measured on standard terms of marks and tests and more success measured on less "objective" bases than students from traditional preparations. A study was made some years later, after the interest and enthusiasm had died down, only to find that most of the innovations had disappeared despite fairly clear evidences of reasonable success. When there was a stop to the infusion of energy, the systems tended to return to rest.

It takes energy, too, for mid-path course corrections. Hagerstown, MD, some years ago was a pioneer in the use of television for instruction. The program got under way before the advent of video-tape recorders. In consequence, the programs were televised live. The system, lacking the injection of resources or the priority to use resources for this purpose, continued to use live television, long past the time when video-taping was a successful and economical approach. The system had lost its ability to change because of decisions it had made about the use of its resources. It was running down.

PLANNING

While it is virtually impossible to be a part of an administrative system without planning, some people do more planning than others. In the field of educational planning, the major line positions — principals and directors of elementary and secondary education — have an operational responsibility as well as a planning responsibility. In consequence the kind of planning that is done is tempered by the time that busy administrators can give to it and the ability of staff members, mostly teachers, to take on a planning function.

The school system administrative organization should be modified to provide a planning function that would respond to demands made upon it by the operating system. This would be a staff, not a line, function, interacting with the direct line of management people responsible for learning in the schools. Interaction is a two-way street.

The major roles of the planning unit would be:

• *Information Broker*. The planning unit should maintain information linkages to research and other information systems so that whatever is done would be done with full knowledge of the state of the art inside and outside the system.

• *Internal Educational Change Plan Development at the Request of Educational Operations Staff*. Prior to decisions to proceed with an action, the planning staff should develop a plan or proposal for a project in cooperation with teachers and line staff. The plan would include:

   ▪ Procedure or description of the project

   ▪ Evaluative and feedback systems which would be a part of any change plan[4]

   ▪ Cost benefit analysis including as principal components direct financial expenditure, direct staff and teacher time reallocation, and indirect costs required of teachers to learn how to operate in the changed role

   ▪ In-service education component

   ▪ Time schedule

   ▪ Prediction of degree of success of the proposed program in achieving the goals, perhaps using simulations to test this predicted outcome.

• *Take Part in Decisions Regarding Proceeding with Educational Change Programs*.

• *Monitor Educational Change*. Along with the operations staff who initiated the change, the planning staff should assist in monitoring the change. This would be done by bringing to the attention of the operation's staff discrepancies that may appear between planned program results and observed results.

Such feedback could result in course correction, speeding or slowing, or abandonment of projects and changes in the goals or targets of the proposed changes.

Information feedback would be made available to the project and to the system. The evaluation component would be an in-

tegral part of the change project from the beginning helping in all ways possible to serve the project and the system.

Provus:[5]

"... holds that every aspect of a program, not just its outcomes, is involved in an evaluation. Evaluation is primarily a comparison of program performance with expected or designed program, and secondarily, among many other things, a comparison of client performance with expected client outcomes. This comprehensive comparison of many aspects of actual events with expected events therefore requires the explication of a detailed picture of an entire program at various points in time as the standard for judging performance. These program standards may arise from any source, but under the Discrepancy Evaluation Model they are derived from the values of the program staff and the client population it serves.

"Similarly, when the values employed by persons conducting an evaluation are compatible with those of the staff and program being evaluated, it is generally possible for everyone concerned to both understand and accept a final evaluation report. When value conflicts exist among clients, practitioners, or evaluators, reports are generally characterized by lack of specificity and debatable conclusions...

"Evaluation can serve at least three major purposes: (1) to ensure the quality of the product, (2) to ensure this quality at minimal cost, and (3) to help management make decisions about what should be produced and how."

• *Initiate Planning for Problems Involving the School System and its Community*. The function of educational planning should include initiating plans for educational change where the educational system interfaces with the community, in the event that such change is not started by the schools. Someone must keep a careful eye on the outer world. The problems described by Coleman II,[6] for example, and by other recent publications,[7] as the flood of students that almost submerged the schools moves into the job market, are the kinds of issues that may be brought to the attention of the school system by the planning group.

• *Develop Community Resources*. Beyond engaging the community to support the schools politically, the forecasts of the future suggest that many school systems may be forced to look to the community for ways in which to buy the services that people want and which they may no longer be able to purchase with public tax money. The school system, to maintain its edge of quality, may need to seek some form of annual or special giving of funds to the schools, may depend even more heavily upon volunteer time, may shift services to community or municipal budgets to free funds for needed educational services, use community resources for education, and engage with the community and teachers periodically in canvassing ways to reallocate faculty time for improvement of instruction. Many of the roles now assigned to the schools may be returned to the parents.

• *Plan and Operate In-Service Education Systems.* Every educational change project plan should have an in-service educational component. By lodging the responsibility of in-service education for such plans with the planning unit, this unit would be better able to deal with the pressing issue of reducing the indirect costs of educational change to teachers. If new roles, procedures, processes can be introduced to and learned by teachers more easily than the present hit or miss system, substantial energy will be released and not lost by the system.

The involvement of teachers and community in the planning of in-service education is of great importance.

• *Operate General Testing Systems.* The planning unit, because of its emphasis on evaluation planning and information feedback, should operate the systemwide testing program.

In the process, the possibility of increasing the service to teachers by provision of data regarding individual student's work at the level of item analysis instead of largely normative data should be considered.

• *Manage a Teacher and Staff Time Budget.* The way in which a teacher's time is used is determined in large part by formal or informal negotiations and traditions regarding teaching load. Other time is available, in modest amounts, that has been devoted to faculty meetings, meeting with children after school, and systemwide involvement in educational change, among other things. This bank of time, possibly increased by community participation in the schools, is a resource of the system that should be managed, in a way to extract

maximum benefit. Faculty should be involved in allocating the resource along with staff.

A budget of this type, which would be most crude as it started, would do a variety of things. It would look in a quantitative way at the various demands on teacher time arising from educational change, for example. The indirect cost to the teacher of changes would be assessed over time. The reduction of overload could be planned. The involvement of individual staff members in in-service education or educational change could be quantified. Probably a number of teachers have been overloaded and some never given a chance to participate. The availability of faculty time could be related to the faculty time for educational change, this could be appraised, and decisions made as to the best use of this resource. Schools could balance the demand for time for administrative and supervisory work with the availability of time. Studying this area, which represents one of the few variables left, may provide illumination as to the needs of the schools in this area.

There is no intent here to set up an elaborate system of monitoring time. Rather, if insights can be obtained, the system would operate with greater concern for the use of time, reducing its casual and off-hand decision-making and taking into account some of the unintended results of action.

• *Provide a Management Information System.* A management information system is at the heart of the planning process because it is from the analysis of interrelated data dealing with the use of resources and the achievement of results that the school system can move to improve its performance.

The management information system must include the data regarding resources and their use as accounted for by the logistics branch. The information system must relate the evaluation of the performance of the system including parts of the system to the use of resources. Projection of the data into the future is required so that the use of resources is related to a forecast profile of achievement and the system can plot what actually happens against what is expected to happen. Above all, the management information system must be understandable for it will become a major element in the management effort to show its constituency what is happening in the schools.

There are competing management information systems represented by complaints directed to administrators and board members or in the conversation at social gatherings. A believable, understandable system in which the school public has confidence is essential.

PRINCIPALS

Along with teachers, principals are given major responsibility under the proposals advanced. In order for the principals to carry out the responsibilities given, some series of tradeoffs are important. These might include:

• The information gathering-reporting function of the principal's office should, except for raw data input from the schools, be handled by central office as a path of a well designed management information system.

• The budget for each school should have enough leeway that faculty can be paid for extra time spent in participation in management.

• The position of the principal should be scrutinized, and where needed, additional help given the principal in order that the incumbent can actually carry out effectively the total job.

• The principals should be supported by in-service education, help from the central administrative staff, and help from outside the system in order to keep the incumbents fully aware of the potentials that exist in their positions.

• The school system must back the principals.

• The system must recognize that what happens in the school is the essential activity of the school system.

Accordingly, what happens in central headquarters or board meetings has little meaning unless it contributes to improving the educational process in the school.

THE SCHOOL BOARD

The school board or school committee, as it is called in some parts of the country, has a most significant role in assuring an effective management model. The role relates to decision-making, of course. The board's ability to make good decisions eventually relates to the board's ability to secure good information in understandable form. As such, the scrutiny of the management information system is a major concern.

The information system, as stated earlier, must be simple enough to enable it to be carried out without undue cost, complete enough so that it can supply information for decisions, reports, and to help the system make corrections in its course, and understandable enough for the general public, should it wish to do so to be well informed. The system must be flexible enough so that new data that becomes needed can be added and old data, no longer significant, sloughed off.

The school board should have a well understood agreed upon policy of management of the schools. If it adopts one that resembles the focus on principal and staff responsibility in each school, the board should be very careful to examine each action it takes so that no unintended result weakens the role of the school.

The board increasingly becomes concerned with the quality of the guidelines within which the schools operate and the effectiveness of the operation of the schools, and less in trying to solve all the problems of the world at the board meetings.

REFERENCES

[1] Drucker, Peter F., "Managing in Turbulent Times," Harper & Row, New York, 1980, pp. 14-28.

[2] Slevin, Dennis P., "The Innovation Boundary: A Specific Model and Some Empirical Results"; Administrative Science Quarterly, December 1971, pp. 515-531.

[3] Thompson, S., "Motivation of Teachers," prepared by ERIC Clearing House on Educational Management and published by Association of California School Administrators, 1979, The Association, 1575 Old Bayshore Highway, Burlingame, CA 94010.

[4] Provus, Malcolm, "Discrepancy Evaluation for Educational Program Improvement and Assessment," McCutchan, Berkeley, 1971, 380 pp.

[5] Provus, Malcolm, "Discrepancy Evaluation for Educational Program Improvement and Assessment," McCutchan, Berkeley, 1971, p. 12.

[6] Coleman, James, Chairman, and Committee, "Youth, Transition to Adulthood," Chicago, University of Chicago Press, 1974, 193 pp.

[7] Special Task Force to Secretary of Health, Education, and Welfare, "Work in America," Cambridge, MIT Press, 1973, 262 pp.

8

MANAGEMENT STRATEGIES FOR HANDLING SCHOOL FINANCIAL AFFAIRS

Frederick W. Hill, Ed.D.

The school business official can develop the kind of yardsticks and checklists that can comfort the community and help the entire staff to make sound general management decisions — if he is up to snuff. Author Hill tells what you should expect, and perhaps demand, from competent school business officials.

Fred Hill, former deputy superintendent of schools in charge of administration and business in Yonkers, Minneapolis and New York City, is a former president of the Association of School Business Officials and one of the country's most distinguished authorities on that aspect of education.

THE ROLE OF THE SCHOOL BUSINESS ADMINISTRATOR IN HARD TIMES

In education, the efficiency expert, the "go by the rule book" supervisor, and the school business officer were often perceived as the "executioners for management." They were the ever-present "axe wielders," always anxious and ready to end the hapless careers of the brightest and the unorthodox; and constantly attuned to punish the minutest deviation from drab and plodding normality. Theirs was a sinister and unpopular role, and they were grudgingly tolerated in a world of ever expanding population, more school children, building booms, post-war baby booms, and a full fledged flowering of the American dream.

Gradually there developed an understanding of the role of management in every human enterprise, and a greater appreciation of the contribution which effective management gives to the success and well-being of those who participate in any human endeavor.

As people began to appreciate that the success of an enterprise was directly related to the skill with which it was managed, there arose a number of persons who began to analyze what successful managers did, and how managers in successful enterprises acted differently from those in unsuccessful enterprises. From these types of studies, it became apparent that "good managers" had specific functions which they performed well, and that poor managers were not aware of their specific functions of management or performed poorly.

Briefly stated, a "good" manager was considered as one who performed the following functions:

1. Planning — To look ahead, anticipating setting up goals and objectives, and plans of action to achieve such goals, evaluating resources and situations, and considering various possible approaches and alternatives, and selecting the best approach.

2. Organizing — Creating and maintaining all the necessary conditions and relationships to achieve the plan. Establishing an organization structure or framework, developing procedures for accomplishing the work.

3. Controlling — Regulating action in relation to the plan. It involves setting up criteria or checks, comparing actual results with the criteria and making needed corrections.

4. Coordinating — Obtaining the proper relation of activities of the people involved, with special emphasis on time and sequence of performance. It refers not only to activities directly under a specific manager's control, but also to relationships and communication with activities outside the manager's immediate control.

5. Directing — Guiding and supervising activities and personnel to achieve the desired objective. It involves directing people as well as procedures. Its purpose is getting things done.

6. Staffing — Providing competent manpower to accomplish established goals.

7. Evaluating — Measuring and judging progress and effectiveness in achieving the plan.

Within the areas of school business administration, these seven functions of management are largely the responsibility of the school business administrator.

MAJOR AREAS OF RESPONSIBILITY

Because the school business officer is part of the policy team, his responsibilities should be well defined. He must be given the authority to act. This authority is vitally important because it allows him to be uninhibited in discharging his responsibilities within the framework of the established, over-all policies of the district. This kind of environment also provides the educational administrator with relief from worry about the functions of school business management. The educational administrator can depend upon the school business administrator to provide information to increase his own effectiveness in public education.

In any given school system, the contributions which a school business administrator can make to the effective operation of the total system will be limited and circumscribed only the the limit of his or her competence and imagination, and by the interpersonal relationships which penetrate the top management staff.

If the staff operates under a team concept, then each member of the team will feel free to bring suggestions, evaluative comments, and objective perspectives to the continuous analysis of ongoing operations. Members of the team will respect each other's specialized expertise, and will not feel unreasonably combative and defensive in an enforced era of reallocation of resources, should the need arise. Such a team spirit will be of special significance in periods of hard-times.

Moreover, if the school business administrator (SBA) has previously demonstrated his appreciation of the importance of the many facets of the educational enterprise, and had made clear that he *understands and operates under the "service concept,"* then his role in hard-times operation can become especially meaningful. When the SBA demonstrates by his action, and those of his staff, that he firmly believes that school business functions are not an end in themselves, but are only of value when they are of service to and contribute to the success of the educational enterprise, then his potential contributions in times of declining resources are great indeed.

An anlysis of the potential contributions which a school business administrator can make during hard times might be approached in many ways. We believe three approaches may be especially useful. They are:

1. An overview of the *"general management decisions"* which the total top team of management should make and to which the SBA would contribute his unique talents and specialized expertise. Without such unique contributions from the SBA, these decisions might be "skewed" in both perspective and impact.

2. An analysis of the *kinds of "check points" and yardsticks* which the business manager might suggest to be applied for the measurement of various tasks or phases of the total evaluational operation.

3. A detailed *listing of specific actions, studies, restrictions and curtailments, and reallocation of resources and services* which could raise the efficiency, enhance the services or reduce the unit costs of specific phases and functions of business operations.

In this chapter, we shall suggest some potential activities and contributions which the school business official may make in each of these three broad categories.

GENERAL MANAGEMENT DECISIONS

In these days of tight budgets, we hear much of cost-benefit analysis. We are bombarded with suggestions for program budgeting analysis and are urged to adopt zero based budgeting procedures. All of these techniques imply the desire of management to look into the various functions performed by the educational enterprise, and to evaluate the costs of such functions in proportion to the goals of the enterprise's over-all activities.

When zero based budgeting is used, it assumes that every function of the enterprise is required to justify its existence, to submit alternatives for various levels of service, and to incur continuing management evaluation of the reason for its existence, and the effectiveness of its result.

Obviously, cost benefit analysis, program budgeting and zero based budgeting are three management techniques which are almost wholly dependent upon the integrity of the data used for decision making — and the scope, accuracy, timeliness and pertinence of the financial data depend almost entirely upon the effective contributions of the business office staff, and these in turn are largely the results of effective leadership given to that staff by the school business administrator.

DECISION PACKAGES

In making general management decisions, it is assumed that the top management staff and the policy making board will consider specific "decision packages," and that the staff specialists and/or consultant experts will work together in formulating the decision packages to be evaluated. Obviously, the school business staff will play a key role in providing the cost histories, current expense operating levels, and potential expenditure estimates needed to analyze the various options and alternatives which will be considered. In addition, the business staff will be most directly responsible for estimating available resources, for evaluating potential new sources of revenue, and for evaluating the cost implications and potential savings involved in any proposed actions such as staff reductions, plant closings, service curtailments, reduced levels or frequencies of operations, and changes in quality and intensity of services presently performed.

In each such decision package, the business administrator would normally be responsible for furnishing not only the pertinent financial information required, but also in many school systems he would likely be responsible for the management of the supportive services and general management information systems. Hence he might also be required to furnish information on the number of students served, the potential "market" indicated by future census estimates, and the estimated cost impacts involved in changing utilization of auxiliary costs for transportation, plant operation and maintenance, capital costs for plant and program changes, and potential "markets" or enrollment trends in preschool, school, and postschool age programs. Every potential change of program has these related cost change potentials as well. Hence the school business official has a unique opportunity and specific responsibility for adding an adequate and proportionate "economic perspective" to general administrative decision making.

In these days when declining enrollments and skyrocketing costs are the rule rather than the exception, nonschool or outside pressure groups can place particular burdens on the SBA. Taxpayer groups demand access to school cost data and financial statements, and are prone to ask for special cost analysis reports of particular functions which may be the "targets" of their displeasure. In these situations the SBA is sometimes construed to be "disloyal" by proponents of a particular program if he releases such cost data, or an axe wielder whenever he does. In fact, he is a public official responsible for the stewardship of public funds, and in most states is required by law to make public records available under various Freedom of Information statutes and regulations.

However, in school districts where the SBA has established a reputation for integrity, accuracy of reporting, and non-withholding of either favorable or non-favorable information, the pressure of inclination to seek out and find "scandalous" information seems generally to peter out and subside. Hence the effective SBA can contribute much to the atmosphere of candor and objectivity in which decision packages are and can be evaluated.

Moreover, where there is a community concensus that school business operations are well run, there is a perceptible lessening of hysterical and unreasonable demands to "clean house" and to throw out the baby with the bath water when school program reevaluations occur.

Hence, whenever tax administration and policy board consideration is given to basic decisions dealing with such important questions as program offerings, facilities changes, personnel reductions, or shifts in levels of service, the SBA may well be and should be the primary source of data for making such decisions, and for furnishing financial as well as educational perspective to the decision making process.

ESTABLISHING PRIORITIES

Another aspect of decision making with regard to basic function and program offerings lies in the aspect of establishing priorities. It is a reality of hard-times operation that there is usually not enough money to pay for *all* desirable and/or necessary operating programs. Moreover, even among necessary programs, the lack of sufficient resources frequently requires the establishment of an order of critical importance. Here especially, the SBA can suggest a higher priority for a leaking roof repair or replacement versus a cosmetic interior repainting. Similarly, a worn out boiler may be of higher priority than a worn out school bus, and a mandated bond and interest payment or other mandated program or contract expense may be of higher priority than either the boiler or the bus. These representative examples merely illustrate the kind of role which the SBA must play, and should play in general administrative or management decisions.

CHECKS POINTS IN MANAGEMENT

Some years ago, Dr. Schuyler C. Joyner, business manager of the Los Angeles school system, and one of the pioneers of modern school business management techniques, suggested some of the critical "check points" which the competent school business administrator should examine if he wished to evaluate the effectiveness of the business services in a particular school system. His ideas are especially appropriate in hard times. Interested readers may wish to contact the Association of School Business Officials for the latest updated statement of such check point lists.*

A competent school business official can devise his own list of "check points" which may serve as gauges of proficiency in evaluating the performance of his own system's business operations.

In a very real sense, these check points are or can be used precisely as the physician checks pulse rate, heart beat, body temperature, blood pressure, urine analysis, blood cell counts, and similar critical measurements in his overall diagnosis of the health of a given patient.

We may therefore think of the school business administrator's use of "check points" as a diagnostic technique to determine the over-all efficiency of his school system's particular strengths and weaknesses, and as a proven methodology for indicating areas where improvements and economies may be generated.

From my own experience, I recommend that "check points" be established in each phase and function of the school business operation, and that gradually a prioritized list of the most critical check points be culled out, so that a good picture of management efficiency can be arrived at very quickly. A random sampling of personal past practice suggests that these check points can best be utilized in the form of specific questions, such as the following.

In Areas of Accounting

1. How soon after the close of a fiscal period can an "operating statement" of financial condition be given to top management? — e.g., immediately; within one hour; one day; three days; a week; a month; irregularly, at extended intervals; at year's end as required by law.

2. Does accounting provide information on a cash basis; accrual basis; encumbrance basis?

3. Does accounting provide information on a state mandated minimum coding or classification basis? Does it provide for program budgeting and constant control of resources? Does it provide a mechanism for periodic transfer or reallocation of resources, or permit responses to critical needs?

In Areas of Personnel and Payroll Procedures

1. How long does it take for a new employee to "get on the payroll" and receive a paycheck for services rendered — e.g., one hour; one day; one week; one payroll period; one month; two months, etc.

2. Has the operation ever missed a payroll date?

3. Are part-time employees, substitutes, and extra pay and overtime pay personnel paid within the same payroll periods as regular salary or wages?

4. Do employees get a regularly updated report on such items as accumulated tax withholdings, retirement contributions, savings deductions, vacation credits, sick leave days and similar personnel fringe benefits on their paycheck stubs? If not, how often is such data furnished?

5. How often are employees paid? — e.g., monthly, semi-monthly, biweekly, weekly — and is a list of payroll dates established well in advance so employees may anticipate and plan their own financial commitments?

6. Do employees get paid a lump sum prior to vacation leaves? Are there procedures for optional pay plans for ten-month workers, etc.?

These check points are merely suggestive. Nevertheless, inasmuch as employee "morale" contributes much to the efficiency and rapport relationships within any organization, it should be obvious that the SBA, by constantly checking and fine

---

*ASBO, 720 Garden St., Park Ridge, IL 60068.

tuning the performance of his operations, can make a very significant contribution to the successful and economical operation of the educational enterprise. In hard times such effectiveness can assume critical importance.

In Areas of Purchasing and Supplies Management

1. Do staff users of supplies and equipment have established schedules and procedures for giving "input" to the periodic updating of supply bid specifications and listings?

2. Do vendors have opportunities to make ethical, professional presentations of their competitive advantages, new products, revised specifications, and construction features?

3. How long a period does it take for a supply requisition for a standard supply item to be processed and the item delivered? — e.g., one hour; one day; one week; one month; one semester; one year; etc.

4. How long does it take for a vendor's invoice to be processed and payment sent to the vendor? Is specific record procedure established for "logging" the progress of business paper through the various departments? Can inordinate delays or log jams be identified as to location, cause and possible remedies?

5. Is there honest open competitive bidding on all classes of supplies and equipment? Do vendors believe or "know" that certain suppliers have an "in" with purchasing?

6. Do out-of-town bidders submit bona fide proposals or is bidding largely restricted to local merchants?

7. Are there genuine efforts made to enforce acceptance of "or equal" bids?

8. Has the number of bidders increased or decreased? Are the changes in number of bidders due to local conditions?

9. Have bidders expressed satisfaction or objection to bidding procedures or bid opening procedures? Are bidders subjected to "post bid opening" negotiations and spec or bid modifications?

Financial Reporting and Records

1. Are staff members given adequate procedures and information — dispensing instructions? Are there established timelines for issuance of important operational reports?

2. Are citizens and taxpayers queries welcomed and given adequate responses? Are records made available under written procedures, so that both inquirers and employees are not harrassed by "public information" processes?

Transportation Services

1. What is the average "on time" arrival of buses in each section of the city?

2. How many complaints on bus service were received this day? This week? This month? This year? How do these figures compare with prior periods or prior years?

3. What is the pupil/bus accident frequency? How does the district's safety record compare with other similar districts? With other periods?

4. Are individual driver safety records, health checks, vision tests, traffic violation records, fingerprints, records, etc. carefully evaluated and reviewed periodically?

5. Have all bus vehicles undergone periodic safety checks and is there a daily driver "condition of vehicle" report? Is all safety equipment present and operable?

Equipment Maintenance

1. Does each piece of equipment requiring maintenance have suitable maintenance tags indicating date of latest service, latest inspection, latest lubrication or cleaning, etc., together with identifying signature of responsible person performing such service or inspection?

2. Are there written and established maintenance procedures and maintenance and operation manuals to inform employees of their responsibilities for the care and proper use of specific pieces of equipment?

3. Are boiler room log books and maintenance and repair requisitions controlled and accounted for? Is an accurate analysis of recurring repair problems made? Are there procedures for junking, salvaging, trading in old equipment?

4. Is periodic preventive maintenance, inspection, and replacement of items like fire extinguishers, emergency lighting,

and power batteries, fire alarm systems, and other safety, health and property loss prevention measures carefully and faithfully administered?

5. Is "life cycle" maintenance and replacement provided for items like typewriters, duplicating machines, vehicles, fluorescent light bulbs, blacktop pavements, roof felt resaturation, etc.?

Capital Investment Protection

1. Is there an adequate cash flow plan established for each fiscal year, with provision for contingency or emergency needs?

2. Is there an over-all borrowing and financing plan, with borrowings maximized in sufficient quantity and long term to attract a number of responsible bidders from outside the local district as well as within it?

3. Is there a long established investment plan which permits the SBA to invest surplus working capital during certain periods of the cash flow cycle?

4. Are surplus funds used to take advantage of genuine bargain opportunities for equipment or supply purchases? Is bidding timed to take advantage of "off peak" price levels?

5. Is there genuine bidding for items such as insurance protection, or is there fee splitting among favored brokers? Similarly, is there only token bidding on borrowing or other forms of purchasing?

These, then, are the types of questions the alert business official will use as "check points" in surveying the entire span of district business operations.

Every facet of his responsibility can suggest a myriad of questions. For example, he or she can look at data processing and ask whether they use batch processing, whether "on-line" answers are available for most management questions, and whether the costs of the information system are a good investment, or if the data could be processed more economically or more effectively by regional data networks, etc.

It would be impossible to list the significant check points in every school system, but by these illustrations it is hoped that the SBA will have a better insight into the way in which such "checks" may be used to give an overview of the operating efficiency of the system and to make improvements therein.

In the same vein, this writer has often suggested that the school business administrator or school business official should have broad familiarity with "yardsticks" or norms which are prevalent in the local area, state or province, and on a regional and national basis regarding cost and expenditure levels, frequency of service levels, and prevailing practices which are directly germane and pertinent to each and every phase of school system operation.

Thus, he will seek information regarding "norms" or expenditure levels not only for his system itself, and for each individual unit in his system, but also for prevailing practices and cost levels at regional, state and national levels. We have proposed, for example, that districts *must* establish "yardsticks" which determine levels of service and which in turn determine levels of expenditures within any given school system. For example, "yardsticks" can deal with levels of service or programs such as:

1. Every pupil shall be offered 'x' years of subject _____.

2. Every pupil shall be transported who lives more than _____ miles from school.

3. Every pupil shall be offered a choice of _____ elective curricula subjects in the year.

4. No pupil shall be permitted to take fewer than _____ subjects, nor more than _____ units or subjects in any one semester.

5. Every school of more than _____ pupils shall have an assistant principal, as well as a full-time principal and an additional assistant principal shall be assigned for each _____ additional pupils enrolled as of _____.

Obviously, the number of "yardsticks" regarding programs offered to pupils may be mandated by federal, state or local laws and regulations or by current contract agreements. Obviously, also, many aspects of any local educational program are determined by the local citizenry acting through the accumulated policy decisions of the local school board and school staffs. These composite decisions form the basis for the "status quo" in each community school system, and they provide the restricted matrix within which the school business officer *must* operate. He may think it ridiculous to provide an expensive language elective, but if that is the policy of the district, his role may and should be to provide accurate cost-benefit figures against which other relative costs are compared to establish system-wide priorities of expenditure.

In addition to providing basic data for program priority decisions, the effective school business officer should be equipped with other kinds of *yardstick* information. One of the types of yardsticks which are most helpful are data dealing with *"consumption norms."* For example, in the particular school system, it would be helpful if the business officer could say things like this:

Consumption Norms

1. On the average, a pupil in grades 1-3 uses ___ soft lead pencils per term.

2. On the average, high school English pupils use about ___ sheets of composition paper per year.

3. A track team uses ___ pairs of track shoes per team member, per year.

4. A wood shop junior high school teacher usually orders about ___ per pupil in softwood project materials per semester.

5. It is reasonable to expect a textbook in ___ subject to last for ___ years before a new adoption and replacement of texts will be permitted.

Staffing Norms

Frequently, budgets may be evaluated in terms of basic yardsticks related to personnel or staffing costs.

6. A custodian should be allowed $___ per square foot for classroom cleaning materials.

7. Custodial manpower should be allocated on the basis of one person per ___ square feet of floor area; or one person per ___ pupils; or one person per ___ acres of grounds; or one person per ___ teaching stations; or one person per ___ faculty members; or one person per composite average of these or other factors.

8. Clerical service should be allocated on the basis of ___ persons per school office; or per ___ persons on school staff; or per ___ pupils in enrollment; or per ___ hours of school operation.

Life Expectancy Norms

9. Truck or bus replacement should be assumed on a basis of useful life of ___ years per vehicle.

10. Typewriters and office equipment shall be replaced upon an assumed life cycle of ___ years.

11. Classroom furniture and specific categories of instructional equipment shall have an assumed useful life of ___ years.

12. Equipment destroyed by vandalism shall not be replaced before the elapse of ___ months, as a deliberate incentive to student opposition to vandalism.

Service Limiting Policies

Yardsticks may be effected by service norms established on district policy.

13. School heating shall be furnished only between the hours of ___ and ___, and ___ heat be furnished in such areas as ___, ___, ___, ___, etc.

14. Operational staffs will be furnished only to perform certain levels of service or function, within established cost yardsticks. For example: ___

Frequency Yardsticks

1. Classrooms shall be cleaned twice per ___.

2. Windows will be washed ___ times per year.

3. Halls will be waxed ___ times per year.

4. Waste baskets will be emptied ___.

5. Cafeteria tables will be washed ___.

6. Toilets will be cleaned ___.

7. Hall lockers will be emptied of trash ___.

8. Furnace tubes will be cleaned ___.

9. Buses will be washed ___.

10. Buses will be greased and oiled every ___ miles.

11. Classrooms will be painted ___.

12. Auditoriums will be swept ___.

Policy decisions establishing these frequency intervals will have crucial impact upon the budget.

Expenditure Norms

Sometimes yardsticks are established purely on a per capita cost basis.

1. An allowance of ____ dollars per pupil will be provided for library books.

2. An allowance of $____ per pupil will be provided for each pupil enrolled in departments, such as math, science, language, phys ed, shop, health, social studies, art, music, etc.

3. An allowance of $____ per square foot or cubic foot will be allowed for heating, lighting, cooling, custodial care.

4. A per capita allowance of $____ will be provided for water, sewerage.

Other Yardsticks

Still other "yardsticks" which the school business official can provide have to do with state, regional, and national cost studies. For example:

1. If on the average of a national study, school systems spend $140 for instructional supplies, and the local system spends $285, should this not generate questions?

2. If on the average it costs $____ per pupil to transport a pupil within the state, and the school system spends significantly more or less, does this warrant close analysis?

3. If a similar school system spends significantly different dollars for a particular pupil service, such as instruction, guidance, counseling, extracurricular activities such as music, art, drama, athletics or language, math, science, electives, etc.

4. Frequently, the school business official will be asked to provide significant yardstick figures related to emotion laden service and personnel questions (especially in such areas as fringe benefit costs and such ancillary board costs for legal fees, negotiating fees, and insurance costs). For example, it is not unreasonable to expect the school business official to provide answers to questions such as:

a. How much does out district pay and how much do comparable or other districts pay for:

    health insurance
    dental insurance
    sick leave
    vacations
    severance pay

    grievous loss or bereavement
    maternity leave
    paternity leave
    clothing allowance
    theft or vandalism losses of staff

b. What is the absence frequency of our district compared to others, by different staff categories?

c. What are typical contract provisions and costs for sabbatical leave, military leaves, political action leaves, union official business leaves?

In the realm of negotiations and personnel benefits, it is the business official who is expected to be able to project costs of proposed salary and fringe benefits packages. This official should also be expected to work with personnel officials in estimating staff turnover, retirements, special leaves, and in projecting estimated costs of proposed staffing changes, including transfers, reductions, additions, or part-time deployments. He is also expected to be able to provide cost-benefit estimates of proposed personnel packages such as accelerated or incentive retirements, sick leave banks, birthday leaves, "snow day" losses, strike penalties, and many other evolving contract and negotiation demands. A costly but popular, and often mandated, insurance covers employee "save harmless" liability insurance — and recently the horrendous implied costs of mandated unemployment insurance benefits, and mandated staffing needs and other costs of special education programs for the handicapped, bilingual and other forms of compensatory education, and equal opportunity and OSHA regulations.

In times of tight finances, these newer forms of monetary obligations can almost wreck a school system, and the school business manager plays a key role in attempting to prioritize conflicting demands for limited resources, and in maximizing every potential source of income to provide support for these activities.

Thus, it may be seen that "yardsticks" can be related to such diverse factors as:

- Mandated programs or services
- Local adopted programs and services
- Expected levels and frequencies of service
- Options, electives and alternative

services
- Prevailing personnel practices, contracts
- Prevailing wage and salary patterns
- Frequency of services expected
- Prevailing fringe benefits
- Priority of competing demands
- Prevailing local economic conditions
- Expectancy level and support level of the local population
- State, federal and private resources available to the school system.

Within these general relationships, the school business official can make significant contributions to the objective understanding of the local citizenry, the school staff, and the school board of the impact of specific yardsticks upon the local educational system, and can thereby provide an assumed more intelligent decision making process to benefit the local educational enterprise.

SPECIFIC AREAS OF CONTRIBUTION

Obviously the list of specific contributions which the school business manager can make in a particular school situation will be directly related to the specific tasks or functions which are within his purview of responsibility.

Such a list should be directly specific for each category of responsibility. A few typical kinds of categorical contributions may serve as an index of what can be done, and thereby give the reader opportunity to interpret or extrapolate potential opportunities for service in a given job situation.

For an overview, it is suggested that the reader peruse Bulletin 21, "The School Business Administrator," published by ASBO, jointly with AASA and NSBA, which lists some 10 pages of basic functions performed within 21 broad categories of responsibilities and duties. Each broad category is subdivided into a number of sub-categories and it requires but little imagination to visualize enhanced opportunities for significant contributions toward economy and efficiency in each of these areas, or in similar unlisted areas which may be the responsibility of a particular school business official in a particular local situation.

The basic areas of responsibility to

which the school business administrator is most frequently assigned, including typical duties, were listed in that publication as follows.

The school business administrator, as a member of the superintendent's cabinet and advisory body, is a part of the team that helps to determine school policy. Therefore, it is important that his responsibilities be well defined and that he be given the authority to act. This authority is vitally important because it allows him to be uninhibited in discharging his responsibilities within the framework of the established, overall policies of the district. This kind of environment also provides the educational administrator with relief from worry about the functions of school business management. The educational administrator can depend upon the school business administrator to provide information to increase his own effectiveness in public education.

In the past, many specific tasks of the school business administrator have been laboriously described and catalogued. However, because of the individual profile of each community, it is useful to concentrate on the major areas of responsibility or functions of the school business administrator which will be performed in cooperation with all members of the staff having related administrative responsibilities.

I.   Budgeting and Financial Planning

Assists in coordinating the views of administrators, teachers and citizens in translating the educational needs and aspirations of the community into a composite financial plan. Understands the effect of the educational program on the financial structure of the community and exercises sound judgment in maintaining a proper balance between the two. Conducts long-term fiscal planning in terms of community resources and needs. Is sensitive to the changing community, particularly in regard to the economy, and is alert to all sources of new revenue and outside events which affect the community. Should be well versed on taxation at all levels. Recognizes that he is constantly dealing with scarce resources and endeavors to employ systems analysis and the concept of planning-programming-budgeting-evaluating systems to all aspects of financial planning in order to provide his district with the best educational experience for each dollar spent or resource used.

II. Purchasing and Supply Management

Is responsible for all purchases, including equipment and supplies for new buildings as well as for existing buildings. Considers the educational implications associated with each purchasing decision, prepares suitable specifications and standards and utilizes good purchasing principles and procedures. Is also responsible for warehousing, storing, trucking and inventory control.

III. Plant Planning and Construction

Works with administrators, teachers and lay personnel in determining and planning for school plant needs and in acquiring school sites and managing school property after the educational standards have been determined. Works with architects to see that needs are properly translated into final plans, with attorneys and financial advisors to effect suitable financing, with bidders to secure economical contracts and with contractors to provide satisfactory building facilities.

IV. School-Community Relations

Helps interpret the educational program to the public by preparing materials for distribution, addressing and working with service clubs, the PTA and citizens' committees, and through contacts with press, radio and television services. Provides the superintendent and other staff members, as well as the board, with facts that help them in their relations with the public. Interprets the business area of educational programs to the public and to the educational staff.

V. Personnel Management

Recruits or helps to secure personnel for all positions in the area of school business management. Handles individual and group problems related to working conditions, benefits, policy and procedure, and provides guidance and information in connection with severance from service for all personnel.

VI. In-Service Training

Organizes and directs a program of in-service training aimed at increasing the skills of school business management personnel and at developing proper attitudes toward the educational objectives of the school district.

VII. Operation and Maintenance of Plant

Has the responsibility for providing, operating and maintaining facilities which will assure maximum educational utility as well as a healthful, comfortable, safe environment for pupils, teachers and the public.

VIII. Transportation

Supervises the operation and maintenance of the school bus fleet to insure safe, economical and comfortable transportation for children.

IX. Food Services

Has general responsibility for the operation of the school food services by providing economical and satisfactory facilities, and efficient management in the operation of the school lunch program, in close cooperation with those staff members charged with the educational aspects of such service.

X. Accounting and Reporting

Establishes and supervises the accounting system necessary to provide school officials and administrators with accurate financial facts as the basis for formulating policies and decisions. Provides the proper safeguards for the custody of public funds and makes possible complete and revealing reporting both locally and statewide.

XI. Data Processing

When desirable, introduces data processing to provide better and more complete accounting records. May establish or assist in establishing appropriate data banks, electronic files, and data processing procedures to provide management information for appropriate decision making, forecasting and evaluation.

XII. Grantsmanship

Assists in obtaining special educational funds from private foundations, from state or provincial departments of education, from state or provincial legislatures and from federal sources such as the U. S. Office of Education. Makes certain that proposals are administratively sound from the business point of view. Insures that records are maintained and financial reports published.

XIII. Office Management

Supervises clerical personnel in the business office(s) and, upon occasion, in other school offices. Reviews form design and updates form requirements as needed. Establishes procedures for record keeping, maintaining all records that prudence and legal requirements demand.

XIV. Educational Resources Management

Recognizes that he is constantly dealing with scarce resources and endeavors to employ systems analysis and the concept of planning-programming-budgeting-evaluating systems to all aspects of financial planning in order to provide his district with the best educational experience for each dollar spent or resource used. Consider the multi-year or long term impact of all aspects of the educational program.

TYPICAL DUTIES

In order that interested school people and lay citizens may have a broader understanding of the kinds of duties typically assigned to the school business administrator, a list of frequently performed functions has been compiled. The list may be helpful to board members, school administrators and others who are concerned with establishing the position of school business administrator in a system which does not have one. It may also be useful in comparing existing assignment of duties in the several types of systems. Because of the great variations in district size, the following functions may be assumed by one person or assigned to several individuals.

I.   Financial Planning
   A. Budget compilation, in coordination with educational planning
   B. Long-term fiscal planning — operating budget
   C. Receipt estimates
   D. Budget control
   E. Fiscal relationships with other government units
   F. Use of systems analysis and PPBES

II. Accounting
   A. General fund
   B. Capital reserve funds and trust funds
   C. Construction funds
   D. Internal accounts
   E. Student activity funds
   F. Voucher and payroll preparation
   G. Inventory
   H. Attendance accounting
   I. Government tax and pension accounting
   J. Special trust funds
   K. Cost accounting
   L. Student stores, book stores

III. Debt Service and Capital Fund Management
   A. Long-and short-term financing
   B. Maturities and debt payments
   C. Long-range capital programs
   D. Investments
   E. Reporting
   F. Bond and note register
   G. Debt service payment procedures

   H. Short-term debt management

IV. Auditing
   A. Pre-audit, or internal, procedures
   B. Determination that prepared statements present fairly the financial position
   C. Propriety, legality and accuracy of financial transactions
   D. Proper recording of all financial transactions
   E. Post-audit procedures
   F. External audits
   G. Reconciliation of internal and external audits

V.   Purchasing and Supply Management
   A. Official purchasing agent
   B. Purchase methods
   C. Stock requisition
   D. Standards and specifications
   E. Purchase bids
   F. Purchase contracts
   G. Purchase of supplies and equipment
   H. Storage, delivery, trucking services
   I. Inventory control

VI. School Plant Planning and Construction
   A. Assists in the establishment of educational standards for sites, buildings and equipment
   B. Plant utilization studies
   C. Projections of facility needs
   D. Design, construction and equipment of plant
   E. Safety standards
   F. Contracts management
   G. Architect selection

VII. Operation of Plant — Custodial, Gardening, Engineering Services
   A. Standards and frequency of work
   B. Manpower allocations
   C. Scheduling
   D. Inspection and evaluation of service
   E. Relationship with educational staff
   F. Operating of related school-community facilities, such as recreation, park, museum, library programs, etc.
   G. Community use of facilities
   H. Protection of plant and property
   I. Security and police forces

VIII. Maintenance of Plant
   A. Repair of buildings and equipment
   B. Upkeep of grounds
   C. Maintenance policies, standards, and frequency of maintenance
   D. Scheduling and allocation of funds and manpower
   E. Modernization and rehabilitation versus replacement

IX. Real Estate Management
    A. Site acquisition and sales
    B. Rentals, leases
    C. Rights-of-way and easements
    D. Assessments and taxes
    E. After school use of buildings
    F. Dormitories, student unions, concessions

X. Personnel Management
    A. Records
        1. Probationary and tenure status of employees
        2. Sick leave and leave of absence
        3. Official notices of appointment and salaries
        4. Retirement data and deductions
        5. Salary schedules and payments
        6. Individual earning records
        7. Withholding, tax and group insurance or fringe benefits
        8. Civil Service and Social Security
        9. Substitute and part-time employees
        10. Dues checkoffs
    B. Supervision of noninstructional staff
        1. Recruitment
        2. Selection
        3. Placement
        4. Training
        5. Advancement
        6. Working conditions
        7. Disciplinary action
        8. Termination of services
    C. Relationship to instructional staff
        1. Good will and service concept
        2. Cooperation in procurement
        3. Cooperation in budget preparation
        4. Information on pay and retirement
        5. Personnel records and reports

XI. Permanent Property Records and Custody of Legal Papers
    A. Security and preservation of records
    B. Maintenance of storage files
    C. Purging of records no longer legally required

XII. Transportation of Pupils
    A. Policies, rules, regulations and procedures
    B. Contract versus district-owned equipment
    C. Routing and scheduling
    D. Inspection and maintenance
    E. Staff supervision and training
    F. Utilization and evaluation of services
    G. Standards and specifications

XIII. Food Service Operations
    A. Policies, rules, regulations and procedures
    B. Staffing and supervision
    C. Menus, prices and portion controls
    D. Purchasing
    E. Accounting, reporting and cost analysis
    F. In-Service training
    G. Coordination with educational program

XIV. Insurance
    A. Insurance policies
    B. Insurable values — buildings and contents
    C. Coverages to be provided
    D. Claims and reporting
    E. Insurance procurement procedures
    F. Insurance and claims record
    G. Distribution of insurance to companies, agents and brokers

XV. Cost Analysis
    A. Unit costs
    B. Comparative costs
    C. Costs distribution studies

XVI. Reporting
    A. Local financial and statistical reports
    B. State financial and statistical reports
    C. Federal financial and statistical reports
    D. Miscellaneous reports
    E. Required legal advertising
    F. Relationships with public information media

XVII. Collective Negotiations
    A. Service on management team when required
    B. Preparation of pertinent fiscal data for management team
    C. Development of techniques and strategies of collective negotiation
    D. Sharing of proper information with employee units
    E. Use of outside negotiators, agencies
    F. Mediation, arbitration, grievances

XVIII. Data Processing
    A. Selection of system
    B. Programming
    C. Utilization of systems analysis
    D. Forms preparation
    E. Broad use of equipment for all pertinent applications

XIX. Board Policies and Administrative Procedures as Related to Fiscal and Noninstructional Matters

NEW AREAS OF RESPONSIBILITY

Because of the complexity of our contemporary society, the school business administrator must view his role as greater than the functions, duties and responsibilities actually assigned to him. One new area involved in his expanded role is that of educational public relations. The school business administrator must be in communication and interaction with decision makers in the community because the business of the school cannot be isolated from the community it serves. In recent years, tax payers have become more knowledgeable about and concerned with the educational process and its financial operations. Therefore, it is becoming increasingly essential for the school business administrator to establish a direct line of communication between the school system and the public.

The school business administrator must assume a prominent role in preparing and providing information to the public concerning school business operations. This type of community involvement can be of significance to the concept of school business administration and have an impact on community decisions on school operations.

In an institutional context the school business administrator must recognize that the institution of the school is only one of many in the community. The school cannot be an isolate, but must work to see that the school goals are consistent with the larger goals of the total structure of the community.

Within a school system itself there exist sub-institutions which require the administrator to exhibit sustained collective action. He must be dependent upon interchange with the larger system — the total school organization and the total school business community organization.

The school business administrator must give evidence of professional competence. There is no monopoly on good business practices. The advice of the school business manager on business affairs of the community should be sought. He should be prepared to assist the superintendent and the board of education in interpreting, presenting and planning school financial programs.

He must realize that the skills he has used in the past are no longer sufficient to do an effective total job. He must learn new techniques and new approaches so that he can effectively and directly contribute to and strengthen the educational objectives of the community.

To be of maximum value to his school system during hard times, the SBA will do at least some of the following:

1. He will examine each function and duty performed by his operation. He will ask, "Is this function necessary? Is it desirable? Should it be reduced, expanded, abolished or retained.?"

2. He will seek to objectively determine if the function or duty can be combined with others, or shifted to a more appropriate department, or held in abeyance for the period of budget emergency.

3. He will suggest alternative levels of performance and provide cost-benefit analysis of changing the frequency or level of performance, e.g., what happens if gyms are swept only twice a week instead of daily? What happens if typewriters are kept for five years instead of three? What happens if ceilings are washed yearly instead of painted at five-year intervals? What happens if textbooks are adopted for five years instead of three? etc.

4. He will promote an atmosphere of team consideration of existing procedures, and will seek frank evaluations of what is currently being done. He will encourage and provide incentives for employee, student, and citizen suggestions on how to change or improve efficiency of operations.

5. He will review present methods of "delivery" of goods and services, and will ask, "Are there other methods by which the service can be delivered, or other agencies which can do it better, faster, cheaper than we can? This kind of questioning will bear very directly on the possibility of contracted transportation, food service, maintenance, repair and operations procedures. Even simple tasks like garbage and trash removal, towel service, uniform laundry, and similar activities will be closely examined for possible economies.

6. He will stand above the swaying pressures of personnel groups, neighborhood and parent groups and proponents and protagonist factions in examining such questions as staff reductions, facilities closings, program and service curtailments, and will honestly and accurately determine and state the costs of various options and alternatives. He will not "juggle" figures or findings, or attempt to

withhold or distort findings which are relative to the consideration of any policy issue. His status should be that of an expert, whose integrity is respected even by those who disagree with him. There is nothing more tragic in public administration than "wrong" policy decisions made by honest and sincere persons upon the basis of inaccurate, incomplete, or deliberately misinterpreted data.

7. The most useful SBA will be able to isolate truly relevant cost data and expenditure trends and will be able to give perspective, not only on present actual total and relative costs, but also upon long-term trends and total potential costs of any service or program, or proposed changes in salaries, fringe benefits, and mandated potential commitments, etc.

8. By providing careful data gathering procedure in an orderly ongoing fashion, and by having competency in the areas of computer utilization, the effective SBA can be extremely useful. Decision questions will be anticipated, and appropriate data gathering methods and procedures provided so that answers can be forthcoming when needed, in a fashion to be of maximum use to the decision makers. Reports of significant trends and operating results can be given historic "trending" interpretations and current comparisons with other districts and state, regional and national norms or patterns can be readily identified.

9. The successful SBA will alert and encourage his staff to be students of their own operations. He will encourage them to analyze their own performances, and will provide emotional and financial incentives for exemplary achievements. Conversely, he will inculcate the habit of self criticism and unit self evaluation, to ensure betterment of production. For example, if it costs only $50 per student to provide shop and laboratory supplies in school A, why does it cost $85 in school B? Or if secretaries in the district type an average of 30 letters per day, why is office X staff only typing 18? Or if it costs $195 per pupil to heat and light junior high school A, why is it costing $238 in junior high school B?

These kinds of self directed questions can have tremendous significance for the improvement of operational efficiency in any district. The *good* SBA will make them happen.

10. Perhaps the final or most effective contribution the good school business administrator can make to the success of his school system's operation lies in the area of interpersonal relationships. He (or she) is first of all perceived of as a "good man." His arrival in the morning is welcomed with smiles by his staff. He has a reputation for fairness and integrity. He is known by citizens and taxpayers as one who "runs a tight ship." Merchants and vendors believe him to be fair and honest in his dealings. He pays district bills on time. He settles disputes fairly, and with a keen sense of human values involved. People trust him. They know he is ethical and will not take advantage of honest mistakes. They believe he is trying to get a buck's worth of value for every dollar spent, and he spends every penny as if it is his own.

With the presence of such an esteemed person, candor is encouraged; more objective and less emotional consideration is given to package decisions, and even those who lose decisions come away believing their ideas have been fairly considered, and they have had a fair shake. They believe the school system is in good hands, and they will support, even in hard times!

There is only one way SBAs can achieve this maximal acceptance of usefulness to the school district — they earn it, by the sum total of all they do every day!

9

ENERGY COST CONTAINMENT:
THE DOLLARS ADD UP

Paul Abramson

Because a school district can't do everything to conserve energy, that doesn't mean it can do nothing. Author Abramson lists a number of uncomplicated steps a district can take that save money as well as energy without dismantling or even harming the educational program.

Mr. Abramson, a distinguished writer and editor on educational matters, is president of Intelligence for Education, and the author of Chapter Four.

It's been less than a decade since the first Arab oil boycott. At that time, in most schools, "energy" was something that was exhibited by good teachers in the classroom. Utilities represented a small line item on the budget that was paid, without much thought, year after year.

Those days of non-concern will never return. But the buildings constructed during that era — buildings that consume a great deal of oil, gas and electricity — will continue in use for another 50 years. And therein lies a problem.

Colorado architect Lamar Kelsey recently estimated that the difference in energy costs between an energy efficient 500-student elementary school designed today and a standard 1960's elementary school of the same size would make it possible to hire six additional teachers!

Obviously, the cost of energy today is a significant drain on the school budget. And it is a drain that provides no educational value whatsoever. One goal of educational leadership in the 1980's and beyond, must be to convert the money that is literally going up the chimney into productive educational dollars.

While it is true that most school buildings constructed in the post-war era are not energy efficient, it is also true that if their electrical and mechanical systems were operated at peak efficiency, a great deal of energy would be saved. Take buildings that were not designed for energy conservation, mix liberally with 25 years of deferred maintenance and add a dash of poorly trained, underpaid head custodians and you have a perfect recipe for energy waste. Bring the systems back up to top operating shape and put trained people in charge of them and you can reduce your costs as much as 40 per cent — with little or no capital spending. What it does take is determination and leadership. And that is what board members and administrators must provide.

Because most of us are laymen when it comes to building construction and operation, it's tempting to pass the responsibility for energy conservation on to somebody else. But energy conservation is not a complicated process. It's a combination of good educational practices and a little common sense. Here are a few rules of thumb that can help you save money without a huge investment of time or capital.

1. Remember that most energy is saved by people, not machines. For many, many years, custodial and maintenance people were the bottom of the employment pile. They were good people who received little training, little recognition and little pay. Today they are running million dollar systems with a potential for savings that rivals that of any other person in the school system.

Custodial and maintenance staffs must be upgraded. They must get better leadership, real training and be given a feeling of responsibility and importance. You wouldn't think of putting a tug boat captain at the helm of an aircraft carrier, but that's essentially what we do when we put untrained people in charge of our school buildings.

2. Develop district-wide energy awareness programs. Once again, it is people who use and waste energy — or who can save it. It's important to impress energy conservation tenets on students, teachers, principals and others. It isn't necessary to turn all lights on when entering a room (nor should they be left on when the room is empty) but in school after school, teachers automatically do just that. Walk into a gymnasium some day and look at the number of lights that are burning. That's a matter of awareness.

There are many ways in which to increase awareness and cut utility bills. Principals must take leadership in their schools and keep after recalcitrant teachers. Students can be involved through poster and composition contests, through class work, through messages sent home on the need for energy conservation everywhere. Engineer Manfred Moses suggests to his clients that energy records be posted in the front lobby of every school building, comparing that building's energy record this year with last and with the records of other schools in the same system. Make it competitive. Set up a contest. Provide an incentive to have the best energy record. It doesn't take much to create awareness — it does save a lot, by bringing energy costs down.

3. Keep records. Records alone don't save energy, but they can document where you really are, how well you're doing. Month-by-month, building-by-building records of energy use and cost, once started, are easy to maintain. Add to that such information as oil deliveries, how much oil is actually in the tank on a particular day each year (i.e. July 1,) and degree day information available from your local utility and you have the makings of a very good, simple and effective energy record system.

4. Reevaluate board policies. School board policies exist today which are anachronisms. For example, in many districts every school building is open and heated five or six nights a week for adult education or recreation programs. Consider consolidating such programs in a single building or even a section of a large building. Run recreational programs with thermostats on night setting.

But that is a detail. All board policies and administrative regulations need to be reviewed with energy conservation in mind. What is really necessary and what can be changed? What makes a contribution to the district program and what is simply a convention or a convenience? Can it be done as well at less energy cost? Is the program really valuable or just something that's "always been done"?

It is not necessary to dismantle useful programs in the name of energy savings. That's penny wise and pound foolish. But it is necessary to insure that what you are doing is truly worthwhile today.

5. Cut lighting levels. One of the great energy (and dollar) wasters of our school systems is the tremendous amount of light we have provided in most areas — classrooms, lavatories, gymnasiums, boiler rooms, everywhere. For many years we were convinced by the argument that more light makes better light. But that ain't necessarily so.

Most of our school rooms are overlit to the point that they can actually cause problems rather than solve them. Thirty-five foot candles is a good reading surface for most activities, but if you take a light meter to your classrooms, you'll probably get readings of 90 foot candles or more.

A major look at the lighting conditions in your schools is a necessity if energy and dollars are to be saved. But don't just take out a lightbulb here and there. Hire expert help to insure that distribution is correct, that task lighting is where it belongs, that controls are set so that lighting can be changed to meet specific circumstances. You'll find that less light often means better sight, better study and learning conditions, and considerably lower electric bills.

6. Use the powers of nature. One way to cut the use of artificial lighting in classrooms is by using more daylight. Open the shades where appropriate and let the sun shine in. Let it shine in, too, in the spring and fall (and sometimes winter) to provide solar heat. And open windows in the spring and fall to provide free ventilation. Nothing smells as good in a classroom as that first whiff of clean spring air each year. And yet, in too many buildings, tightly shut windows and drawn blinds keep the delights of nature out of our classrooms — and increase the costs of lighting, heating and ventilating those rooms.

7. Don't tinker with what you don't really understand. The electrical and mechanical systems of most schools are fairly sophisticated. Run correctly, they can save a great deal of energy. Tinkered with, they can be thrown out of whack altogether. For example, cutting off ventilation air by blocking unit ventilator dampers probably costs more than it saves. Running the summer cycle of a centrally air conditioned system in the winter may cause freezeups. Most maintenance personnel are good hands-on people. But they are seldom engineers. They may know and care about the buildings' electrical and mechanical systems, but then they may know and care about the educational program, too. But when something has to be done to make mechanical systems or educational systems work better, it's wise to bring in an expert to help. Or *do* you let custodians determine your reading and math programs?

8. Use some common sense. The object of schools is to provide education, not to conserve energy. Your job as an educational leader is to provide that education in as economic a manner as possible, consistent with good educational practice. It's better to study in a room that is not overheated

and is free of glare. There's no educational value in heating or lighting an empty school. Ventilation systems need not run when nobody is there to use them. There's no point in running two furnaces when one will carry the load. None of these wasteful practices has anything to do with good education, nor does running more efficiently compromise education in any way.

But other changes may be less benign. Heating a greenhouse may be expensive, but it also may be the difference between an excellent course and a dull one. Keeping a school open after hours to support a recreation program may be the difference between winning and losing budget votes. Keeping an office area at a comfortable temperature may increase efficiency.

Your job as an educational leader must be to judge all proposed changes in terms of educational effectiveness. Use expert help, but don't let the energy expert tell you how to run your schools. After all, the best way to save energy in our school buildings would be to shut them down entirely. But that does seem like a rather drastic remedy for a serious, but not yet fatal, condition.

10

IMPROVING PEOPLE POLICIES: THE ONLY WAY TO GO

Stanton Leggett

Increased productivity, teacher involvement, learning on the job, performance objectives, career planning — these are some of the worthwhile goals that the superintendent and board can achieve if they go about it that right way. The pay off is people who work smarter and stay longer and are satisfied if not happy.

Consultant Leggett, the author of several chapters in this book, was awarded the 1981 award as Planner of the Year by the Council of Educational Facilities Planners. Additional background appears in the introduction to Chapter Seven.

One of the more delightful ironies of our time must be Peter Drucker's forecast[1] that the organizational and management structure of business enterprise will increasingly come to resemble that of a university. No one knows more clearly than university presidents that there is a continuing question at any time as to who is actually running the institution. It was not whim that caused Cohen and March[2] to describe the management model of a university as an "organized anarchy."

But Drucker's comment has significance to managers of educational institutions in that he is recognizing that the command model of the military, the stereotype of "efficient" management, is no longer appropriate when the workers are well educated. Knowledge workers, as Drucker terms them, are potentially most productive, most expensive, and most difficult to manage. Inherently their loyalties are divided between their disciplines and the institution that employs them. Unless the institution cultivates the knowledge worker, the discipline will be the primary focus of loyalty.

In education, an extraordinarily high percentage of workers are knowledge workers. Obviously, all teachers, counselors and educational administrators are duly certified, licensed professionals. Schools increasingly employ systems analysts and programmers; MBA-type management people; audio-visual specialists; electronic specialists; heating, ventilating and air conditioning specialists at a technician or sub-engineering level; and so on. Custodians in charge of expensive and complex physical plants are required to have a high order of technical competence. Aides are frequently highly trained professionals waiting for openings in the professional staff. Cleaners, bus drivers and crossing guards are about all that are left of a simpler model and most of these are part-time employees. Secretarial and clerical workers are in a class by themselves, with the able representatives of the category often working at levels far above their classifications, exercising judgment, making decisions, and often operating the establishment.

Knowledge workers are smart. The possession of skills of a discipline gives the knowledge worker an independence exhibited sometimes by employment for a time to set up a program or to accomplish a goal and then moving on. The mobility of knowledge workers in education is relatively limited at the moment as readjustments to enrollment declines occur, but they remain independent characters. Knowledge workers tend to be underemployed in that often the opportunities do not exist in the employment setting to use even reasonably fully the capacities of the worker. Finally, and particularly with younger people, the knowledge worker places great value on some kind of self-fulfillment in work.

INCREASING PRODUCTIVITY

The manager, attempting to deliver more and better service with the same amount of staff (also known as increasing productivity), must be acutely aware of the setting in which the principal institutional resource — the people who work there — is used. The policies used to improve performance must take into account the nature of the professional or technical employee and the problems involved in the duality of the goals of a discipline and the goals of the institution.

Increased productivity means working "smarter" not longer or harder. This is true of all endeavors. It is especially true in education. Drucker[3] maintains that in an enterprise using a formidable number of knowledge workers, the manager, having created a setting of relative psychological security, arranges for the following to happen:

1. Since the knowledge worker knows more about his or her job than almost anyone else, the manager turns to the knowledge worker to find out what helps or hinders the performance of the task and does something about the findings.

2. The manager helps the knowledge worker take responsibility for the achievement of higher levels of performance on the task.

3. The manager helps the knowledge worker to continue to learn. This means the slow, solid, unspectacular process of

learning how to improve performance when the job is already well done.

MULTI-CHANNEL COMMUNICATION

To carry out these injunctions, the school system managers must improve communications with the staff. There must be channels of communication for suggestions and for complaints that are fully used and where the views of each worker are respected. The development of a multi-channel communication system, one through the hierarchy of teacher-principal-central office or custodian-principal-central office or through areas of specialization such as teacher-subject and discipline council or supervisor-central office or cleaner-custodian-supervisor-central office, are among the routes that should be used. Advisory committees of many kinds including, when appropriate, parents and students are a way of increasing the opportunities of communication. The availability of the managers on an informal basis adds to the effectiveness of the network.

A multi-channeled communication system is an essential prerequisite to expecting increased responsibility on the part of knowledge workers. The network must operate in two directions. The interlocking nature of the communication network can contribute to building the quality of colleague rather than that of employee.

INCREASING ACCEPTANCE OF RESPONSIBILITY

How the knowledge worker is treated will determine to a considerable extent how the teacher or programmer or secretary or principal perceives his or her place in the system and, hence, responsibility in the system. The manager must ask what factors in the employment setting must be adjusted in order to cause an employee to seek responsibility for improved performance.

As in learning, the employee should have a fairly clear and believable idea of his or her level of beginning performance. There should be a clear understanding on the part of the employee as to an acceptable standard of performance toward which to work. There should be a variety of ways in which any gap between present performance and expected performance can be eliminated. For example, in helping a new teacher increase performance to an acceptable level work with colleagues or supervisors, including perhaps micro teaching or clinical supervision, may prove helpful. Inservice courses can be used when these are closely focused on the teacher's needs. Visitation of other classes, the assistance of a senior teacher, reading the research in a field, and similar moves can be made.

The combination of known goals, tasks to be accomplished to reach the goals, and a suportive environment in which help is given in many forms, builds confidence, knowledge and skills and eventually leads to the desired performance. Too many systems lack a clear and objective process for upgrading performance to desired levels. In addition, even fewer provide a systematic way to encourage teachers or other employees to exceed acceptable performance standards. True, superior principals have long been effective in raising faculty expectations. The role of the principal is critical. The system can help by its support of the principal and by creating new avenues for the exercise of responsibility and rewards for the exercise of responsibility beyond the level of acceptable performance.

TEACHER PARTICIPATION IN DECISION-MAKING

An example of the efforts of school systems to increase the participation of knowledge workers in accepting responsibility of setting and achieving higher standards of performance is the San Jose Teacher Involvement Project.[4] The project, as evaluated by Stanford Research Institute, was judged successful, received the support of the staff and was effective in producing improvement in the school system.

The study and the ultimate development of the strategy suggested 13 areas for teacher participation in making decisions about the operation of the school in which they worked. The following table shows these areas.

Possible Areas for Teacher Involvement in Decision Making

1. School Budget and Expenditures
   - policy for instructional accountability in purchase of new equipment and materials
   - procedures for supplying all classrooms with necessary basic supplies
   - procedure for planning and obtaining faculty input on learning resources purchases
   - allocation of school budget to program areas
   - petty cash instructional funds for each teacher

2. Inservice Training and Faculty Meetings
   - mandatory inservice requirements, i.e., advance notice of program and content
   - teacher role in determining scheduling, program, content
   - assessment of teacher training needs, e.g., use of aides and paraprofessionals
   - teacher-designed inservice training for teachers with appropriate resources

3. Principal/Teacher Relations
   - policies defining equitable, consistent and effective personnel management policies
   - development of guidelines for acting on parent concerns regarding teachers
   - guidelines for grievance procedures at the school level
   - reciprocal accountability
   - guidelines for principal consultation with all related teachers prior to action requested by a parent

4. Certificated Support Personnel
   - guidelines for staffing of school special programs and projects
   - parameters for use of specialist re ongoing programs
   - clarification of job responsibilities for counselors, vice principals, nurse, psychologist, etc.
   - policies and procedures for teachers to obtain services and refer students to counselors, vice principals, attendance officer, psychometrist, etc.

5. Parent/Teacher Relationships
   - guidelines for teachers to select their own representatives to parent/community organizations and service clubs
   - policies for appointments and visitations
   - consultation with involved teacher prior to action at other levels
   - teacher involvement in design of special programs, open houses, fairs, expositions, etc.

6. Teacher Personnel Policies
   - equitable policy for distribution of extra-duty assignments
   - procedure for changes in level and combination of personnel or subject in teaching assignments
   - policy for involvement of teachers in decisions relating to school assignments and programs
   - environment and conditions enabling teachers to instruct in style best suited to them
   - policy to accommodate individual differences and teaching styles of certificated personnel

7. Student Personnel Policies
   - equitable student personnel and discipline policies
   - fair assignment and transfer policies based on individual student needs and differences
   - instructional resource options to accommodate individual student learning styles
   - scheduling procedures sensitive to student socioeconomic and ethnic needs
   - policy regarding psychological referrals and their impact on other students and teachers

8. Evaluation
   - procedure for open information feedback to staff on both positive and negative outcomes of continuing projects/programs
   - pre-evaluation consultation with staff to avoid duplication of effort and needless data collection
   - coordination of A127 project objectives and Stull objectives to meet *minimum* standards
   - reciprocal evaluation

9. Curriculum Content and Philosophy
   - policies for teacher involvement in developing innovative programs and discontinuing existing programs
   - teacher role in defining curriculum and educational philosophy (open education, modular scheduling, team teaching, etc.)
   - method of articulation between and among programs
   - time and opportunity to study results of potential new programs and projects within and outside the district
   - coordination of school rules and curriculum emphasis with recreation and other after-school programs

10. Instructional Materials
    - procedure for allocating instructional resources
    - evaluating and obtaining complete curricular packages for full instructional benefit
    - equitable policies for student use of library/media materials

11. Instructional Methods and Grouping

- policies for teacher load, staffing patterns, class composition, scheduling patterns
- options for implementation of a variety of teaching and learning styles

12. School Procedures
   - guidelines to limit classroom interruptions
   - guidelines for messages and referrals
   - methods for obtaining assistance in proposal writing
   - distribution of association mail

13. School Priorities
   - procedure for setting priorities
   - teacher participation in generating items for priority setting

The levels of involvement that were seen as possible are shown in the following table.

Levels of Involvement

1. *Recommendation:* The faculty or staff council would act in an advisory capacity to the principals, suggesting policies and ideas.

2. *Information:* The council would be informed of the principal's decisions and in turn inform the rest of the faculty of these decisions and what they required of the teachers by way of action and implementation.

3. *Consultation:* The council would be consulted by the principal for its recommendations before the principal took action.

4. *Approval:* The council would be consulted about decisions and have the right to alter, approve, or reject decisions of the principal.

5. *Authorization:* The council would initiate decision making, with the principal offering ideas and suggestions to the council and carrying out the decisions of the council.

The faculty in the schools where the process was undertaken, for the most part, selected from among the first three levels as the basis for their participation. However, some school staffs opted to work at the authorization level, accepting greater risk and responsibility. Obviously, with experience the degree of risk that would be acceptable, given intelligent management, would be expected to rise. Outside stresses also can affect the operation of a change of governance of this sort. The passage of Proposition 13 and the reduced budgets resulting have exacerbated the tension of collective bargaining and reduced the effectiveness of the program.

The areas of major faculty interest in involvement are shown in the following table. (See next page.)

Curriculum and teaching methods were the greatest concern of the faculty participants. The increase in interest in budget in recent years reflects the pressures that Proposition 13 has had upon the schools.

Any school system has an interesting problem of weighing autonomy and authority in each school as against system wide priorities and concerns. The multi-channeled communication system and the use of good staff work in relating the concerns of the school with the concerns of the system are critical factors in success in operating a complex organization.

If, in the long haul, the faculty acceptance of responsibility makes the faculty participation group for each school into the equivalent of a quality-control committee or a continuing in-school pressure for increasing the level of performance, the results will be well worth the effort. This seems to be one of the most promising avenues for improvement particularly when linked to system-wide efforts to support the expectations of each school.

CONTINUED LEARNING ON THE JOB

Learning to do better that which you already know how to do well means the establishment of a learning system as a part of every job in the school system. It is well known that learning on the job is the most effective way to increase vocational or professional skills. A school system should be more effective at this process than any other enterprise.

The five year plan, outlined by Andrisek in a previous chapter, shows how central importance can be given faculty learning on the job in effecting curriculum improvement.

Expenditures for in-service education of teachers tend to decline in direct proportion to decline in enrollments. As funds dry up, the in-service education program tends to be considered an expendable item.[5]

When improvement in the performance of staff is so important and training of staff is so central to the accomplishment of the goal, the effective manager will find ways to continue and improve learning on the job. The use of central office staff in more specific and more goal-oriented ways may be at the heart of the program.

JOB SECURITY: HAVE A PLAN

One essential element in any managerial effort to increase performance of a school system is the creation of a sense of security on the part of its staff. The staffing process should contribute to this sense of security to assure the new permanent employee that there will be an appropriate employment slot with the system for the foreseeable future.

Tenure or continuing contracts are a fact of legal life in schools. The development of a community of interest between staff and administration is a vital prerequisite for staff loyalty and the willingness of the knowledge worker to increase his or her use of energy or, more important, to use it more intelligently for the institution. While in some circles lifetime employment is looked upon as an abdication of the right to fire employees and therefore an invitation to laziness and inefficiency on the job, it should be noted that below

the top administrative level, most entrepreneurial organizations attempt to retain their employees and indeed often find ways to change jobs to adapt to the changes of employees over time. A prime example of the policy of lifetime employment has been the group of larger industries in Japan. Interestingly, the record of productivity increases in Japanese industry has been much higher than that of the United States. Most of the increase has come about because of the development of working environments in which workers who are smart enough are motivated to find ways to increase their own productivity.

It is essential in a time of declining enrollments for the school system to plan ahead in its use of staff so that no permanent teachers will be hired who must, in a few years, be fired. This same sense of job security should prevail in all aspects of the system. A good plan will look ten years ahead. It will assess the needs for teaching staff based upon carefully made and frequently updated enrollment estimates. These estimates then should be translated

INVOLVEMENT AREAS OF INTEREST TO RESPONDENTS

Involvement Area	% Endorsing as Most Important		
	1975 (Rank)	1976 (Rank)	1977 (Rank)
Roles of certificated and classified support personnel ...	16.5 (7)	12.0 (7)	11.4 (7)
Guidelines for teacher/parent relationships.............	5.3 (8)	4.9 (8)	7.2 (8)
Curriculum content and philosophy....................	43.1 (1)	51.0 (1)	50.6 (1)
Instructional methods and grouping	32.8 (2)	33.7 (2)	39.8 (2)
Student personnel policies and discipline..............	29.8 (3)	27.7 (3)	21.7 (4)
School budget and expenditures	17.0 (6)	19.0 (6)	25.9 (3)
Inservice training and faculty meetings	25.3 (4)	21.7 (4)	19.3 (5)
Teacher personnel policies	24.9 (5)	20.7 (5)	16.3 (6)

Source: Stanford Research Institute, 1977, Table 12, p. 29.

into available job slots. The plan should also estimate the changes that will take place in the present staff over time. The experience of the school system in recent years in retirements, deaths, resignations, and other separations from the service can be used to forecast changes in numbers of staff by position. Again frequent updating of these forecasts will improve the accuracy of the estimates.

Estimating future staff needs is particularly important in secondary school teaching positions where, in most parts of the country, enrollments may be expected to decline sharply over the next ten years. As an example, in Independence, OH, a recent study[6] showed the following estimated changes in numbers of sections of science by discipline in the high school in 1982-83 and 1989-90 compared to the number of sections in 1979-80. The course enrollments were expected to drop to 84 per cent of 1979-80 enrollments for the 1982-83 year and to 53 per cent of 1979-80 enrollments for the 1989-90 school year, based upon systemwide estimates of grades 9 to 12. It would be possible to make estimates by the year in which most students enrolled in a subject, such as 9th grade enrollment estimates related to earth science enrollments.

If each teacher is assumed to teach five courses a day, to simplify the example, using the system's staffing patterns, 4.6 science teachers are required in 1979-80 while in 1989-90 only 2.2 teachers will be required. Even by 1982-83, only 2.8 teachers will be required. Clearly, faced with this kind of information, were a science teacher to resign in 1980-81, the school administrator should consider many factors before deciding to replace the resignee with another full-time permanent teacher. These factors would include the situation in science in the lower grades, the anticipated number of staff in science who could be expected to leave, the certification of teachers now in the system, and that of prospective candidates. If openings in mathematics were anticipated, a candidate who was certified in both science and mathematics would be useful to the system and would, under such circumstances, be relatively assured of continuing employment. Even if the system could manage its science staff to avoid any layoffs as enrollments declined, it is clear that the broader the certification or preparation of a teacher, the better chance the system has to protect the individual's job. One role of the system would be either to hire teachers with broader certification, interests and training, or to plan with present staff to broaden each teacher's areas of competence.

A similar situation prevails in non-

EXCERPT FROM: TABLE 16

ESTIMATED NUMBER OF SECTIONS BY SUBJECT AND COURSE, 1982-83 and 1989-90, BASED ON 1979-80 EXPERIENCE, GRADES 9-12, INDEPENDENCE, OH

| | 1979-80 | | | 1982-83 | | 1989-90 | |
| | No. Enrolled | No. Sects. | Avg. Sect. Size | Est. No. Enrolled 1 x .84 | Est. No. Sects. | Est. No. Enrolled 1 x .53 | Est. No. Sects |
Subject / Course	(1)	(2)	(3)	(4)	(5)	(6)	(7)
Science							
Earth Science.....	112	6	18.7	94	5	59	3
Biology	104	5	20.9	87	4	55	3
Chemistry	47	3	15.7	39	2	25	2
Physics..........	24	2	12.0	20	1	13	1
Electives-Sci......	47	7	6.7	39	2	25	2
SUBTOTALS:	334	23	14.5	279	14	177	11

teaching roles where both projected numbers of jobs and some estimates of the way staff remains with the system will mean a more intelligent hiring policy. Where enrollments are dropping and the system anticipates closing schools, one example of an approach to maintaining job security for its present employees would be to develop temporary and alternative ways of providing the service. If it is expected that an elementary school will be closed in time, when vacancies occur in the system-wide cleaning staff, for example, it might be useful to fill the vacancies by contracting with an outside agency for cleaning services in a school. This would involve concentrating the school-employed cleaning staff in the remaining schools. If one of the schools is closed, the contracted cleaning service could be terminated and the school-employed cleaning staff could be redistributed over the remaining schools.

EVALUATION OF PEOPLE AT WORK

No person employed by an organization likes to think of himself of herself as a faceless worker, one of 500, or 20, or "them." Every employee is "me" surrounded by others doing the same task or interconnected work. The "me" in the worker wants to be important. One of the goals of employment is the flowering of "me" over time, as the organization allows "me" to grow into an effective person performing an important task that is appropriate to "me" in terms of my self-fulfillment.

The organization, while it wants to be assured that all employees work to an acceptable level of competence, has a great stake, also, in the flowering of the individual into a person in the organization who works "smarter," or stated another way, who is highly productive on the job.

The question tends to be raised as to what constitutes an acceptable level of performance of a set of tasks that make up a job. A test of some kind is called for.

In education, the use of tests as a weapon of power over students has a long, long tradition. Few enough students are motivated by the joy of learning and a fair number of students are moved to learn by the threat of tests. There is little surprising in the fact that teachers resist being tested themselves, no matter how the testing is done.

There is little doubt that evaluation of staff to determine whether or not individuals maintain an acceptable level of performance on the task is a basic requirement of any operating institution. Thomas,[7] in his illuminating review of this area, describes a performance evaluation system using four steps, as follows.

> Performance standards are established. Frequently standards are expressed as objectives.
> Standards are monitored to assess progress made toward meeting performance standards.
> A remediation process is established to help employees meet standards.
> Validation of achievement is established by judgment, tests, observation of products, observation or other device.

For the manager concerned with the general area of productivity or helping staff to work smarter, two factors are important. One is that performance standards can be raised slowly and carefully with the cooperation and participation of the staff involved. This is an appropriate and ongoing process. Standards, however, are necessarily set at a level below the work of the best employees. Such standards may, over time, raise the average performance somewhat. To the manager looking to increase the effectiveness of workers, there should be ways open to motivate the best to improve and to increase the number of workers operating well above performance standards. Most systems underemploy their workers: they do not challenge the employees to work at a level that utilizes their real competencies.

A school system should expect all employees to meet the agreed upon performance standards. If these are not met, efforts should be made to help employees build skills to meet standards. If this fails, the system can withhold salary increments, transfer employees to alternative locations, separate them from the system, or use some combination of measures to assure that ultimately the performance standards are met.

Beyond this base line, the system should have a variety of alternatives or choices that motivate much of the staff to operate above the acceptable level of performance. A manager can be evaluated on his or her success in the percentage of employees observed objectively by others to be performing at well above average levels.

Among the choices possible include increasing the numbers of levels in the hierarchy of positions, relating performance on the job to a career ladder including opportunities both within and without the system, and creating "stretch objectives" including individually negotiated goals, working conditions and salary that can result in the individual making a greater than ordinary or acceptable contribution to the meeting of the goals of the system.

To deal with choices, complexity of organization, stretch objectives or contracts with the system, the number of levels of performance standards must be increased. The system should focus on keeping superior teachers in close contact with students. While some will seek other jobs in a career ladder, the system, through stretch objectives, contracts, and other devices, should try to improve productivity of its teachers and not to reward teachers by making something else out of them.

The development, as a major management effort, of a carefully and thoughtfully developed career plan for each employee can contribute mightily to a more effective school system. The cost is low and the benefits are high.

WHO MAKES AN INDIVIDUAL CAREER PLAN?

Ideally, each employee has an individualized career plan that is worked out with representatives of the administrative staff. A team should be involved, possibly organized as are the following examples:

New social studies teacher
- supervisor of social studies or senior social studies teacher
- principal
- personnel department

New cleaner
- a foreman of cleaners
- representative of maintenance and operations staff
- personnel department

Another part of the career planning staff should be the major central office Personnel Evaluation and Compensation Committee which meets frequently to review all individual career plans and revisions and updating of plans.

INDIVIDUAL CAREER PLANS

Exxon likes to say its strength is its people. So does just about every other company. But few come close to matching Exxon's amazing attention to nurturing new leaders. Three dozen or so times a year, on Monday afternoons, the men who make up the management committee meet . . . as the compensation and executive development committee. At those sessions, the rulers of the Exxon empire personally review the professional progress of the company's top 500 or so managers and the pay of the top 3,000. Comparable committees in the affiliates extend this process right down to the first line of supervision throughout the Exxon system. The goal: to spot talent early and nurture it.[8]

It is doubtful that there is a school system in the United States that focuses the attention and time of its senior administrative staff to any extent paralleling that attributed to Exxon on the growth and development of staff members. Yet education is a personal service in which the effectiveness of the entire operation is much more dependent upon the growth and development of staff members than an industry that sells products.

INDIVIDUAL CAREER PLAN: HOW IS IT STARTED?

Each full-time and some part-time employees should have developed a tentative career plan upon entry into the system. This obviously will be revised many times. But the individual employee should learn in the process how to set goals and how to accomplish goals. In order to learn this process, most individuals need some support, largely in terms of people who are accustomed to the planning process and who are aware of the many alternative courses of action that are possible. The support personnel most significantly represent the institution's concern for the individual: the fact that a group of people, in addition to the immediate supervisor, believe in and are doing all they can to help the individual reach the goals that he or she has set.

A Group Helps Plan. The composition of a group to help a cleaner or a teacher or any staff member with his or her career planning is important. The personnel office is the one involved and has the problem of recording data, keeping records up to date, and reporting. The immediate supervisor — a principal or a custodian, for example — may be included. A senior colleague in the same position can be involved such as a senior social studies teacher or supervisor if the teacher is in that discipline or a foreman of cleaners or a senior skilled cleaner.

Data available for the planning include all the data accumulated upon hiring, results of any testing used, and an early or preliminary evaluation. The committee or a skilled interviewer should, in informal conversation, secure from the individual some understanding of the individual's perception of his or her strengths and weaknesses together with aspirations. The individual should, using a form that may suggest items to be considered, have a preliminary plan or goal statement for consideration. A substantial amount of information should be available to the individual in order to illustrate the kinds of opportunities available in the system and outside the system. The development of career plans that look to the individual's eventual placement outside the system should be considered an expression of a reasonable alternative course of action to be appraised in the same fashion as any other course.

The information about the system could well include a series of alternative career ladders which are parallel and more generalized plans. The variety of choices available to an employee should be described. Opportunities for trying out various roles leading to career path choices should be presented. A forecast of available openings expected in the system would be realistic information to evaluate.

Plans for Teachers. Since one of the key employees is the teacher, the information provided regarding that position is important. Education is a very flat organization. There is little hierarchy. The system has no great interest in developing an attitude on the part of teachers that classroom work is only a way station on the road to satisfaction elsewhere.

In consequence, for teaching and other positions where there are a large number of posts and where much of the satisfaction and earnings must be related to the level of performance at that post, the system should develop a series of descriptions of superior performance and a wide variety of ways for the individual to be recognized as performing beyond the acceptable levels.

The first goal, for any person in any position, is to reach the acceptable level of performance as established by the system. In this effort the evaluation system will be most helpful in showing strengths and weaknesses. The available ways to improve performance in terms of the diagnosis of skills or knowledge that need to be

A new social studies teacher might develop a plan in which the process of meeting the system's acceptable level of performance is the first order of business. Based upon evaluation, the new teacher may be enrolled in a workshop on creating a workable classroom environment. A senior teacher with strong skills in focusing a class upon learning may also be important in helping the new teacher strengthen skills in this area.

Once the teacher and the system are agreed that acceptable performance requirements have been met, the career plan should be focused on moving to a superior level of performance. The evaluation system, organized to discriminate among a number of levels of performance, can be most helpful in directing the efforts for improvement. Parallel to working to strengthen skills in the classroom can be in-service education programs closely focused on teacher needs; formal course work in higher education, if the offering is pertinent; and a variety of experiences in school-wide and system-wide improvement of teaching in general and in social studies in particular.

The school system, using faculty as a measure to increase faculty responsibility for performance, should offer opportunities for the teacher to gain more control over the uses of professional teaching procedures and the understanding of the subject discipline in the schools. Such opportunities as textbook selection and review and revision of curriculum are important. The changing role of social studies to include environmental matters which are social rather than scientific problems, the problem of teaching awareness of the complexity of the world setting, the matter of adding economics to the curriculum and the use of data processing as a formidable scholarly tool in the social studies represent areas of inquiry that should be ongoing in terms of the involvement of teachers in the discipline.

In terms of teaching, per se, the faculty should have ample opportunities to take part in many aspects of school organization and operation that impinge on excellence of instruction. The growth and development of the entire evaluation system alone, particularly in the area of describing with increasing clarity varying levels of teaching performance in writing and in the development of hierarchical models of questioning using oral recordings or in TV taped models shown in order of quality of teaching, for example, are ways in which teachers will be helped to grow in their own teaching skills as well as in setting standards for their colleagues.

Another level of involvement of faculty would come with the development by individuals of specific stretch objectives, negotiated with the school system, to develop, carry out and evaluate a project that will contribute significantly to the achievement of the goals of the institution.

CAREER PLANNING FOR A CLEANER

Similarly, a cleaner hired by the school system to work at cleaning buildings on a shift from 4 to 12 p.m., for example, is expected to learn first how to meet the acceptable standards of performance in cleaning. The cleaner has a list of tasks, should receive specific training in performance of the tasks, and should be evaluated. Based upon the evaluation, strengths should be capitalized upon and weaknesses given attention. This is an early part of the plan.

The individual may have trouble arriving at work on time, regularly. The system should have a well developed, tested procedure, slowly to develop job attitude and sense of responsibility so that the worker does make it to the job on time each day. The participation of other cleaners in setting up procedures; the awareness of the load put on those who do get to work when one is absent; the help in organization necessary to achieve responsibility and the use of the working group to sustain members all may be part of the helping hand offered by the system.

The system must have the expectation that all people can learn and learn well whether students or employees or board members. Again, using the cleaners as an example, ample opportunity should be available for moving to a higher level of performance and to move up a career ladder. There are foremen and custodial positions, with increased responsibility, pay and sense of contribution.

The reexamination of levels of standards, the use of superior cleaners as models to instruct new people into the system, experimentation and evaluation of new procedures and equipment, and increased responsibility of cleaners for the performance are paths used to get the most out of staff willingly.

REVIEW OF CAREER PLANS

A central management group at a high level should periodically review the complete career plan of each individual. The personnel of the school system should know that this is being done and should know how the personnel committee will use the material.

There are a number of uses. The personnel office should attempt to generalize from the plans, showing where the system's efforts to help faculty may best be focused and to find out if the communication systems are working. Some generalizations about the individual employees' reactions to the planning should be forthcoming. The plans would also allow considerable insight into the effectiveness of the evaluation system. The management committee obviously will be looking for talent that may be exhibited in this process, although not all talent will surface through this one approach. The management committee on personnel is constantly concerned with the assumptions of responsibility for results by the staff and the plans should give some indication. There is a budget problem in making available funds for the support and payment of staff, creating and meeting stretch objectives. Finally, the overall management interest, including that of the Board of Education, is to evaluate the individual career plan as a complex technique to improve productivity — to help employees work smarter.

"STRETCH" OBJECTIVES

The use of "stretch objectives" or contracts for performance between individual staff members and the system, is a significant tool for the manager and allows the ambitious employee an opportunity to get out of the lockstep of the usual salary schedule.

A transportation supervisor who, by proposing combining the joint thinking of his or her staff of drivers, the computer services, and some real originality in scheduling buses using more express routes, for example, may set up a situation in which the stretch objectives are a significant reduction in bus mileage. The evaluation of this contract with the system is easy and the employee should enjoy the benefits of having accomplished much more than would be possible under acceptable performance of duties.

In Hinsdale, IL, elementary school district a teacher has contracted to deliver advanced mathematics instruction to large groups at various locations by Bell telephone voice writer system in direct competition with traditional teacher taught small class instruction and has been highly successful in any way that the instruction can be evaluated. There are many more examples.

In a recent study[9] of salary problems in Columbia, SC, the following points were made about stretch objectives.

> As some school systems stop growing and begin to decline in members, the existence of a reward system which can be to some extent independent of experience oriented salary structures becomes more important. In an expanding system, there are a relatively large number of openings and effective employees can be rewarded by promotion. . . .

Another tool in the management by objectives system is the use of 'stretch' objectives in determining the rewards of some employees. As stated, each person should have as a focus of work a set of objectives to be accomplished. These are, by definition, reachable by reasonably diligent effort. Stretch objectives go beyond the standard objectives. There is risk in that the stretch objectives are not necessarily readily reached by the exercise of reasonable diligence. A substantially higher level of effort, more effective use of skills or knowledge, a superior ability to develop a successful strategy, and a remarkable ability to persuade others to contribute to the effectiveness of the strategy may be among the elements of success in reaching stretch or risk objectives.

Stretch objectives are such that, if realized, an employee has made a significantly increased contribution to the success of the organization in meeting its goals. The stretch objectives should be set in the same general way as other objectives but may involve the approval of several levels of supervisors. Stretch objectives should not be easily reached. They are intended seriously to 'stretch' the effectiveness of the employee. A percentage of employees undertaking to reach stretch objectives should perform well at their positions but may fail to reach the stretch objectives.

The funds available for use for stretch objectives will necessarily be limited. In consequence, the use of such an approach by managers should be at strategic locations where the greatest benefit to the unit in reaching or surpassing its own goals may be realized.

One question relates to the way the rewards for meeting of stretch objectives may be incorporated into the regular pay schedule of the recipient. Obviously, one burst of energy should not necessarily result in the employee's enjoyment of the proceeds for life. A number of possibilities exist, depending upon the nature of the contribution made to the system. One is a one-time payment. A second approach is to incorporate part of the reward into the employee's permanent salary and to continue to renegotiate contracts for services beyond the ordinary level of the permanent job. A third device is, on the basis of successful meeting of stretch objectives, to consider upward reclassification of the position. A fourth might be to increase the maximum salary for the job to reflect the increased responsibility involved. Whatever form of payment is used, it should be agreed to in advance.

The school system should incorporate into its salary policy additional and flexible salary or personnel tools adding to its presently available procedures of relatively automatic schedules and occasional reclassification of employees. The judicious and selective use of measures designed to reward significant contributions to the system at any level and the fair and consistent process of relating evaluation of employees to pay scales and continued employment will broaden the present strategies available. Some kind of broadly based participation in the monitoring of the process by employees, managers, and representatives of the public may be the best control.

EVALUATION OF EFFORTS

As in any planning exercise, a key element is periodic evaluation of efforts to reach goals. As a result, the plan is changed to conform to new information and to reflect changed or modified aspirations. The periodic evaluation against performance standards may show areas where additional effort should be used. The evaluation feedback to the employee constitutes basic data that supplement the personal perception of how well he or she is doing.

The course correction in goals may also be mixed with modifications of procedures to be used. An employee who does not seem to be able to correct weaknesses may be moved to a different operating unit to reduce the possible impact of personality clash or bias in the career program. In-service education may be adapted. Greater or less responsibility may be assigned or personnel transferred or put in another setting to avoid declining levels of performance for any reason.

BRANCHING — OR ALTERNATIVE ROUTES

In any system involving a large number of knowledge workers it is essential to increase the number of choices available to each employee. The current employee is concerned with satisfaction on the job and with the ability to grow and develop as a human being, a process to which a good job contributes. The system should have a variety of resources ready. One of these is an alternative career.

An example of an alternative career can be a hypothetical social studies teacher who, after 15 highly successful years as a teacher, develops a plan to go into public relations. The system offers opportunities to learn this craft, working as an adjunct of the school system's staff. In time, the teacher may move into the public relations staff of the system or into a position outside the system. The system, within the realities of potential openings, should do whatever it can to react constructively to employees' career changes.

Retirement is, of course, one of the career alternatives open to those qualified for the change. The notion of retirement at a specific age is slowly dissolving. The idea of partial retirement is attractive to many. School systems, faced with potential RIF, could do well to explore the part-time employment of staff where this relates well to the career plans of the individual employees.

COMPENSATION AND BENEFITS

Each person employed by the school system should be expected to reach acceptable levels of performance of the task for which they are hired. The level of performance may well be stated as more or less measurable objectives.

The salary paid the employee is the reward that is earned for reaching objectives. The school system should try to make this reward as high as can be justified and secured. Failure to meet the objectives should be a subject of concern both of the employee and the supervisor. By monitoring the process, it should be possible to give notice to the employee of anticipated difficulty in meeting objectives. The system should provide support for the employee to help him or her to meet the objectives. If objectives are not met, withholding of a salary increment or separation from the system may be appropriate responses.

Successful experience on the job is important, but on the other hand longevity in a position may or may not be a blessing. A salary schedule most frequently has a series of steps between the entry level to the class of job and the top salary in that grade. To some extent the series of steps indicates the fact that during the time the job is being mastered the employee is of less value than after the job has been mastered. The length of time to master the job is a function of the complexity of the job, given an acceptable employee. However, research suggests that for most people the major learning experience takes place in the early period of time on the job.

Once a person has mastered a position,

it is to the employee's advantage and a matter of equity for the employer to move the employee as rapidly as possible to an appropriate salary for the position. Far too often salary schedules are a means for postponing appropriate salaries, stretching out over years the final arrival at a proper pay for work performed. The intelligent system looks toward the provision of shorter schedules with relatively few steps. It is this schedule that increasingly is the subject of negotiations with unions or associations of employees.

The question arises as to what happens after the employee reaches the top of a short schedule. In times of economic instability, employers have been accustomed to making salary adjustments beyond those called for in a schedule in order to adjust to increases in the cost of living. Beyond the top of the salary range for a position classification should be a moderate number of positions in higher classifications for which personnel, suitably equipped with skills and performance characteristics, can compete for fewer openings. A hierarchy of jobs is to be preferred to a single job classification. The use of stretch objectives, as suggested earlier, is another tool of upward mobility. Opportunities outside the system should also be recognized as a valid alternative for the employee.

Employee benefits are a large part of the cost of a position. In the past, an employee benefit system was thought to be equitable if all employees had the same benefits. Now with so many families having two workers, schools system should look at some other measure of equity in which the amount spent per employee of the same category is the same, but the benefits vary.

To this can be added the opportunity to add voluntary, or employee-paid benefits to the benefit package. When the school system can secure additional benefits or voluntary benefits under its group purchasing power, the employees have a markedly increased number of choices to make with respect to benefit packages, so arranged that each family kan make its own decisions as to how to allocate money for benefits. Where both husband and wife work, depending upon the plans available, the wife's life insurance may be increased while the husband's contribution to retirement using a voluntary thrift plan may be given most emphasis.

The system that is intelligent in creating choices and in helping employees get good advance on the allocation of benefit money is creating a more responsive and concerned group of employees.

REFERENCES

[1] Drucker, Peter F., "Managing in Turbulent Times," Harper and Row, New York, 1980, p. 133.

[2] Cohen, Michael D. and March, James G., "Leadership and Ambiguity: The American College President," A general report prepared for the Carnegie Commission on Higher Education, McGraw-Hill, New York, 1974, p. 2.

[3] Drucker, *op. cit.*, p. 24.

[4] Crockenberg, V. and Clark, W. W. Jr., "Teacher Participation in School Decision Making: The San Jose Teacher Involvement Project," *Phi Delta Kappan,* October 1979, pp. 115-118.

[5] ASCD, "Effects of Declining Enrollments on Instructional Programs and Supervisory Practices in Public Elementary and Secondary Schools," The Association, 225 N. Washington St., Alexandria, VA 22314, 1980.

[6] Leggett, Stanton, "Alternative Futures, Independence, OH Public School System," Stanton Leggett and Associates, West Tisbury, MA 02575, page Ind 42.

[7] Thomas, M. Donald, "Performance Evaluation of Educational Personnel," *Phi Delta Kappan Fastback* No. 135, Phi Delta Kappa Educational Foundation, Bloomington, IN, 1979, pp. 15-17.

[8] Parisi, Anthony J., "Inside Exxon: Managing an $85 Billion-a-Year Empire," *New York Times Magazine,* August 3, 1980, p. 18.

[9] Johnson, C.; Kaye, S.; and Leggett, S., "An Analysis of Some Structural Problems of the Salary Program, Richland School District No. 1," Stanton Leggett and Associates, West Tisbury, MA 02575, 1980, p. 4.

11

HOW TO RETRAIN YOUR STAFF TO IMPROVE PERFORMANCE

Arthur Shapiro, Ph.D.
and
Kitty Chase Kirby

A mood of despair must not interfere with what needs to be done by staff to maintain quality education and, indeed, improve our current performance levels. The authors offer guidelines for rethinking what we now offer and re-shaping it so that it works.

Arthur Shapiro is professor of educational administration and director of the Knoxville Graduate Center at the University of Tennessee, Chattanooga. Formerly professor of education at George Peabody College for Teachers, Professor Shapiro also has served as a superintendent of schools and principal. He has written widely on educational administration. His co-author, Kitty Chase Kirby, is director of Adult Educational Services at the University of Tennessee, Chattanooga, and a frequent contributor to journals of higher education. Ms. Kirby is now completing her doctorate at the University of Tennessee.

With the multitude of pressures and forces affecting education this past decade, we have been in a state of depression — financially and emotionally. Staff morale is drooping in many places. It's time to wake up and do something about it besides feeling sorry for ourselves.

Unfortunately, we can't alter our programs and systems with new blood and new ideas as we used to. Like the Roman Empire, then, we face a period of decline and stasis *if* we permit it. However, we cannot permit our present mood of depression to override our responsibilities.

And because our personnel are growing older and we can't bring in newer people with fresh ideas, we *must* improve our staff. With the rate of change of technology and knowledge, it is absolutely essential to improve performance even to maintain quality education, let alone improve our performance substantially.

Let's face it: we have problems in doing this well. We don't do a good job in in-service education generally, which produces a great deal of staff cynicism. The model we often use in in-service education of doing something *to* faculty *by* others violates everything we know about effective teaching and learning by not involving the learner actively in the learning process. The second problem is that because of the crunch on financial resources, we must develop staff by utilizing our own administrators and teachers in the process. And they can't do the job effectively with the traditionally ineffective model we currently use.

As Murphy predicts, when we need staff growth the most, we seem to have the fewest resources to accomplish the job — but do we?

RETHINKING OUR MODELS

We presently have an assortment of traditional models to reeducate staff. One is for the individual to take courses at a university, either for pay increases so that courses are usually taken to satisfy that goal or in a program to achieve an advanced degree.

Neither approach seems to change behavior substantially, develop needed skills, foster changes in attitudes or substantially increase effectiveness of the staff. The authors have noted a number of principals who have taken doctorates, have re-entered their old system, and like China with invaders, have been absorbed. The placid waters of the organization remain undisturbed, new ideas usually do not surface, and the initial energy and enthusiasm of the principal dissipates.

Sometimes school districts themselves may build in university-involved in-service programs. The university typically utilizes its own faculty and occasionally a person from within the district. The result of this approach is that teachers and administrators often feel they are participating in a "canned" program. Rather than being willing participants in a freely chosen educational endeavor, they see the program as an extension of the power of the central office imposed upon them.

Another frequently used approach is to provide an inspirational outside speaker to motivate faculty. Unless a follow-up is arranged, the lift fades after a time and little may come from this model. As Whitehead notes, education has three phases: Romance or motivation, Precision, and Generalization. This last model utilizes merely the first.

ALTERNATIVE APPROACHES

Since the purpose of in-service education is to improve faculty's skills, or to increase their knowledge, or to raise questions for thinking or to question present attitudes and values, we are speaking of staff development, of human growth and change. And we know enough about this enterprise to realize that it is no simple matter.

For example, the preceeding models treat staff growth as a useful end, but obviously develop neither educationally sound nor systematic approaches. There is little sense of urgency or high priority regarding the matter. If the staff's professional growth is important it ought to get top priority and be approached both professionally and systematically. Programs have to be developed thoughtfully reflecting our best thinking and knowledge about the educational process — in this case, of faculty (including administration).

Our first step is to review needs in relationship to present performance. What should they be able to do well, but can't? And how do *faculty* view the matter? Do *they* share the assessment of present adequacies of skills, knowledge, attitudes? Are priorities perceived in common? Or, are there discrepancies in perceptions of priorities, purposes, skills, and abilities?

We are speaking here of organizational change in very highly sensitive areas — of our own self-perceived adequacies and inadequacies, of our feelings and sensibilities about ourselves as professionals, about our own competencies. Since our most important identity as adults lies with our jobs, we tend to be instantly and often angrily defensive about any perceived slights or innuendoes about our inadequacies. Consequently, honest in-service attempts which inadvertently tap into this defensiveness may produce a range of surprisingly defensive reactions of anger, apathy, withdrawal, cynicism, etc.

To achieve any degree of success with any designed, systematic program, with any group of people, certain assumptions have to be made:

> The people involved (in this case, faculty)
>> are intelligent and competent
>> are professional
>> can be trusted
>> are concerned about quality instruction
>> are willing to share knowledge

Failure to make and use these assumptions leads us to treat the people involved with little respect and as inept. It results almost inevitably in defensive reactions, in faculty feeling that they are not respected and that something is being imposed upon them to improve them. Faculty have to feel respected for their competence and professionalism, and they have to be involved. They have to *feel* that they will have a major voice in the process; without this they can't develop ownership in the enterprise and will turn it off. If we don't own, we don't care. And the program won't work. Faculty must believe that they need development in certain areas and become

committed to the process or little will happen, except more alienation and reduced administrative and faculty effectiveness.

Hammons & Wallace* listed 16 ways to kill a college faculty development program which could apply to any level of faculty.

1. Fail to provide an acceptable rationale for why a faculty development program is needed.
2. Fail to assign responsibility and authority for planning.
3. Fail to involve faculty in planning.
4. Fail to provide sufficient flexibility (develop a single program).
5. Fail to balance institutional priorities and individual needs.
6. Fail to make participation voluntary.
7. Fail to have administrative staff participate in staff development activities.
8. Fail to include part-time faculty.
9. Fail to reward participation.
10. Fail to exercise common sense scheduling.
11. Fail to consider the instructional techniques to be used in the program.
12. Fail to mix internal and external resources.
13. Fail to publicize adequately the program.
14. Fail to evaluate the results.
15. Fail to provide adequate funding.
16. Fail to provide critical nonmonetary support for the program.

If we could build a model or models that neutralize these errors, a strong and effective program could be developed. The approach that must be taken is for sufficient involvement to take place that faculty "buy into" the process and the program and become *committed* to their *own* development.

Therefore, we should not plunge blindly and immediately into the process feeling that the program has to be off and running as of last week. We should do it right the first time or our errors will haunt us for years. We must develop support by identifying key leaders in key social systems in each school and ask them to come together to discuss faculty needs for further professional development. The program, then, has to be built on those needs. We have to ask faculty (including administration) what do they perceive are the major problems they face, what are *their* major needs,

*James O. Hammons and Terry H. Smith Wallace, "16 Ways to Kill a College Faculty Development Program", *Educational Technology*, December 1976, pp. 16-20.

and in what areas do they feel highest priority for development?

If done properly the faculty, hopefully, will come to view development activities for their own development rather than the system's. If faculty identify through this process their need for in-service, for their own professional development, they will be more supportive, "buying into" the process.

In short, the program must be faculty-based and inspired, or it will fail. Such an involvement process generally will overcome the "threat factor" of inservice programs, particularly in light of some of the suggestions made in the remaining sections of this chapter.

In designing faculty development programs we ought to practice what we preach about education, even if we use it on ourselves. That is, we have to diagnose each separate individual staff member's (including administration's) individual skills, attitudes, and cognitive achievement in order to determine his/her unique educational needs. The next step, of course, is to prescribe and design appropriate learning experiences for *each* staff member. We are borrowing from Dewey, starting with each staff member's perceived interests, needs and abilities and then designing individualized experiences with and for them. We might consider developing a learning contract with every person in this process.

This approach allows for choice of activities by the staff — the greater the personal control over choice, the greater the personal involvement.

Choices can include:
content
format
group or individual

Content can be learning a subject, a method of teaching, a process, or a concept.

Format ranges over the process by which staff development occurs. It includes attending conferences, workshops, and learning contracts which the staff member assumes. It also can include organizational arrangements such as a supportive committee of colleagues who work with the individual assisting him/her in developing and evaluating the program

she/he experiences. In that model, the faculty member, and perhaps the administration, might nominate three peers to be a resource, assisting in establishing goals and follow-up experiences to implement those goals. Of course, evaluation of achievement and further designed experiences would follow as a feature of a continuous program.

ACTION ITEMS

The following diverse models, options and approaches comprise some of the armamentarium of alternatives we already possess and can be utilized in programs designed for each individual.

1. If people are interested in developing any kind of program such as a reading program, an individualized program, team teaching, etc., it may be appropriate to visit one that has a reputation for high quality. A caveat is that if the change is to be instituted within the school, key social systems and people ought to go. If one person visits a program she/he has to convince the rest to adopt the change. If many go, they do not have to be convinced. It is helpful, even critical, if the model they visit has a dissemination feature.

2. If the change is complicated it might be useful not merely to visit the program, but to work with the people operating it for a week or so. Apprenticeships have a place in education in the 80's.

3. Create an internal organization within the system whose job it is to provide a wide range of experiences in content, process, skills, etc. In short, develop a teacher center with a curriculum library of materials, books, programs, kits, and workshops. Provide space and resources for teachers to develop their own materials and tap into human and program resources. Such centers exist in Nashville, TN, and Little Rock, AK. Smaller districts may wish to form consortia to develop interdistrict coopera-

tive programs, such as the Mid-Ten Teacher Center, a consortium of ten centers in Middle Tennessee. Federal and other moneys may be available for this enterprise.

4. An alternative to this idea is the Training and Development Center, such as the Elk Grove, IL Training and Development Center that served a great range of districts demonstrating programs such as Madison Mathematics, Instructional Learning Centers, etc. Districts wishing to tap into the demonstration programs were given supportive assistance in trying the ideas out by staff consultants.

5. Peer tutoring. Research on supervision reveals that the most effective and frequent supervision is lateral, with teachers helping other teachers and principals helping peers. Other terms for this include internships and mentoring. Institutionalizing this process can be helpful to those who are able to take this form of collegial assistance and are interested in this as one of their options.

6. Another effective approach to self-improvement is team teaching since teachers, feeling that they are on display, usually try very hard to be at their top form in team situations.

7. The Management Academy concept. Differing from the traditional concept of returning to graduate school full time the management academy is located in the school district, and provides on-the-job training for administrators and would-be administrators. Experiences are structured by university faculty, staff and local personnel resources to improve on-the-job performance. Dade County, Miami, FL, has such an entity. The academy is designed to meet unique local needs, therefore coming close to the criteria developed earlier in this paper.

8. The peer group model. In this model the peer group is not design-ed to be an in-service development resource. Rather, the peer group undergoes the same treatment, namely, viewing one's own teaching on video tape. Needless to say, no administrators can be involved because of the threat factor; the teacher decides when and where to video tape and has sole control over the tape. Generally, in this model a university consultant is useful to bring in process resources so that the teacher and group can observe their own individual teaching with some sort of instrument which can help make sense out of the classroom interaction. The authors have seen a modified Flanders matrix utilized (CERLI) as well as others. The group functions as a very gentle support and objective, outside Greek-chorus type commentator. This process, of necessity, must be outside the evaluative process, or the threat becomes so great that learning becomes much more difficult.

9. The curriculum structure. This structure consists of teachers and administrators from all levels and fields through a school or a system organized to support program change. In short, it is an internal institutional vehicle designed to move change through the system on a *routine* basis. Most of the time we treat any change of a single program as extremely difficult, putting all our resources behind it and pushing and pressing for that one change. When it is adopted we are practically worn out and wonder if all that effort is worth it (realizing that we usually have to monitor and protect the change). This model proposes that we build organizational expectations, norms, that change is natural, comes from within from operational (teacher and local administrator) levels and is based on their expertise. In short, a change is treated as normal and desired, even routine in a quality system.

FIGURE 1

Curriculum Structure

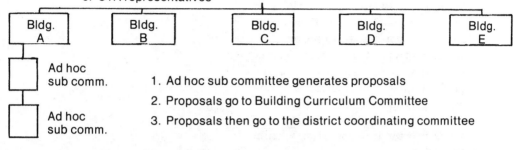

Curriculum Coordinating Committee

1. Two representatives from each Building Curriculum Committee
2. Administration
c. CTA representatives

| Bldg. A | Bldg. B | Bldg. C | Bldg. D | Bldg. E |

Ad hoc sub comm.

Ad hoc sub comm.

1. Ad hoc sub committee generates proposals
2. Proposals go to Building Curriculum Committee
3. Proposals then go to the district coordinating committee

FIGURE 2.

Curriculum Structure

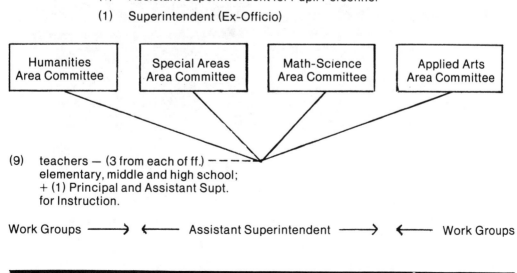

Curriculum Steering Committee

(5) 2 representatives appointed by CTA President
     and 3 teachers to be selected at large (1 elementary,
     1 middle school, 1 high school) by Ass't. Supt.
     for Instruction, one Principal, & CTA President

(4) Chairmen of Area Committees

(3) Principals

(1) Director of Research

(1) Assistant Superintendent for Instruction

(1) Assistant Superintendent for Pupil Personnel

(1) Superintendent (Ex-Officio)

| Humanities Area Committee | Special Areas Area Committee | Math-Science Area Committee | Applied Arts Area Committee |

(9) teachers — (3 from each of ff.) — — — —
     elementary, middle and high school;
     + (1) Principal and Assistant Supt.
     for Instruction.

Work Groups ⟶ ⟵ Assistant Superintendent ⟶ ⟵ Work Groups

Figures I and II present two curriculum structure models. To give the structure clout the system has to build norms about these expectations, and has to permit the curriculum structure a strong say in recommending program changes and allocating money for that purpose. Absent such provisions, the structure will not attract the key reference people and will not perform its appropriate function. Another method of giving the structure clout is to base promotion on performance in developing and designing proposals and shepherding them through the curriculum structure and into operation within the system.

We have not advocated a formal structure, a Staff Development Committee of some sort to direct the entire effort. Rather, we propose decentralizing the operation, implementing it informally through key social systems based on staff willingness and not on coercion.

12

COST EFFECTIVE APPROACHES IN VOCATIONAL EDUCATION

Alan P. Woodruff, Ed.D.

Vocational education traditionally has been a tender topic among educators because it is often more expensive than successful. Consultant Woodruff offers some guides and directions that can help districts find their way out of high cost areas and into other areas that cost less and do more.

Dr. Alan Woodruff is a national authority on vocational education. He is the author of Career Education Facilities, *published by Educational Facilities Laboratories, New York City, and in demand as a writer and lecturer on this topic.*

*When you don't know where you are going
any road will take you there*

(Ancient proverb)

Before a school system can assess the cost-effectiveness of alternative approaches to providing vocational education it must specify its objectives.

Until relatively recently vocational education meant only one thing — the development of job skills which lead to successful entry into the work force. Based on this definition, which emphasized the job skill development aspects of vocational education, the only valid measure of program effectiveness was job attainment.

Early in the 1970's educators began thinking of vocational education in terms of its educational value as well as its value as a program for the preparation of students for employment. The emergence of this viewpoint was paralleled, if not caused by, the development of the "career education" movement. This movement, which first received federal support as a result of the efforts of US Commissioner of Education, Sidney Marland, focused on the development of skills in the affective as well as the cognitive, domain. In so doing it sought to develop awareness of occupational alternatives and an understanding of the world of work.

Many of the concepts of career education were initially rejected by traditional vocational educators. However, the impetus of career education lead to an expansion of offerings in "exploratory" vocational education. Like career education, programs of exploratory vocational education focused less on the development of salable skills and more on the needs of students. For these programs the use of job placement as a measure of program effectiveness has no meaning. The development of programs of exploratory vocational education required (a) changes in existing vocational education programs, (b) the development of closer coordination between instruction in vocational education and general education, and (c) an expansion of the role of guidance services as an integral part of the educational process.

The emergence of programs in career education and exploratory vocational education was furthered by an increased recognition of the findings of more than a decade of research which showed that, in hiring for entry level positions (the positions for which vocational education purports to train) industry is more interested in an applicants work attitude and *ability to develop* appropriate skills than with the skills which *have already been developed* in a vocational educational program. This perspective reflects three important facts. First, industry is as concerned about worker dependability and the ability of a worker to perform consciously and safely as with the workers initial skill competency. Second, most entry level positions require a worker to develop and apply only a limited number of skills — not the entire range of skills taught in a vocational education program. Third, most industries require employees to learn to use their own equipment and to follow procedures which are not generally taught in vocational-technical education programs.

Furthermore, follow-up studies of vocational education program graduates show that an average of less than half take a job in the field for which they were trained and that, after two years, over half have changed jobs and are working a position unrelated to their initial training.

A recognition of such findings highlights a need which could be met through redesigned vocational education programs. Specifically, these requirements suggest that vocational education programs should:

- Emphasize the development of *work* skills — e.g. good attitude, safe work practices, low absenteeism, etc. — as well as *job* skills — e.g. the technical skills of individual jobs.
- Emphasize the development of *transferable* skills — e.g. general skills required in a variety of jobs — rather than *job specific* skills.
- Emphasize the development of an ability to *develop skills* rather than the ability to *perform specific tasks*.

Traditional programs of vocational education — e.g., separate self-contained shops and laboratories and one dimensional lock-step curricula and instructional program organization — are based on the development of competencies in the total range of technical skills which are applied in a single occupation. While many of the skills which are taught in one occupational training program are applicable to many jobs, most vocational technical education programs are organized to develop these skills only in the context of their application to a single job or occupation.

A recognition of this fact, and the needs discussed previously, suggests that the relatively high cost upper levels of job specific vocational education programs should be truncated and greater emphasis placed on the development of more generally applicable aspects of each program. Such a redesigned program is depicted graphically in Figure A.

Programs of vocational education — as traditionally organized — lack the flexibility to respond to the diverse objectives of students and, in many instances, to rapidly changing needs of the labor market in which graduates are expected to compete. As a consequence, traditional vocational education programs have been criticized for their failure to effectively meet their purported goals of preparing students for successful entry into the job market.

Programs of vocational education — as traditionally organized — also cost up to four times as much to operate — when measured on a cost per student basis — as do programs of general education. This high cost differential is the result of a combination of extremely high initial facilities and equipment costs — which may be up to twenty times the cost of a general education classroom — low student-teacher ratios, higher costs for materials and supplies, higher energy costs, and a multitude of other factors. The high initial investments required for vocational-technical education programs has been a major deterrent to the development of adequate, diverse programs of vocational-technical

FIGURE A

Content Structure of Traditional Vocational Education Program

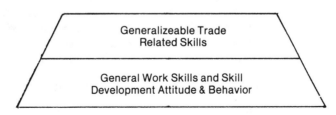

Content Structure of Proposed Vocational Education Program

education — especially in smaller school systems.

The limited flexibility of traditional vocational-technical education programs, and the limited diversity of programs which can, because of their high cost, be offered in most schools, severely limits the cost-effectiveness of most vocational-technical education programs — particularly when program concepts currently in use are examined in the context of what is needed and what could be.

In the early 1970's, the concept of "cluster based" vocational education was introduced as one means of addressing both the cost (and cost-effectiveness) problems of traditionally organized instruction in vocational education and the need to offer instruction in programs which more effectively responded to student needs for career exploration. The cluster concept of vocational education was also intended to promote greater flexibility in instructional offerings and, hence, increase the cost effectiveness of the total vocational education investment.

Vocational education programs developed on the basis of the career cluster concept reflect two concepts of the interdisciplinary relationships which exist between the task requirements of most jobs.

The first of these approaches is based on the notion of "trade clusters". Examples of trade clusters range from programs in such broadly general clusters as building trades — in which students learn skills in woodworking, construction, electricity, plumbing, painting, masonry, etc. which may be applied to jobs as diverse as building construction, remodeling, and maintenance — to narrowly defined clusters such as electrical trades in which students gain experience applicable to such diverse fields as residential wiring and industrial electrical control systems.

The second of these approaches is based on the notion of "skill clusters". Skill cluster curricula reflect the commonalities in functional skills which apply to many jobs in distinctly different occupational clusters. Skill cluster programs may be developed to reflect the core skill requirements in areas ranging from general mechanics — where students learn basic skills which

are required in jobs ranging from industrial machine repair to auto mechanics — to general metals fabrication — in which students develop broadly applicable general skills in disciplines such as welding and sheet metal fabrication.

As indicated by these examples, cluster curricula — which should not be confused with curricula clusters* — are neither generic nor rigidly defined. Rather, they may be defined by any combination of learning elements common to any combination of occupations. Since the concept of cluster curricula is not based on the notion of preparing students for specific jobs, the content of the cluster curricula reflects an analyses of the general applicability of skills rather than the application requirements of specific jobs. Thus, cluster curricula may also be thought of as "common denominator" curriculum as illustrated in Figure B.

While the concept curricula was intended primarily to provide breadth to the student's basic vocational preparation, it brings with it numerous advantages in terms of program cost and cost-effectiveness.

First, since the emphasis of cluster curricula is on the development of basic skills, vocational education programs based on the cluster concept do not require the purchase of the sophisticated, high cost equipment which is needed to develop the advanced, specialized skills required in specific occupational specialties.

Secondly, in focusing on the development of skills having diverse applicability, the cluster curriculum is able to serve the needs of more students having diverse interests and to prepare students for a greater diversity of occupations. Thus, cluster curricula programs of vocational education are more responsive to both student needs and the changing needs of the market place.

---

*In the early 1970's the U. S. Office of Education identified 12 occupational clusters into which all programs of vocational education could be grouped. These "curriculum clusters" are: public service, transportation, manufacturing, natural resources-production, natural resources-control, commerce/finance/distribution, communications, construction, recreation, arts and humanities, health and welfare, education and research.

These advantages of the cluster curriculum are of particular significance in small schools which would, were they to employ the traditional approach to vocational education instruction, be forced to limit severely the range of programs offered.

In addition to reducing initial program costs and increasing program cost-effectiveness, the cluster curriculum adds flexibility to program choice and creates a teaching environment which promotes individualization of instruction. That is, while designed for diversity in basic skills development, the organization of instruction in cluster curriculum programs permits each student to concentrate on any individual aspect of the program which is of particular interest to him or her. Thus, the capability to offer specialized job specific training need not be a casualty of the effort to increase program diversity, flexibility, and cost-effectiveness.

The capacity of vocational education programs to expand the level of specialization offered without incurring the high cost of specialized course offerings was greatly expanded throughout the '70's by the introduction of a vast array of training and simulation devices which could be used to teach basic concepts. These develop basic skills using equipment costing only a fraction of the cost of equipment which the student is likely to encounter in industry. Such devices provided the "hands on" equivalent of audio visual instructional aides whose use had been rapidly expanding since the late 1960's.

Audio-visual training systems and trained/simulators may consist solely of a projector and slide-tape or film sets which provide step-by-step instructions for performing individual tasks; or may be total training systems in which complex operating equipment — such as an air conditioner — is displayed in modules in which all components are fully exposed for easy study and for easy access to facilitate the repair of "faults" which may be programmed into the system.

Using such equipment, and the plethora of instructional software developed to support it, students are able to develop highly specialized skills through what, in its extreme cases, amounts to virtually independent study. Thus, large measures of program diversity — in both breadth and depth — can be purchased at relatively low cost.

The use of trainers and simulators was initially criticized on the basis that it was artificial and did not really result in the development of occupationally relevant skills. However, research has shown that this method of instruction can be more ef-

FIGURE B

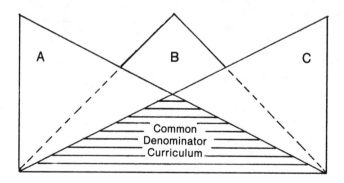

Job Specific Curricula (A, B, C) and a "Common Denominator Curriculum"

fective than the traditional approach of learning by repetitive performance in the development of an understanding of basic skills and concepts. Research has also shown that the use of trainers, simulators, and media aides can significantly reduce the time required to master basic principles and can, when used to develop basic skills, contribute to increases in the overall quality and cost-effectiveness of programs using traditional approaches to vocational education.

Some schools, particularly small rural schools where there is insufficient demand to justify a diversity of vocational education programs as traditionally organized, have gone so far as to develop what amounts to vocational education "libraries" which consist almost entirely of audio visual aids, trainers, and simulators. In such programs, vocational education is a highly individualized effort with teachers serving as facilitators and aides rather than the primary source of instruction. The use of such an approach to vocational education promotes the development of skills in independent learning and, hence, enhances the development of a student's ability to *learn* as well as his or her ability to *do*.

Late in the '70's, federal legislation initiated a new wave of innovation in the preparation of students for the transition from school to work. This initiative, which was promoted by the Youth Employment Demonstration Programs Act (YEDPA) administered by the US Department of Labor, stimulated the development of a broad array of partnership agreements between schools and industry. These programs represented a major expansion of the earlier concepts of work-study and cooperative education programs. Rather than emphasizing occupational skill development, these programs focus on the development of work readiness attributes such as attitude, and job choice decision making, and the development of an understanding of the employees obligation. Unlike other approaches to vocational education, which now generally use *employability* rather than *employment* as the measure of program effectiveness, these programs are concerned solely with the fostering of student employment. This approach to vocational education was initiated in response to research findings which showed that the single most important determinant of employment, as opposed to unemployment, is a previous history of successful employment.

Where skill development is offered as an integral part of those vocational education programs it is generally provided as a joint effort of the school and the participating employer and is limited to the development of only basic entry level skills. Where vocational skills are developed in programs in the schools they generally require only minimum investments. Rather than concentration on the development of cognitive skills required for job performance, school based services generally emphasize placement assistance, the development of interviewing skills and job survival skills, and the provision of remedial education.

The use of this approach to serving the occupational preparation needs of students embodies many of the principles of career education while focusing specifically on the attainment of these specific objectives of traditional notions of the fundamental objectives of vocational education — employment.

13

SHARED PROGRAMS WORK IN CHICAGO

Donn Wadley, Ph.D.

Responding to the plea of local industry for a better qualified work force, Chicago has started and broadened a shared-cost effort that provides on-the-job experience and training.

Doctor Wadley is director of program development for the Chicago public schools. Staff under his direction designed, developed and implemented the education programs he describes. Descriptions of other new community programs developed in Chicago and elsewhere are available by writing: National Clearinghouse for Options in Public Education, Chicago Public Schools, Center for Urban Education, 160 W. Wendell, Chicago, IL 60610.

Better qualified people should mean more production at less cost. That's what industry is telling educators, and we must listen.

With that in mind, the Chicago public schools developed a program that combines academic preparation with career preparation. This new program was designed to minimize the duplication of costs expended by the school system and business/industry.

Early in 1977, the Chicago public schools opened four Career Development Centers in the corporate space of the Continental Bank, Illinois Bell Telephone, Holiday Inn-Lake Shore, and the air terminal at Midway Airport. The purposes of this partnership were 1) to provide high school students with an extensive and intensive learning experience in a corporate site, and 2) to provide corporations with a direct hand in the design, development and implementation of an educational activity that would produce better prepared students and eventually, employees.

Since 1977, an additional 16 firms, agencies, institutions, and universities have joined with the Chicago public schools in this partnership. More than 7,000 high school students have annually participated in the Career Development Center Network program.

Only juniors in high school were selected to participate in the original four centers. Since then, the program has developed to include freshmen, sophomores, and seniors in a four-year sequential program that incorporates investigation, exploration, development, and preparation for careers.

The Career Development Center program prepares high school students with on-site experience and training that leads upon graduation to either 1) job entry, 2) preparation for further technical training, or 3) for higher education and university study.

SOPHOMORE MODEL

The high school sophomore program was designed to provide students with general career orientation and avoid the possibility of their graduating with little or no knowledge of careers and their future. Each sophomore Center permits students to become acquainted with the functions of key departments through actual visit, use of presentations, audio-visual and direct speakers, question and answer sessions and written booklets and other materials provided free be each Center partner. Students also learn about the high school subjects that would best prepare them for each career path.

Visits to community resources such as a business, government agency or industry enable those sophomores who are interested in careers of a wide variety to learn first-hand about the opportunities and job related activities. The sophomore model engages approximately 30 students by Center unit, they visit each Center during a two-week cycle during the year. During Week No. 1, pupils spend a full day at the Center for a general overview. During Week No. 2, selected students (based upon interest) return for five half days of specific career awareness activities tailored to their interests and representative of the spectrum of careers in the specified occupational area. Every third week a new cycle begins. The program operates on a 10-month basis. As many as 600 students may visit each sophomore center during the year.

No academic credits are earned, but the curricula of the sophomore program relate career awareness experiences to the various academic subjects in which the students are enrolled or will be enrolled at their home schools. Sophomores who participate in these career activities are eligible to enroll in the junior year program of career development.

General goals of the sophomore program are:

1. To provide meaningful career awareness opportunities for students in specific areas of business, industry, and government.

2. To provide opportunities to visit selected business and government institutions within the Chicago area.

3. To offer relationships with individuals who can aid students by providing career information.

4. To participate in studies dealing with self-awareness, educational atti-

tudes, and appreciation of work.

5. To allow students from schools throughout the City of Chicago to meet at learning sites that provide interesting career awareness and business education experiences.

JUNIOR MODEL

In the junior year program, juniors are scheduled for a full semester, one-half day every day in a business or institution site. Learning opportunities are provided through real experiences in the business. The individual student is guided through the real business activity in a series of Learning Modules. These Learning Modules are self-directed activity booklets prepared jointly by the teacher and his/her corporate partner. The student is expected to perform in his/her activities as closely to the employees of the business as is possible. This activity includes case studies, independent study contracts, "thinking through" seminars, simulation exercises, search for real solutions to real problems.

Students often make appointments to meet with company personnel, community representatives, city employees and any other person who might help in the solution development. As much as possible, the students emulate the regular routine of the employees in the company. An example of the exploratory/investigative activities was the research of students at the City Hall Career Center who studied the issue of rezoning residential areas. The students canvassed the neighborhood on the issue, learned of the proposed zoning from the City Hall department, and then prepared a proposed recommendation. The report was used by the Chicago City Council in evaluating the rezoning request.

Students in the junior year program earn academic credit by using the resources of business, industry, professional organizations, cultural institutions, and urban universities as learning laboratories to develop appropriate concepts, understandings, skills, attitudes and habits.

General goals of the Junior Year Career Development Centers are:

1. To develop a partnership between the private/public sectors of the city and the Chicago public schools for the purpose of creating an education program that guides the students in career preparation and skill development.

2. To provide an educational option that offers the student an opportunity to take a credited sabbatical leave from regular studies in order to use the resources of business, industry, professional organizations, cultural institutions, college and universities, and government agencies as learning laboratories for developing concepts, skills, understandings, and habits related to career development.

3. To give the student who plans to pursue a tentative career goal at college or in an advanced technical training program, or career entry upon graduation, the opportunity to test his or her career choice in a non-threatening, realistic setting.

4. To expand the career education options and learning experiences for students enrolled in Chicago secondary schools.

5. To provide the businesses and industries, government agencies, cultural institutions in Chicago with secondary school graduates, technical school graduates, who possess the abilities, skills, attitudes and habits characteristic of reliable, productive employees.

SENIOR MODEL

The Senior Year program of Career Development Centers offers a selected program at a few selected sites. The program only accepts seniors who participated in the junior year program and who have shown aptitude and interest. The half-day daily program for one semester provides one-to-one experience in a Center of the student's choice. The activity follows on from the junior program, but with highly intensified experiences. The student earns one and one-half credit units for participation.

In all the centers, the physical facilities, equipment, instructor/employees and materials of the business are the items used daily in the production of real goods and services. The students, in all cases are apprentices learning directly about and from those persons who produce those goods and services.

The cost savings to the board of education are considerable. On the converse side, there are cost savings for the businesses, industries, and other institutions of the city through early preparation for career employeeships. Costs of job entry training at the corporate level is reduced through this program where salaries, benefits and the associated costs of real employees are virtually non-existent. In my opinion, this form of vocational/career education provides the best of real world skill development at the least possible cost per student unit.

Costs of the program to the board of education include the salary of a full-time certificated teacher, student transportation costs from their high school to the "office" and return, paper supplies, telephone. Costs borne by the business/industry/institution include the classroom "office" space, accessibility to employees, business liaison partner, and business related materials used by the students.

The advantages of this program from the student's perspective can best be described by their own comments. Brian, an 11th grader enrolled in the Banking Center stated that, "I found out that banking is more than just exchanging money, it is a business that makes money for the owners, can found a new company and provides many persons with jobs and income. I can actually see the relationship between my study at school in mathematics and government and the work in the bank. In school we just talk about school stuff, but at the bank I found it much more interesting to talk about ways of making money. I really was interested in knowing more about the Stock Market and in this program I had the time and guidance to meet, and study the Stock Market. I intend to continue to study so that I can become an employee of a bank after college." Arletta is a 12th grader now, but she was "employed" in the Montgomery Ward Retail and Merchandising Center. "I did not really know very much about business, certainly not about the retail business. I thought for some time that I would like to be a clerk in

a store some day, but now I know that I want to study fashion design. I have had the opportunity this semester to meet some designers and find all about the design business. Ms. Barber told me that my interest in art and drawing was an important asset. She gave me a lot of her time this semester introducing me to her friends and some of the people she works with. It was really fun to go to school this way and still earn graduation credits."

Sandi and Robert were 11th graders from different high schools who met at the Blue Cross/Blue Shield Health Studies Center and collaborated on a report dealing with medical care services for high school students. The report was particularly concerned with the preparation of teachers and coaches for athletic related injuries. The report required tremendous amounts of interviewing, reviewing medical records and case histories, and a fair amount of hard writing. They both indicated at the conclusion of the semester that they intend to continue their study in the field of health and medicine. Robert will likely be a doctor in the years ahead; and Sandi, well we will all be interested in learning about her life's career.

Over and over again during the closing sessions of each Center the students indicate a thankfulness for the experience, the sharing and concern shown them by their teacher and the business partners and the quiet understanding of what is ahead of them. The feeling one comes away with from these sessions is that these young people, from all walks of life and representing the full spectrum of economic, social and ethnic segments of the city, have a sense of purpose and direction to their lives. Each one of them appear to have taken on the elements and characteristics of those persons they have assciated with over the 20 weeks of internship. The business representatives express joy and enthusiasm for the program and especially the students. It has given all involved a new sense of purpose and a feeling of success in this partnership. In the final analysis, it has done a great deal toward reawakening the belief in our young generation and hope for the future of this country and its free enterprise system.

TABLE I

Freshman/Sophomore Career Development Centers

Center	Site
Air Transportation	Midway Airport, FAA, related businesses
Data Processing	Standard Oil, related businesses
Entrepreneurship	Chicago Association of Commerce and Industry
Hotel/Motel Management	Lake Shore and Mart Plaza Holiday Inns
Industrial Occupations	Washburne Trade School
Insurance Centers	Kemper, Continental, Allstate, State Farm, CNA and other agencies
Marketing and Retailing	Montgomery Ward and Company
Military Occupations	Washburne Trade School
Urban Energy and Utilities	Peoples Gas
Urban Government	Chicago City Hall

Junior/Senior Career Development Centers

Air Transportation	Midway Airport, FAA, related businesses
Architecture	University of Illinois, related businesses
Design	Illinois Institute of Technology, related businesses
Economics and Business	Continental Bank and Harris Bank
Energy/Environment	EPA, related businesses
Government and Inter-Nation Studies	First National Bank, related businesses
Health and Life Sciences	Blue Cross, related businesses
Hotel/Motel Management	Lake Shore and Mart Plaza Holiday Inns
Law and Justice	U. S. District Court
Management Studies	Arthur Anderson & Co., related businesses
Maritime Studies	Shedd Aquarium, related businesses
Retailing/Merchandising	Montgomery Ward and Company, related businesses
Urban Communications	Illinois Bell Telephone
Urban Studies	University of Illinois, related businesses

14

HOW TO MEET FEDERAL REQUIREMENTS FOR EDUCATION OF THE HANDICAPPED — AND REMAIN SOLVENT

Charles W. Fowler
and
Robert O. Guth

You can meet the federal requirements if you think them through and relate them to your district, but it can be tricky going. Here are suggestions that can reduce district expense for this necessary service without creating conflict between parents of the handicapped and nonhandicapped over increasingly scarce financial resources.

Doctor Fowler is superintendent of schools, Fairfield, CT, and a popular lecturer and writer on school board — administrator relationships and problems. Doctor Guth, Director of Special Education and Pupil Services in Fairfield, has pioneered new and effective ways of delivering high quality special education services at lower cost.

Second only to the 1954 Brown decision, the most significant intrusion by the Federal Government upon local public school decision making has been in the area of special education. Since many states had weak or no legislation to require education for the handicapped, the act, Education for *All* Handicapped (PL 94-142), was passed in 1975. The emphasis is placed on the word "all" and brings forth a concept of zero rejection by the nation's public school systems.

Two other important concepts in the law are the terms "appropriate" and "education". Definitions in the law are not clear and, unfortunately, many people see "appropriate" as "ideal" or "the best possible". This can cause problems. To remain solvent, districts should define "appropriate" as "fulfilling the needs of a child in an *adequate* manner even though it may fall short of the most "ideal" method of accomplishing the same task. With a non-handicapped student the "ideal" may well be a 1 to 1 teacher-to-student ratio; however, there are other "adequate" approaches. Considerable money has and will be spent in the struggle to define and provide "appropriate" education.

Another term that needs further definition here is "education". A few years ago, education was conceived as reading, writing and arithmetic but now has taken on many other facets. In the education of the handicapped, it will include those survival skills and self-help skills that the human being will need for daily living. The question comes — does it include custodial care? Is "education" the changing of diapers of an eighteen-year-old who is so profoundly retarded that he is unable to sit up? Is it feeding a twelve-year-old who does not have the motor skills to handle a spoon after six years of intensive training? Is it trying to prevent a seventeen-year-old from tearing out her hair or scratching her arm until it bleeds after already spending over $100,000 in tuition for special education? Is it providing a nursery environment and stimulation for a one-year-old Down Syndrome child?

These questions need to be answered in defining "education" and the responsibility of the public school systems. If custodial and medical facets of child care are defined as "education" then 94-142 may indeed cause insolvency for the Local Education Agency (LEA). These costs are most properly the responsibility of other state agencies and of the family and its health insurance carrier. Currently, the concept of education is rapidly expanding to include all facets of living for the handicapped child from birth to 21. Public school systems are being asked to accept the responsibility of education beyond the limits of what they would normally expect in reading, writing and arithmetic. This may be acceptable, but a line must be drawn between survival skills and custodial care if we are to remain solvent. Unfortunately, if we are left without a definition which limits public education's responsibilities, huge sums of money will be spent in the name of education and results will not be seen. Down's Syndrome and other severely handicapping conditions will not be reversed or ever contained or compensated for by "education".

It would make more sense for other state agencies that have the responsibility for the entire life span of handicapped persons to be given responsibility and the funding to care for them. Then, if education is needed, these agencies can buy services from the public school system. Currently, the philosophy is the other way around. Therefore, another way to remain solvent is to encourage legislators to delimit the definition of "appropriate" and specify what constitutes "education".

Another concept causing fear and consternation to professional staff in public education is that of "least restrictive environment". Some schools have misused the concept and have interpreted it to mean that every handicapped youngster must be in a regular class. This is untrue and not the intent of the federal legislation. It only means that the youngster should be placed as close to the regular program as appropriate for his education. The youngster in a 24-hour, 7-day-a-week residential setting can be in the least restrictive environment if that is the appropriate program for him. School systems must manage and monitor the concept of least restrictive environment so that it is not misused. Youngsters must be prevented from being placed in programs where they are not receiving appropriate services just because of the fear and the overreaction to the least restrictive environment concept.

The original reason for writing this part of the law is to prevent classes of nearly normal youngsters from being placed in basements and substandard situations and thereby not able to reap the benefits of the normal education when it is feasible. It is designed as a correction of an abuse of exclusion that has plagued education for some time; but, again, LEAs must not overreact or misuse the concept.

EXAMINATION OF HIGH COST ITEMS

The most costly item in special education is the out-of-district placement for the multi-handicapped and those severely and uniquely involved children who cannot be educated in the public school system. Here, the public school system may be the victim of the private school entrepreneur and must pay the price that is demanded. Often it is for inferior or substandard programs, but frequently the public school has no choice since they themselves are unequipped to offer appropriate service.

There are several ways to reduce the costs. One is to examine constantly the out-of-town placements to see if there are several youngsters of the same or similar category that might be attending separate institutions. Study the amount of tuition and transportation paid and see if an appropriate program could be developed in the local school system for less money. Many times a school system can establish such a program and the surrounding towns will be willing to send their youngsters since the LEA tuition will probably be cheaper than the private program.

Another cost saving strategy is to monitor regularly the out-of-district placements. Sometimes school systems are paying for services that they are not receiving. Visits need to be made on a regular basis to each out-of-town placement to monitor the program to see that the youngster is in class, to talk with the staff and observe student living conditions. Considerable time needs to be spent visiting on a formal and informal basis. The school system will

need to invest some dollars in personnel and their expenses to accomplish this task. However, in the long run, it will probably reap dollar benefits since discrepancies will be found and children will receive a better program if the private agency knows that it is being carefully monitored. Another result of visiting is that the staff will see that the youngsters are not that difficult to handle and that the private school isn't doing such exotic things that cannot be duplicated in the home district.

Another way to maintain solvency is to encourage legislators to develop programs in state sponsored facilities for those severely involved youngsters whose handicaps will probably not be reversed by education. Many states have programs for the mentally retarded already, but few have adequate facilities for the severely emotionally disturbed or the autistic. Youngsters having such irreversible or severe handicaps will need lifelong care. States must establish adequate facilities that are safe from budget cutbacks to care for these children. If this does not occur, then school systems will be left with the responsibility to purchase high cost private programs wherever they might exist in the country. Costs of this nature will be astronomical for one school system. They should be shared by all the citizens of the state if LEAs are to remain solvent.

NEED FOR EFFECTIVE IDENTIFICATION AND PLANNING PROCEDURES

Federal legislation requires that each public school have "meetings" to plan the education of the child. Each state has specified the nature, details, responsibility and membership of those meetings, and have frequently exceeded the minimal federal requirements. This chapter will refer to the meetings as "Planning & Placement Teams", or PPTs.

It may be interesting to compare the membership requirements of the PPT made by individual states with the Federal Regulations as contained in the Federal Register of August 1977. The required membership is:

1. A representative of the public agency, other than the child's teach-

er, who is qualified to provide or supervise the provision of special education.

2. The child's teacher.

3. The child's parents.

4. The child, if appropriate.

5. Other individuals, at the discretion of the parent or agency.

6. Evaluation personnel (those familiar with the evaluation of that child and with the results).

Since the membership of the PPTs are usually made up of Pupil Services personnel, whose interest in life is to assist the handicapped and other problem children, there is a tendency to overreact and overdo the requirements of such a meeting. It is important to establish a chairman of the meeting who has a perspective of the whole system in mind. Frequently a building administrator or his assistant, who has an understanding of pupil services concepts but who also has the perspective of the entire system, can be an effective chairman. These planning teams have considerable power as they can formulate an individual education plan which is an agreement between the system and the parent to provide certain services and, if appropriate, to make certain adjustments in the teaching and education of the child.

One caution for PPTs is to resist the desire to over-identify. Some youngsters have learning problems but they are not eligible for Special Education. Among these is the slow learner who may have an IQ between retarded and average range who is having difficulty in school. Frequently these youngsters are identified as learning disabled when they are not. The culturally-deprived youngster could qualify as learning disabled but is really culturally deprived and needs services from Title I and other state grants that provide services for this category. The child who has been a victim of a poor educational experience may have learning problems. Many times a youngster who has frequently moved around, or because of inappropriate education, has deficit areas in basic skills. This youngster must be looked at carefully and not labelled Special Education, even though he may have a deficit. He will respond to special tutoring or other remedial programs as soon as his situation is stabilized and need not enter the "Magic Kingdom" of Special Education.

Larger systems may have decentralized PPTs and organize one in each school. It may be advisable to have some kind of representation from the central office on each of these PPTs in order to provide on-the-spot inservice training, interpretation and monitoring of the process. Frequently coordinators of speech and hearing, school psychology, special education and other part-time leaders in the Pupil Services Department can fill these roles. They can assist in resisting over-identification and over-placement.

Another major way to avoid excessive special education identification is to individualize the regular curriculum. Instead of hiring Learning Disabilities Resource teachers and establishing new resource rooms, some dollars can be spent in training the regular classroom teacher to adapt and individualize their program so that the youngster with minimal special needs may be educated in the regular program. Teachers who are competent in individualization can prevent the need for even the beginning referral for special education. In addition, the individualization skills will aid all children, and pay dividends by improving the general level of education in the community.

In addition to the caution about over-identifying the learning disabled youngster, we must also be careful about the seriously emotionally disturbed child. Federal law does not require services for the socially maladjusted or minimally disturbed. However, many states are widening their interpretations to include all levels of the emotionally and socially maladjusted. LEAs must be careful not to over-identify since over-identification of the emotionally maladjusted or disturbed creates very grey or hazy situations. These youngsters do need services but other programs such as social work, guidance counseling, school psychology can meet these needs without identifying the child as a special education student and devising IEPs. Articles like those in *Exceptional Children* (Raiser and Van Nagel 1980)[1] suggest that we include these marginal youngsters under the term "learning disability". Since they should be served, and until someone comes up with another definition, the author suggests that the learning disability category be used as a catch-all phrase. This approach has the potential to cause insolvency especially if special education services are expanded into areas where they are not required. The needs can be best handled by less formal approaches without incurring the expense of a special education bureaucracy.

LEGISLATION

Attention to legislation is another important way to maintain solvency, and the confidence of local legislators must be cultivated. Staff should be assigned to monitor legislation, know the proposed bills, participate in special legislative committees, develop contacts in the legislature and, in general, develop "legislative literacy". Probably legislative acumen is the best defense to prevent 94-142 insolvency.

LITIGATION

This is beginning to be an important aspect of public education. The first requirement is to have a good lawyer who will study school law and represent the school system with enthusiasm. Larger systems may wish to hire an attorney as an assistant to the Superintendent rather than have a part-time consultant. School law is becoming an intricate subject and is developing a case background that needs careful study and understanding by an expert. A professional staff member in each of the major departments involving legal problems (such as special education and personnel) needs to have the time to be the technical advisor to the attorney. This person should have the responsibility to gather information, help the attorney formulate the case, point out important aspects of the law to him. The attorney must be willing to work with the staff prior to the case and do the necessary preparation. Frequently, in many areas, private legal firms are establishing specialties in parent advocacy. These firms hire lawyers whose only job is to be the parent advocate and they become very specialized and skilled in

knowing the intricacies of the law which can be used to require maximum services from and maximum expenditures by the local school system. Thus, you have an attorney who is very familiar and trained in this aspect of the law facing a school system attorney who may see two or three cases a year and may not gain the necessary experience and background to be a successful litigant.

Hiring competent experienced attorneys is an investment against insolvency. Equally important is giving staff the time for preparation so that the case can be brought to a successful conclusion. Along with preparing for the case, wisdom needs to be applied to try those cases which the school system has a chance at winning rather than spending time and money when a negative decision is almost guaranteed. A book by Barbara Bateman can be valuable (Bateman, 1980).[2] It is short and has many excellent ideas to assist in having a successful hearing (see references).

Once a hearing process is underway and you have explored every possibility of resolving the case without compromising the integrity of the program or the school system, then "all stops must be pulled" since it is a total confrontation. Sympathy for the parent will cause losses.

Every method and piece of information available must be used to establish and strengthen the school system's position. The staff needs to be carefully prepared to give testimony. It is prudent to ask the staff to write a report of their contact with the child and then for the attorney to develop his list of questions from that report. Staff need to be cautioned that they answer questions accurately but succinctly. Elaborate answers are an open invitation to rigorous and successful cross examination. The school attorney should prepare the witnesses in a pre-hearing training session. In preparation, it is advisable for the attorney to talk informally to every person who has had contact with the case in order to look for advantage points and identify weaknesses that may be exploited by the parent's attorney during the hearings. Very frequently weaknesses will be uncovered which may lead you to work out a compromise or settlement; be prepared to handle them when the Hearing is in process.

During the Hearing, use every possible technical advantage to insure a successful outcome. If the other side have not fulfilled some of the regulations of submitting evidence, do not be a "good guy" and allow that to be submitted, particularly if it can be damaging to your situation. Question such things as visual aids and people who the plaintiffs might bring in as being appropriate to the case. Exercise the five day notice required by federal regulations if the opposition brings surprise witnesses and testimony. Be sure the attorney cross-examines each of their witnesses so that they are pressed regarding the validity and accuracy of their statements. Frequently, parents bring in expert witnesses who believe that just because of their presence everyone will be awed and will listen. These experts need to recognize that if they do testify that they will be cross-examined for the record. If, during the conduct of the Hearing, members of the staff think of questions, this should be communicated to the attorney by note, and not by surprise testimony. A good attorney will be building a case by his questions and surprise information will disrupt his structure.

If an administrator begins to suspect a legal case is in the offing because of programming difficulties for a student the staff should be required to prepare detailed documentation. Letters confirming telephone conversations, memos to record, letters trying to effect compromises, detailed personal calendars, a log of events in the child's folder, are invaluable in case presentation.

Naturally, the above will cost money in clerical time, but it is an investment against bankruptcy. At least one eastern school for autistic children is charging $59,000 per year in tuition. Win one case and you can purchase several secretaries and still have a profit.

MAINSTREAMING BACKLASH

With Special Education youngsters being identified and continuing in the regular classes, many teachers are complaining about the demands the youngsters are making in their rooms. Many teacher unions are asking for smaller classes or for a weighting system for these students so that they count as more than one regular youngster. Many times these are the same youngsters who have been successfully taught by regular classroom teachers for years without any help. Now, with the new law, we have a panoply of services and the teachers have substantial additional help. At the same time, however, they are asking for smaller classes because of the demands of these "Special Education" students. Needless to say, there are some additional requirements but they are not overwhelming. There is a tendency to overreact to the mainstreaming concept, but we need to be cautious that Planning and Placement Teams do not provoke the regular classroom teacher by demanding more than is necessary.

Naturally, some teachers do a better job than others in mainstreaming youngsters with them. This can cause an overload and a regular classroom teacher may be justified in complaining that they have several youngsters when a colleague has none.

Administrators should be encouraged to give the informal "rewards" that they have available to support the teacher who has more mainstreamed youngsters. Such ideas as commendations on evaluations, fewer teaching duties, and other "perks" that might be available in the system could be useful. Naturally, one must be careful not to cause resentment by those who are not receiving such support. Teachers are very sensitive and desire to be treated exactly alike in all circumstances. Evaluations should identify teachers who find it difficult to mainstream youngsters and self-improvement goals need to be established for them so that they can improve their ability to teach such youngsters.

Inservice training is essential for the classroom teacher in order to have them understand the Special Education program. Inservice training is needed to help teachers become more sensitive to the needs of handicapped students. In such inservice programs, a teacher can be asked to simulate a handicap using such experiences as listening to instructions on a tape with considerable background noise or by trying to hit a ball with the nondominant hand; this can help staff understand the feeling of having a handicap. The inservice course can then continue by aiding the staff in developing programs to remediate or compensate for the handicap that has been experienced. In this way, the regular classroom teacher can understand that Special Education services are not exotic and magic techniques that no one else can do, but really are only good teaching methods implemented on an individualized basis and can and should be devised by all staff. The author's local school system has developed such a six hour course for all professional staff (Cessna, Christiano, Guth, 1979)[3].

The entire faculty should receive information regarding the federal, state and local procedures for Special Education programming. These presentations need to be positive in tone and not a "scare" experience. Many times a presentation can degenerate into "all the things we must do now because of the new law". Experiences of this type can provoke teachers into seeking relief through their labor contracts. Inservice experience for the regular staff needs to be carefully planned and monitored by the top leadership in the district so that the narrow line between awareness and fright is observed.

Emphasis should be placed on the fact that the Special Education teacher is not a "magic person" and that Special Education teaching techniques are only good teaching techniques. It is evident that the best Special Education teacher really is a master regular classroom teacher who has learned some of the phraseology and vocabulary of Special Education. Miracles are not going to happen because it's a Special Education Resource Room or class. In fact, most miracles with these children happen in the regular classroom. The regular staff needs to be aware of this and accept the fact that they can probably do as good a job as a Special Education teacher, given the small class size and individualization.

A regular teacher must realize that resources are extremely limited and every time a Special Education staff member is added, there will probably be fewer resources for the regular program and class size may thus increase. LEAs should design budgeting systems that can make this concept clearly evident to the classroom teacher. By presenting classroom teachers with the decision, "do we need an additional Special Education Resource teacher and less regular classroom teachers with resulting higher class size or can we, as regular classroom teachers in reasonably-sized classes, make the adaptations and changes necessary to implement a special needs program?" The federal legislation does not require that Special Education be given in a Special Education room by a Special Education teacher. If the child's needs can be met in a regular room, and a Planning & Placement Team writes an IEP that prescribes such a program to the parents' satisfaction, the program can and should take place in the regular classroom.

RESOURCE PROGRAM

A good resource program is an excellent strategy in keeping solvent in the face of 94-142 and such a program clearly meets the intent of the law. The Resource Room must be staffed by a highly qualified teacher, because this person not only provides direct instruction to students but also can assist the regular staff member in working with special needs youngsters in the regular room. It is important to require that a regular program handle the child's problem first and definite evidence is required before the child is moved to a Resource or more intensive program. Reward the Resource teacher with a good physical facility, adequate materials, and respect and concern for a reasonable teaching schedule. Multiply the Resource Teacher's efforts by giving them the assistance of an aide, student helper, or the best volunteer you can find. Don't hesitate to use an older Special Education student to teach a younger one. Much is gained in ego-building for the older youngster and sometimes the child's experience can produce a teaching technique that never was considered by the adult teacher. Have a Resource teacher move out of the Resource Room and do some supportive work directly in the regular classroom. It offers the opportunity for indirect demonstration teaching and will multiply the resource teacher's efforts.

The selection of the Resource Teacher is critical. If possible, try to secure a person who has been very successful as a regular teacher and has gained the necessary certification after a regular classroom experience. Caution should be taken in hiring a new BA graduate who was recently certified. Many times such certification programs have had only one course in reading and one course in math, and it is possible that they may have done their student teaching in other settings besides the Resource field. Many school systems end up with having their most difficult youngsters handled by their most inexperienced and poorly trained staff. Dollars spent in buying experience in the Resource Teacher is an excellent investment to prevent the need for more intensive class placement or even private placement, because a Resource program was improperly implemented. The Resource person needs skills in relating to parents and interpreting the child's problem and progress. This person can be instrumental in preventing Due Process proceedings and demands for more intensive programs. Time and money spent in selecting the right person is a good hedge in maintaining solvency under 94-142.

PAPERWORK

PL 94-142 can require and cause bankruptcy through paperwork, clerical time and administrative support if the LEA is not careful. Many PPTs, in their effort to meet the requirement of 94-142 and to be in total compliance, overreact to Federal and state laws. Some systems have IEPs that are 10 to 12 pages long, while other LEAs are able to meet the same requirements in one page. You can imagine that if each year an IEP of 10 pages is completed (and sometimes in the difficult years it may mean more than one IEP) and you multiply that by the number of students in Special Education, one could easily see the volume of paperwork that will need to be created, maintained and, hopefully, able to be retrieved. It can be helpful to find a non-Special Education staff member, or even an outside consultant, who will review your state and Federal requirements and compare them with the methods you have devised in implementing the law, and it may be possible to formulate a design and a paperwork flow that will be much less than one conceived by the pupil personnel staff in your system.

With the new developments in word processing and computers, it is possible to reduce the volume of paper work into electronic processing. Catalogs of goals and objectives needed for IEPs can be developed and easily accessed by word processing or computerization. The IEP itself is a concept that can easily be computerized since the child's basic information is on the IEP and it can be retrieved electronically and is easily edited and brought up-to-date. In this way, an IEP can actually become a working document and prevent increased cost in clerical and paperwork time. If an IEP is computerized, it also then allows accessing of the data for class rosters, program lists, and other management tools that can be useful in monitoring and maintaining the program. The potential also exists for transmitting all required reports to state and federal agencies electronically, thus avoiding hours of local staff time.

LIMITING MANDATES

Administrators must be cautious to limit the local program to actual mandates and should constantly monitor their state agencies to be sure the state adheres to the minimum requirements of the Federal law. There is a tendency to expand upon the "Special Education" theme and to create new programs when they are only "suggested" and not required. Sometimes documents come from state or other agencies stating that we need to meet a certain mandate and even use citations. On checking the citations, one will find that the mandate is only implied and not required. For example, Federal law requires that all handicapped children be evaluated and programmed. In the Federal requirements, ages 3 to 21 must be served, and it does state, under "comments" in the Federal Register, that we should evaluate and identify ages 0-3 so that when a youngster becomes 3, they can be adequately programmed. However, some states are now suggesting permissive programs for 0-3. Resist! Most states will have other agencies that will serve this young child rather than the public school. If LEAs enter this field, they will find the other agencies relinquishing their programs or charging the LEA for the services that are now provided free of charge. It would be better to help the other agencies expand their role and range of responsibility for this age group rather than launching a program in the public school setting. A constant effort must be maintained to compare Federal and state requirements and working through State Education Departments and legislators to be sure that the state does not exceed the requirements in the federal legislation.

THIRD PARTY PAYMENTS

The law states that the insurers of families with handicapped children are not relieved of their responsibility and frequently this source of funding is overlooked. However, even though the LEA can't force a parent to use health insurance programs, they can strongly encourage it and many times will be successful. The use of Title XIX and Medicare is also possible for such services as speech, physical therapy, occupational therapy and psychology. The bureaucracy connected to these programs is frequently overwhelming and will need careful attention in working through. However, it is a source of funding that can help an LEA keep solvent in the face of 94-142.

DISCRETIONARY GRANTS

Many states have discretionary grant funds beyond their usual Title IV allocation. These are given for special projects that the state is interested in pursuing and promoting. Frequently they are funnelled through regional cooperatives. If the state's interests coincide with an LEA program, they can be a ready source of funds. Informal contacts need to be made to state agencies to ascertain the possibility. However, caution must be exercised as outlined above in establishing programs beyond the mandate. Grant proposals also must be scrutinized and the amount of time they will take in clerical and administrative support. Sometimes what looks like a windfall in funds can easily consume its weight in additional administrative services that do not expand or aid your financial situation.

IT IS POSSIBLE

Programs for the handicapped can, in fact, be offered without presaging educational bankruptcy or creating conflict between parents of the handicapped and non-handicapped over increasingly scarce financial resources. The secret lies in skilled leadership of special education programs and procedures insuring intelligent and reasonable compliance with Federal and state regulations — but no more. Emphasize resource programs and moving children out of intensive classes as soon as possible. Encourage all staff to consider themselves as "special" educators — using techniques of diagnosis and individualization that benefit all students. If necessary, be prepared for hearings and courtroom appearances and work to win; you have a responsibility not only to provide for the needs of the handicapped but to see that those needs are balanced against the needs of all other children in the community.

REFERENCES

[1]Raiser, L. and Van Nagel, C. The Loophole in Public Law 94-142. *Exceptional Children,* 1980, 46, 516-520.

[2]Bateman, B. *So You're Going to a Hearing,* Northbrook, IL. Hubbard, 1980.

[3]Cessna, C. , Christiano, M. , and Guth, R. *The Special Education Inservice Program.* Fairfield Public Schools, 1979.

15

SPECIAL EDUCATION FOR THE GIFTED

Ronald Simcox, Ed.D.

Of all the single purpose causes in education, this one may be the most neglected — and the most important. Superintendent Simcox describes some of the better approaches and offers his views on a program that can work without bankrupting the system.

Dr. Simcox is superintendent of schools, District 181, Hinsdale Public Schools, 55th and Grant Streets, Hinsdale, IL 60521.

The "more is better and most is best," philosophy of the 1960's and 1970's is over. While many doom and gloom futurists toll the knell of the parting way of life for our society, more positive thinkers view the future as a new challenge. The Robert Theobalds of the world (Futures Conditional, *et al*) view the options during the 1980's as a chance to live better and improve society in the bargain. These forward looking forecasters of the future suggest that through careful use of scarce resources, people can improve their quality of life. It's a Mies van der Rohe "less is more" philosophy.

Within this general context, you've already been informed of various aspects of managing schools. This section explores some of the possibilities for managing the education of gifted and talented students. This will be done within the "less is more" framework, with the further parameters that research, knowledge and best practice provide.

IDENTIFICATION

Two major areas should be explored in discussing the education of gifted and talented students — identification and program. For our purposes, we can use the definition used by the U. S. Office of the Gifted and Talented to define these children.

> "Gifted and talented children identified by professional qualified persons, are those who by virtue of outstanding abilities are capable of high performance. They require differentiated educational programs and/or services beyond those normally provided by the regular school program in order to realize their contributions to self and society. Children capable of high performance include those with demonstrated achievement and/or potential ability in any of the following areas, single or in combination: 1) General intellectual ability *and* 2) Specific academic aptitude/talent."

Early work by Terman and others as reported by Getzels and Dillon in the "Second Handbook of Research on Teaching" concentrated on single measures of intelligence to identify gifted and talented youngsters. Great strides have been made since those early days in better understanding the nature of giftedness and in the availability of better and more measures of various elements of giftedness.

Most experts in educating the gifted now agree that there are many different facets of giftedness which must be examined in order to shape future programs. Dorothy Sisk and Joseph Renzulli wrote on this point in the Winter, *1980 Gifted Child Quarterly*.

The early work of Havighurst with his notion of developmental tasks, Benjamin Bloom with the concept of a taxonomy of educational objectives and Guilford's structure of intellect have provided groundwork for the recent thinking of Calvin Taylor (structure of the intellect) and Mary Meeker. These ideas all made a contribution to more clearly defining the nature of giftedness and solidifying the notion that the "whole" may not be as important to examine as the individual parts. It is the parts that vary within the person that must be addressed programmatically to have an impact on fully developing the student.

This approach to program mandates an identification procedure that delineates various talents. This approach also has the potential of offering the most benefit to the students and the school. According to Taylor, "Talent search and development should occur in the classroom. It takes no extra time and practically no extra expense." In hard times, when many districts are searching for ways to cut corners, it is extremely difficult to initiate new programs or refine existing ones. To accommodate the gifted children, an effective yet economical approach is necessary. The multiple talents program preceded by a procedure for identifying these specific talents is one that shows promise.

In accordance with current best thinking concerning identification as set forth by Paul Torrance, Joe Renzulli and Dorothy Sisk, districts must use many measures, not just one, to identify multiple talents. As an example, one district's newly revised gifted and talented program calls for the Otis Lennon Mental Ability test; Metropolitan and California Achievement tests; Renzulli-Hartman Rating Scale; Structure of Intellect Learning Abilities Test by Mary and Robert Meeker; and limited use based on particular needs of: Ross Test of Higher Cognitive Processes; Torrence Test of Creativity; Stanford Binet and WISC individual intelligence tests; and teacher observation and judgment. The Institute for Educational Research located in Glen Ellyn, IL, has done some definitive evaluation studies of identification procedures and new programs. There are many other individual measures reviewed by the Institute that, when used in tandem with each other will produce a comprehensive identification program. Suffice it to say, that with the general distrust by some citizens of education generally and more particularly gifted education; the increasingly activist nature of community groups and individuals; and equal rights provisions of the constitution and state laws; it makes sense to diversify the identification procedure in order to achieve a comprehensive, fair program. This approach will also provide for greater acceptance by school district parents, students, faculty, administrators and the Board of Education.

PROGRAM

Several issues need to be examined in connection with programming schools for gifted and talented students. Federal legislation (PL 94-142) has had a significant impact on gifted education as well as special education. Pull-out programs versus mainstreaming has recently become a significant issue in establishing community and teacher acceptance for gifted education. The impact of technology has also caused the opinion makers in gifted education to do retakes on what is feasible concerning the best quality educational opportunities available for gifted and talented students. Multiple-talents approaches to programming for gifted students are gaining in acceptance philosophically and substantiated through a growing body of research and use.

Two of the most significant aspects of PL 94-142 for special education students are the provisions for mainstreaming and individualized educational programs (IEP's). Mainstreaming will be examined later in this section when pull-out programs are discussed. IEP's have had a terrific impact on students, teachers, and schools since they were prescribed for all special education students in PL 94-142.

IEP's

Individualized instruction has been a goal of some educators for a decade. Until recently, however, most programs gave only lip service to the concept. With the 94-142 mandate came the great incentive as well as the provision and resources for training and retraining staff. This same concept, when used as a major element in gifted education, provides a new means of attaining quality programming for able students.

Research has told us repeatedly and unequivocally that children learn at different rates of speed and their interests are varied. It is then incumbent on the schools to provide programs that take advantage of these facts. Since gifted youngsters are even more dissimilar than alike as compared to regular students, more individualized approaches to education are required to benefit the gifted and talented — hence the need for using IEP's. Since faculties are becoming more familiar with the logistics of using IEP's with special education students, it should be much easier to adapt this individualized approach for gifted students. Eventually, all students could be handled more effectively through the use of IEP's and individualized programming.

A number of problems must be dealt with in implementing an individualized program for gifted and talented or any students. Funds and time must be made available to train and retrain teachers, develop new individualized program materials, and work on an individual basis with students and evaluate their products. One of the great pluses of the use of IEP's and its prime feasibility is that the model is already established for special education. The wheel has been invented and simply needs to be refined for use with gifted and talented or regular students.

PULL-OUT VS. MAINSTREAM

In the past, advocates of special programming for gifted students have pointed to research studies which show that "acceleration" in all phases of schooling shows positive results. These same researchers indicate further that neither grouping nor regular classroom enrichment experiences have consistently provided positive results among the gifted. Improvement in achievement has occurred when the curricular program, methods, or teachers fit a particular learning situation most effectively.

Many existing programs, and most programs operating in the past that have been successful have been "pull-out programs". Students have been grouped together for parts of the program in order to facilitate scheduling with special teachers, engaging in new and innovative curriculum, and participating in experiences where special methodology was employed.

These special programs have elicited a great deal of criticism since they tend to be considered by the public as elitist. A number of very promising programs have been terminated prematurely or never expanded due to this phenomenon. Educators have come to realize what many believe to be the essence of good administration — acceptability of programs for gifted is the art of the possible.

In this regard it must be remembered that society, in general, benefits from all education, be it special, gifted or regular education. Inasmuch as this is true — a case can certainly be made for pull-out programs that have the acceptability of the community and teachers. More importantly, new programs must be generated that will stand the rigors of research efficacy while being acceptable to the community and faculty. Because mainstreaming carries with it the acceptability earned in its association with special education, it holds a great deal of promise for acceptability. Equality of opportunity, as well as civil rights and other equality principles are moving educators inevitably to a consideration of innovative ways to serve needs of gifted and talented young people. Mainstreaming has the potential for meeting many of these needs and generating greater community acceptance.

TECHNOLOGICAL ADVANCES

The advent of microcomputers, low cost use of minicomputers with on-line cathode ray tube input, and economical in-house printers has opened new possibilities for educating exceptional children. The use of IEP's has generated a problem for special educators in planning individualized lessons, offering options for various types of programs and students, monitoring progress of all programs including evaluation and recording achievements, and generally managing instruction and assisting program implementation.

Through the use of the computer, identification of multiple talents can be facilitated and the results recorded and systematized for easy retrieval. Options for various instructional programs can be provided for individual students to use in the computer assisted instruction mode. IEP goal achievements can be recorded, evaluated, stored and retrieved as needed thereby streamlining and making viable an otherwise cumbersome and laborious process.

Simulations available on most micro or minicomputers, allow gifted and talented students or any students to sample slices of real life without sacrificing time or being placed in potentially destructive situations which usually accompany these activities. These simulations can provide the necessary environment for experimentation and creative expression vitally needed by gifted and talented students. Through simulations, individuals can be accommodated without fear of destroying the communities' acceptance of the total gifted, special or regular curricular programs.

MULTIPLE TALENTS APPROACHES

As mentioned previously, Guilford's Structure of Intellect models, and the subsequent development by Meeker of the SOI profile have worked to diagnose various intellectual abilities among gifted and talented students. Meeker has published a set of workbooks to be used by teachers to aid the instruction of students according to the abilities identified in the profile. (Workbooks available at the SOI Institute, El Segundo, CA.) This approach provides a differentiated technique for educating gifted students. It is in accord with current best thinking that giftedness is not a single faceted characteristic, but a multifaceted set of abilities that are recognized and developed.

Calvin Taylor has developed this same idea in a number of school systems across the United States. Through his *talents unlimited* approach, he has encouraged and trained teachers in all regular classrooms to search for and identify talent and develop that particular talent in the classroom. In this era of limited resources, this program has proved very successful and has the advantages of taking very little time and expending few dollars. The program existed as a Title IV-C project in Peotone, IL, and has been adapted to other districts where interest was indicated.

Multiple Talent teaching, while less rigorous than the SOI approach has the advantage of simplicity of identification and implementation. It is meant to be used by classroom teachers with a low budget. It has proven to be a very successful vehicle for handling gifted and talented students in a way that is acceptable to the community and teachers. Since it is a mainstream type of program it has not been tagged with the elitist criticism. Philosophically it is attuned carefully to the voices of leading experts on the education of gifted children who say that we must educate for a variety of abilities and interests. The day of single-minded gifted programs is over.

A PROTOTYPE PROGRAM

Managing schools in hard times brings to mind at least two different notions. One is that hard times refer to money and the lack of it. The other idea is that the impact of accountability and pressure groups inside and outside the schools cause a series of new and serious problems (hard times) which must be dealt with in much different ways than in the past.

Some of the issues have been explored in identifying gifted students, diagnosing their diverse needs, and implementing programs for talented children. Let's examine a prototype program that builds in some of these concerns. It should be noted that this is only one example that works. There are undoubtedly numerous others which have been devised or are yet to be devised which will be equally as effective and fit the criterion established for an individualized, multitalented approach to gifted education. The following plan is currently being used in the Hinsdale Public Schools, Hinsdale, IL, under the direction of the Coordinator of Gifted Education, Mary Ellen Madden, who designed it.

This program for gifted and talented youth is mainstreamed so that opportunities are provided for interaction with intellectual, as well as age and grade level peers. All students identified for the program are mainstreamed for most of the school day. Intellectual peers are scheduled into the same language arts block for a minimum of two hours per week. Cluster grouping, appropriate to the curriculum is used to accommodate the needs of identified students. Differentiated materials and activities are employed as needed to meet individual needs of students.

Individualized Educational Programs (IEP's) are written for each identified student by a teacher assigned to guide him/her. IEP's are based on knowledge of each student's unique needs. All individuals concerned with the student's well being; i.e., the student himself, teachers, and parents agree on objectives and goals at the beginning of the year. Changes are agreed upon and implemented as needed depending on changes in the student's behavior and achievement. Provisions for student/teacher conferences are provided on a weekly basis. Flexible scheduling arrangements are available for all identified students when it is necessary in achieving their specific learning objectives. Each school's learning center affords opportunities for independent learning by all students. Structure of Intellect profiles are shared with parents so that objectives may be pursued out of school as well as in school.

The curriculum is differentiated to accommodate a program for gifted students that allows both teachers and students to develop learning alternatives, while remaining compatible with general district educational objectives. General areas of concern in the Hinsdale Extended Learning Program include:

- communication and general language skills on an advanced level
- cognitive and effective learning experiences
- research skills
- independent study techniques
- higher level thinking skills
- intense concentration on topics of interest
- improvement of basic skills when there is recognized need
- application of concepts
- original work.

Four goal areas are common to the program at all grade levels:

- thinking skills
- communication skills
- research skills
- SOI abilities.

A hierarchy of learning skills are prescribed for participants at each grade level. Learner objectives, activities, and evaluation procedures are shared and/or individual as required.

The approach to teaching thinking skills incorporates the use of Calvin Taylor's Talents Unlimited program for all student's and Bloom's Taxonomy of Higher Level Thinking Skills. The Structure of Intellect program overlaps both of these and provides differentiated teaching opportunities.

Objectives in the communication skills area correlate with general education language arts objectives. However, goals for gifted and talented students are aimed at an accelerated introduction of skills combined with a degree of mastery or depth of understanding different from requirements for other students.

Research skills are taught early and extended with expectations that expand as the student grows and matures. Appropriate tasks are pursued by students according to their own development.

IEP's include learner objectives, activities and evaluation procedures for each child. Individual as well as shared goals for each student are pursued. IEP's are shared with teachers, students and parents in an effort to have a coordinated and comprehensive approach to the program. Parent observation forms and student interest inventories assist in this effort. Results are recorded on the IEP so that progress can be tracked from year to year. The program aims to provide differentiated experiences for each student to the degree needed. (Differentiated curricula, materials, and activities are defined as those which go beyond regular program concerns expanding the depth, breadth, understanding and creativity of students involved.)

Teachers use and develop materials to provide experiences uniquely different according to the IEP's and learning styles of the students. Effort is made to use some materials that cut across subject matter and grade level lines to provide continuity. The school's learning center is a key source for individualized materials appropriate for each student's achieving his IEP objectives.

Specific materials used in the programs include: *Basic Thinking Skills, Brain Stretchers, Classroom Quickies, Critical Thinking I and II, Deductive Thinking Skills, Inductive Thinking Skills,* and *Analogies* published by Midwest Publications, Troy, MI. SOI materials include: *East Whittier Curriculum Guides* (E. Whittier, CA), *Foxtail Press Units and Lessons* (El Segundo, CA) and *SOI Learning Prescriptions* (SOI Institute). Evaluation instruments used in the program are: Ross Test of Higher Cognitive Abilities, Piers-Harris Self-Esteem Inventory, SOI Abilities Test, and pre and post tests for specific materials studied.

Teachers who have training and/or special interest in working with high ability students are used exclusively with this program. Each building is responsible for assigning teachers for the program — one teacher for each grade level 2-6, two teachers each for grades 7 and 8 at the junior high. Program teachers are responsible for preparing IEP's; however, additional staff members may be required to meet some special student objectives. Learning center teachers are a vital part of the program and offer the promise of continued assistance to faculty and students in the program. Each program teacher has access to a regularly assigned substitute teacher for a minimum of one and one-half hours per week to support the program and aid in meeting the needs of the identified gifted and talented students. Substitutes and early retirees are also used to administer and score some of the identification measures associated with this program.

Several regular inservice training sessions for all teachers are held each year to inform the staff about the characteristics and needs of gifted and talented students. Special workshop sessions are held periodically for teachers and learning center personnel directly involved in the program. District workshops, graduate courses in gifted Education, Area Service Center training sessions and presentations, ECA, TAG, NAGC conferences, and general district presentations, are all used to improve teachers' skill in working with able children.

Progress of students is evaluated by:

- pre and post tests in appropriate areas
- standardized or validated tests
- student products evaluated according to established criteria
- student teacher records
- self evaluation.

Program evaluation includes:

- reports from an exterior evaluation group based on planned evaluation tasks (Institute for Educational Research)
- student, teacher, parent attitudes
- success of individual students in the program.

The preceding program description is an effort to illustrate a workable gifted program that operates in accordance with current best thinking concerning educating gifted and talented students. It has the advantage of being successful in what it purports to do and is well accepted by the faculty and community. As mentioned earlier this program represents only one example of an individualized, multiple talents approach to education. There are many others which can be equally successful if they are personalized for the district, community, teachers, and students as this one was.

In this chapter, identification procedures as well as program possibilities have been explored. The use of a multiple talents approach has been emphasized within an individualized instructional program setting. The areas of mainstreaming, IEP's, new technology, and multiple talents teaching have been examined for use with able students. A prototype program has been suggested which is currently in use, successful, and accepted by the community. Hopefully, this discussion has offered some new and better ideas for managing programs for gifted and talented students in hard times.

SELECTED BIBLIOGRAPHY

Bloom, B. S. (Ed.) *Taxonomy of Educational Objectives, Handbook I: The Cognitive Domain.* New York: David McKay Co., 1956.

Getzels, J. W. and Dillon J. T. "The nature of giftedness and the education of the gifted", from Travers, R. M., Editor, *Second Handbook of Research on Teaching.* Chicago: Rand McNally, 1973, pp. 689-731.

Guilford, J. P. "The structure of intellect", *Psychological Bulletin,* 1956, pp. 52, 267-293.

Guilford, J. P. *The Nature of Human Intelligence.* New York: McGraw-Hill, 1967.

Guilford, J. P. "Three faces of intelligence", *American Psychologist,* 1959, pp. 14, 469-479.

Headbring, C. and Rubenzer, R. "Integrating the IER with SOI with educational programming for the gifted", *The Gifted Child Quarterly,* 1979, p. 23 No. 2, pp. 338-344.

Meeker, M. N. *The Structure of Intellect: Its Interpretation and Uses.* Columbus, OH: Charles E. Merrill, 1969.

Renzulli, J. S. *The Enrichment Trial Model: A Guide for Developing Defensible Programs for the Gifted and Talented.* Mansfield Center, CT: Creative Learning Press, 1977.

Renzulli, J. S. and Smith, L. H. *A Guidebook for Developing Individualized Educational Programs (IEP) for the Gifted and Talented.* Mansfield Center, CT: Creative Learning Press, 1979.

Taylor, Calvin W. "Multiple talent teaching", *Today's Education,* 1974, March-April, pp. 71.74.

16

HOW TO USE A MICROCOMPUTER TO MAKE BETTER DECISIONS

Stanton Leggett

Chances are good your district has a number of microcomputers in its schools that headquarters staff could use quite independently of any central computer system you already have going.

No stranger to school administrators, Stanton Leggett is perhaps the nation's best known and most resourceful educational consultant. A distinguished author and lecturer, he has worked in hundreds of school districts and colleges in most states and in a half dozen countries on a wide array of projects running from Administration through Zoning. His office and home is West Tisbury, Martha's Vineyard, MA 02575.

HOW TO USE A MICROCOMPUTER TO HELP YOU MAKE BETTER DECISIONS

Computers are no strangers to American schools. Student records are kept, tests scored and analyzed, schedules made, salary checks written, accounts kept, and students taught, to mention a few uses. However, the most strategic use may well be in marshalling data for decision making in a way that makes possible careful examination by the school executive of alternative courses of action.

The microcomputer is inexpensive. Hence it is possible to use it independent of a central computer system, thus getting the work out of the traffic jam. A large computer needs a traffic jam of steady work to justify its cost. The software for microcomputers will increasingly be available to do sophisticated work for a manager. A microcomputer program in cash flow management can pay off quickly both in reduction of managerial time and in actually getting more dollars out of money. New software ranging from the advanced Visicalc to "The Last One" to highly flexible data base management systems are making programming easier and may end up eliminating much of costly custom programming.

The shift of emphasis from massive data handling, which remains as a chore well done by the machines, to insightful probes into cause and costs, is in process and as experience is gained, will flourish. It will flourish because the tool will prove to be worth the trouble. As an example, look at the possibilities inherent in the use of microcomputers or any other computer for that matter in the analysis of work orders.

MANAGEMENT OF WORK ORDERS: AN EXAMPLE

A work order is a request from some authorized person operating or using a building for the performance of some task necessary to keep the building in good operating condition, such as to fix a leak in the roof, or to improve the effectiveness of the building as an educational tool, such as by building an outdoor weather station for sixth grade science.

The work order contains important data, other than its use as a system to get tasks accomplished. It will tell what building is involved, the date the work order was initiated, and the type of problem the work order was intended to meet. Eventually the date the work order was assigned to be undertaken, the person or crew to whom the task was assigned, the date the task was completed, the cost of accomplishing the task, and a follow-up evaluation of the quality of performance of the task should be added.

In most school systems, these data exist merely to accomplish the task. It is possible to make a powerful analytic tool out of the data. A person can be assigned to analyze work orders. A machine, when properly instructed, can analyze the data systematically and report, allowing the saved time of the person to be spent doing something to improve the system and to reduce its costs. The equation of cost and benefit must offset the cost of a person analyzing the data manually against the cost of time on the computer, some allocation of cost of software to record and manipulate the data, and the cost to enter the data in the computer. In a computerized system the data regarding the work order would be entered in the machine, an increase in work over using copies of the original work order. The computerized system would require entering of data concerning the time of completion and cost of the work order, comparable to that required in a manual system.

The advent of low cost but powerful microcomputers, the increasing ability to purchase appropriate software programs, and the simplicity of programming simple machines, all contribute to reducing the investment necessary to computerize the system.

The beginning of the program can be simple, such as determining the average elapsed time in getting work orders completed. The system can then be added to in complexity, perhaps next determining the average elapsed time in completing work orders by category of task. Window shade repairs may take 15 working days. Broken window glass can be replaced in one day, except for large pieces which must be special ordered. Plywood is placed over the opening in one day. Roof leaks, on the average, could take up to five days to complete.

A complete system might end up with a daily printout of outstanding work orders, in which management by exception is used as the approach. If the system has determined that task A takes three days to complete, the printout might not report any task A assignments that were made three or fewer days before. All task A assignments outstanding more than three days could be printed out, together with the name of the person or crew to whom the assignment was made, the building, and any other required information. The manager of the maintenance program would have a systematic way of keeping track of assignments and completion concentrating on the exceptions to normal practice.

For planning, summary data for month and year have great value. These are categorized below.

1. **Elapsed time before work orders were assigned.** Data can be accumulated to show how long it took to assign a task to be accomplished. If there were a backlog of work orders, the manager could examine the causes. Were too trivial tasks being accomplished by work order by the central crews and too little simple preventive maintenance being accomplished by the building crew, work agreements willing? Would systematic preventive maintenance help reduce work orders? Should some items be purchased rather than built by the system? Was the individual school budget charged for all additions to the educational quality of the school? Could productivity be improved? Were repairs being made when replacement would be more cost-effective? Should contract work be used? Should more staff be hired?

2. **Elapsed time between assignment and completion of work order.** This series of data, developed by category of task, provides benchmarks against which to measure task time. A manager may examine a category where the time of completion seems overlong. Comparison with other systems, discussion of problems with the work staff involved and skilled observation of the work in process could produce ways to improve performance. Perhaps the purchase of some labor-saving equipment

could be justified. Specific training of the work crew and development of time-saving procedures may improve the productivity. It may be that there is a pattern of delay caused by lack of parts. The system may improve its stocking of parts or may replace equipment when parts are no longer available.

3. **Classification of elapsed time between assignment and completion of work orders.** Fine tuning of the analysis of elapsed time might introduce a series of variables. Did it take longer to accomplish a task dependent upon season? Roof top equipment may be harder to maintain in certain seasons. When the same task was assigned to different crews, was there a significant difference in elapsed time? If so, what was the reason? Did one crew take longer but produce higher quality results so that no return trips were involved?

4. **Assignment of work orders and resulting costs to individual buildings.** Each work order, upon completion, should be assigned a cost based on labor, including fringe benefits, parts and an allowance for overhead. These costs can be summarized by type of task and summarized by building.

A detailed file, expressed in a computer printout, of work done on a building, and including contract work, would provide most valuable data for the manager. If one building has a history of unusual cost per square foot of space for maintenance, such a history would lead to decisions as to replacement of major components, such as a roof or an electrical system, or to consider whether or not the building should be taken out of service by replacement or use of other facilities.

5. **Evaluation of effectiveness of task performance.** One simple way to evaluate effectiveness of work would be a computerized query to the originator of each work order inquiring as to the satisfaction or lack of satisfaction with the work done. Supervisors of buildings or supervisors of maintenance crews when visiting a building, could be given a printout of tasks accomplished in the school during a recent period of time and could inspect the work. The conditions surrounding the perform-

ance of the task should be taken into account. Not even the best can find a roof leak the first time in all cases.

The simple point of all this about work orders is that by accumulating and organizing data, using low cost equipment and easily accomplished programming (even if you must humble yourself by begging students to do the programming for you), the manager moves from a person dealing with crises to a person with a plan that anticipates problems and reduces the number of crises.

The data are available to improve productivity and quality. By accumulating information about a building the long-range replacement needs for parts like roofs or systems like power can be determined and planned. By analyzing the frequency of various categories of work orders and the cost of responding, the key areas for preventive maintenance where payoff is highest can be identified. The computer is a manager's tool. The cost of computerization at the level necessary to do the job should be included in the cost analysis of each job, as a separate part of overhead.

HOW DECISIONS ARE MADE ABOUT SCHOOL BUDGETS

There is an old fashioned equation in most school budgeting that says that expenditures may not exceed income. School systems find themselves in different positions with regard to the equation. For a few systems, the sum of the approved expenditures determines the income. The necessary money is raised to accomplish the tasks described in the estimated expenditures. For an increasing number of school systems, a limited income will determine which of the many tasks the school system wishes to accomplish may indeed be undertaken. Most school systems fall in between with modest leverage on income which is pressed both by inflation and by the hope to add to or to improve some programs.

Virtually all school systems are required to make decisions that will serve the purpose of educating students best within the reality of the income-expenditure equation. While many school budgets are still rewritten last year's budget with adjustments, increasingly budgets are developing around such accounting procedures as program budgets and zero-based budgets.

Essentially, instead of grouping costs around such categories as instructional salaries, instructional materials, maintenance and operation, and the like, for the system as a whole, the costs are grouped around a part of the system such as a task to be performed or an operating unit of the system. An elementary school will be a budget classification. The costs of teachers, clerks, librarian, principal and all other staff will be assigned to the school. An allocation for instructional supplies, library books, AV materials, and the like will be included. The cost of maintenance of the building and custodial operation may be included. Energy costs are part of the school's budget. Allocated to the school also is its share of overhead. Ultimately the cost of operating the system is the sum of the costs of operating each unit of the system.

These data become difficult to assemble manually. Manipulating the information so that many alternatives can be handled becomes so time consuming as to be impractical.

17

DECISION PACKAGES: THEY ANSWER "WHAT IF . . ." QUESTIONS

Stanton Leggett

What will it cost in 1985 or 1990 to operate each school in your district if you change staffing or modify services? You don't know. Well, you can find out — and with surprising accuracy, barring an earthquake or similar mishap. Consultant-author Leggett charts a course that shows how to develop the information you need for decision making and for deciding among several options.

Stanton Leggett is the author of four chapters in this book and its chief editor.

Some of a school district's projections must inevitably be on a hope and pray basis. But the number of these is much lower than a lot of administrators think. The by guess and by gosh school of management is going to disappear if it has not already done so. The computer will see to that. Not the big fancy ones. But the relatively inexpensive micro-computers that are within the price range of individuals as well as school districts. The programs we are going to describe can be adapted to any micro-computer. Most districts have these in the classroom if not in the central office. No matter. They should be put to use wherever they are on behalf of the district. If you don't now have access to such a computer, you will soon. I promise. Trust me.

Here is how to use it. Let us start by calling all of the materials necessary for making a decision a *decision package*. Now we need a few more arbitrary definitions so we can assemble our *decision package*.

A *decision package* describes any function of the school system in terms of the necessity for performing the function, the resources necessary to perform the function, and the level of performance required, and may be used by the school system in the decision making process.

There are three variables:

1-A. Necessity of the Function.

Some functions of the school system must be performed. School must be operated; usually for 180 days a year. Certain subjects must be offered. Other state requirements must be met. Some federal requirements exist, notably in dealing with handicapped children and in coping with children whose native language is not English.

Above these requirements, necessity is relative, varying from community to community; person to person. A scale from absolutely necessary to not at all necessary is appropriate when dealing with this variable beyond the level of mandated functions.

The decision package must present the rationale for the function. The judgment exercised by the school system is to determine how necessary the function is by placing the decision package in order of importance.

1-B. Necessary Use of Resources.

The decision package should provide present and estimated costs of performing a function based on varying levels of performance. The estimates should be complete, particularly where large units of the system are involved, and should include direct and indirect costs and allocation of overhead costs. What you are doing is to line up the resources that must be committed by the system in order to accomplish the task.

1-C. Necessary Level of Performance.

For most functions the level can vary from limited performance to complete performance. The level of performance of the maintenance and operation function of a school system can vary from cleaning occasionally and repairing when crisis strikes to a well-done job marked by considerable investment in preventive maintenance.

There are usually a wide variety of ways to provide a service. The decision packages can describe a number of alternative ways to perform each function and can give a reasonable estimate of cost.

HOW TO MAKE A DECISION

Theoretically, decisions are made in two steps. The first is to rank decision packages in order of priority. This is easy where the resources at the disposal of the school system are sufficient to allow the purchase, in one form or another, of most of the packages desired by the constituency. Assigning priorities is painful when the resources will not be sufficient to provide for the major necessities.

Assigning priorities to decision packages is not a free process. Legally mandated functions, in a society that governs itself by laws, must be given highest priority. This is the case even if the unintended consequence of a mandate of one function takes resources away from the performance of an equally important but non-mandated function. A function such as paying off bonded indebtedness must be of highest priority since the district has promised to pay back the borrowed amount with interest. Agreements with employee organizations or commitments to the community may place external priorities on functions or levels of performance.

The second step in the theoretical decision making process is represented by the following equation:

Estimated revenues equal estimated expenditures where estimated expenditures is the sum of the cost of decision packages at the level decided upon and accumulated in the order of priority until the total cost approaches and equals the estimated revenues. Where there is greater fiscal freedom, the sum of the cost of the necessary decision packages describing functions to be performed at the level required will determine the revenues to be raised.

DECISION MAKING AS TRADE-OFFS

Real decision making is not the clean process described above. While the general outlines are true, a great deal of compromise and use of trade-offs combine to reach a budget or to set a long-range financial plan. In this process, the decision making profits from the analysis of a substantial number of alternative ways to provide services and a substantial number of sub-packages, also at varying levels of performance.

The use of computerized information is strategic since with a carefully thought out and flexible data processing approach, it is possible to develop many alternative courses of action and to provide data regarding these courses of action. If the process were done manually, the time and energy available limit the number of alternatives that can be examined. The computer, by doing the drudgery, allows the critical energy to be devoted to the development of creative alternatives and the refinement of the costing, prioritization and evaluation of the decision packages.

EVALUATION

After decisions are made the format of the decision package offers the opportunity of more precise evaluation of performance of functions with respect to the re-

sources allocated to the function. If one of the decision packages accepted is to institute a new science program, the costs of texts, materials, equipment, space, teacher retraining and testing the results should be included in the package. At the end of some period of time, the effectiveness of the new science program should be evaluated and the continued assignment of resources to the program should be made contingent upon reasonable proof that the program was an improvement.

EXAMPLES

Using data from Independence, OH, the cost element of a decision package that estimates the total cost of operating its high school in the future was developed. Independence is a school system with above average wealth per student. It is a small system, with much of its available land used. The system has been declining in enrollment and will continue to do so. It is estimated that the high school will drop from its present enrollment of 451 students in grades 9 to 12 to 241 students by 1989.

Independence operates a primary school for grades kindergarten to four with about 175 students enrolled. It will rebound a bit from its low enrollment as births increase. The middle school will decline from 223 to 154 students by 1989. Obviously the major variable will be the reduction in enrollment.

The decision package of the high school is developed in a series of scenarios ranging from reducing costs, to business as usual, to spending more to maintain a broader program, smaller class size, and an enriched learning environment. The alternatives are developed by the author, not by the school system. Costs are expressed in 1979 dollars to make 1989 costs comparable. The costs can readily be converted to estimated 1989 dollars by adding an inflation factor.

TOTAL COST OF OPERATING A HIGH SCHOOL IN 1989

A scenario, Business as Usual, is used to develop the staffing required for the high school in 1989, if the high school were to decline in enrollment from 451 students in the base year, 1979, to 241 students in the estimate year, 1989.

The number of teachers required in this scenario was estimated using the current ratio of teachers to students now in use in the system. The adjusted number of teachers shown in the scenario is the resultant of a slight increase in class size, using 25 as a desired class size instead of 23 average and raising the minimum size class to ten students. Offsetting this change was a forecast of the number of sections that would be generated by the estimated number of student enrollments in each subject. The number of sections was adjusted to meet state requirements. For example, the state of Ohio required at that time that each accredited high school offer and actually provide three courses in homemaking. It would be necessary to violate the minimum class size of ten to meet this requirement.

A computer program that estimates future numbers of sections in each subject using a series of variables is an effective tool. This program is not illustrated but has the capability of giving information regarding the following kinds of variables, in each case with the variable number of students enrolled in the base year and the estimate year considered:

- How many sections would be required in each subject in the estimate year with the reduced number of students if students enrolled in the same pattern that they did in the base year?
- How many sections would be required in the estimate year in each subject if the students were restricted in the number of courses they could take?
- How many sections would be required in the estimate year in each subject if all students were required to take five majors or solids?
- How many sections would be required in the estimate year in each subject if the pattern of course offering were changed?

Some of these estimates of sections in each subject require some arbitrary allocation of students to subjects but the total number of teachers required will probably be fairly accurate.

The cost estimates following show the mathematical projection of staff if all staff decreased in direct proportion to the decline in enrollment. The "adjusted" column is a scenario, since judgments are made in line with the intent of the scenario. The first cost estimate is "business as usual." For example, in this case, although the decline in enrollment suggests less than a full-time librarian, the scenario is adjusted to provide one.

The total cost of operating the high school is shown in a series of sub-items:

a. Staffing
b. Costs related to the number of students
c. Costs of library and AV services, excluding salaries
d. Costs related to building use, excluding salaries
e. Share of administration and overhead

In this approach, the sum of the total costs of all three schools in the system equals the total cost of operating the system.

The decision packages can express options. For example, following are two different levels of staffing of the same high

---

DECISION PACKAGE: COST ESTIMATE

Cost of Operating Independence, OH, High School with Declining Enrollments, 1979 and 1989, All Costs Expressed in 1979 dollars

	School System		High School	
	1979	Est. 1989	1979	Est. 1989
Enrollment...............	873	592	451	241

school in 1989, with the same estimated decline in enrollment. The first scenario cuts staffing below "business as usual." Incidentally, in each case the mathematically projected decrease in staffing is shown as a kind of base figure. The rationale for the reduction from the base exists and, in more detailed presentations, can be included.

Following the rationale of the scenarios, the other related costs can be adjusted up or down, to provide the total cost.

Staffing

STANTON LEGGETT & ASSOCIATES
INDEPENDENCE HIGH SCHOOL BUSINESS AS USUAL IN 1989

POSITION	BASE NO.	1979 COST	EST. NO.	1989 COST	ADJUST NO.	1989 COST
TEACHER	32.5	804180	17.4	429728	16.4	405802
OWE TEACHER	0.5	12372	0.3	6611	0.5	12372
CAF AIDES	2.0	7824	1.1	4181	1.1	4303
PSYCHOLOGIST	0.5	12372	0.3	6611	0.3	7423
NURSE	0.1	2474	0.1	1322	0.1	2474
COUNSELORS	2.0	61228	1.1	32718	1.0	30614
COUNSELOR SECY	1.0	11813	0.5	6312	0.5	5907
LD TEACHER	1.4	34642	0.7	18511	1.0	24744
LIBRARIAN	1.0	22580	0.5	12066	1.0	22580
AV AIDE	1.0	3912	0.5	2090	0.5	1956
LIBRARY AIDE	1.0	3912	0.5	2090	0.5	1956
PRINCIPALS	2.0	62384	1.1	33336	1.0	31192
GEN SECRETARIES	3.0	35439	1.6	18938	1.5	17720
CUSTODIANS'	2.0	37336	1.1	19951	1.0	18668
CLEANERS	8.0	16384	4.3	8755	6.0	12288
CAF WORKERS	6.0	21288	3.2	11376	3.0	10644
	64.0	1150140	34.2	614598	35.4	610642

Category of Cost		Cost 1979	Estimated Cost 1989 (in 1979 dollars)
A. Staffing, including Fringe Benefits		$1,150,140	$610,642
B. Costs Related to Number of Students			
Educational Supplies and Books	$35,200		
Guidance Supplies and EDP	21,741		
Principal's Office Supplies	7,000		
Repair Educational Equipment	4,500		
Internal Printing	2,400		
Permanent Improvement	20,900		
TOTAL:		91,741	
1979 Cost per Student $203			
1989 Cost with 241 enrolled			55,430
C. Cost of Library and AV, excluding Salaries			
Books	$10,500		
Subscriptions	2,500		
AV Supplies	8,000		
AV Films	2,100		
Permanent Improvements	3,500		
Share, Undistributed Costs	2,350		
TOTAL:		28,985	
1979 Cost per Student $64			
1989 Cost with 241 enrolled			15,424

Category of Cost		Cost 1979	Estimated Cost 1989 (in 1979 dollars)
D.	Costs Related to Building, excluding salaries		
	Total Cost of maintenance and operation ÷ total area of buildings x no. sq. ft. in high school	110,346	110,346
E.	Share: Administration and Overhead		

E1. System-wide costs, 1979

Debt Service.......................... $156,775	
Payment to County (Sp. Ed.) 78,500	
Other Administrative Costs 130,230	
TOTAL: 365,505	

E2. Share to high school, 1979

1979 Cost per student .... $ 418		
1979 Cost with 451 enrolled	188,518	

E3. System-wide costs, 1989

Debt Service....................... 0	
Payment to County................. $ 52,595	
Other............................. 130,230	
TOTAL: 182,825	

E4. Share to high school, 1989

1989 Cost per student	$ 308	
		74,228

SUMMARY

Estimated Cost in 1979 dollars for Independence, OH, High School in 1989 Using Scenario: Business as Usual

	Category	Cost 1979	Est. Cost 1989 (in 1979 dollars)
A.	Staffing salaries and fringe benefits	$1,150,140	$610,642
B.	Costs related to number of students	91,741	55,340
C.	Costs of library and AV, excluding salaries ...	28,985	15,424
D.	Costs related to building, excluding salaries..	110,346	110,346
E.	Share of administrative and other costs	188,518	50,369
	TOTALS:	$1,569,730	$842,211
	H. S. Enrollment	451	241
	Cost per Student	$ 3,480	$ 3,495

DECISION PACKAGES FOR PROGRAMS WITHIN SCHOOLS

The school system could examine its policy with respect to the offering of foreign languages, as an example. Among the alternatives that could be considered, for example, in a school system that offers three foreign languages from first grade to twelfth grade are:

1. Continue present program
2. Improve present program by adding languages and more AP courses
3. Offer three foreign languages
   3A. first to twelfth grade
   3B. seventh to twelfth grade
   3C. ninth to twelfth grade
4. Offer two foreign languages
   4A. first to twelfth grade

STANTON LEGGETT & ASSOCIATES
INDEPENDENCE HIGH SCHOOL CUT IN 1989

POSITION	BASE NO.	1979 COST	EST. NO.	1989 COST	ADJUST NO.	1989 COST
TEACHER	32.5	804180	17.4	429728	14.0	346416
OWE TEACHER	0.5	12372	0.3	6611	0.0	0
CAF AIDES	2.0	7824	1.1	4181	0.0	0
PSYCHOLOGIST	0.5	12372	0.3	6611	0.1	2474
NURSE	0.1	2474	0.1	1322	0.1	2474
COUNSELORS	2.0	61228	1.1	32718	1.0	30614
COUNSELOR SECY	1.0	11813	0.5	6312	0.3	3544
LD TEACHER	1.4	34642	0.7	18511	0.0	0
LIBRARIAN	1.0	22580	0.5	12066	1.0	22580
AV AIDE	1.0	3912	0.5	2090	0.0	0
LIBRARY AIDE	1.0	3912	0.5	2090	0.0	0
PRINCIPALS	2.0	62384	1.1	33336	1.0	31192
GEN SECRETARIES	3.0	35439	1.6	18938	1.0	11813
CUSTODIANS	2.0	37336	1.1	19951	1.0	18668
CLEANERS	8.0	16384	4.3	8755	6.0	12288
CAF WORKERS	6.0	21288	3.2	11376	2.0	7096
	64.0	1150140	34.2	614598	27.5	489160

STANTON LEGGETT & ASSOCIATES
INDEPENDENCE HIGH SCHOOL HIGH COST LEVEL WITH LOW ENROLLMENT

POSITION	BASE NO.	1979 COST	EST. NO.	1989 COST	ADJUST NO.	1989 COST
TEACHER	32.5	804180	17.4	429728	23.0	569112
OWE TEACHER	0.5	12372	0.3	6611	0.0	0
CAF AIDES	2.0	7824	1.1	4181	2.0	7824
PSYCHOLOGIST	0.5	12372	0.3	6611	0.5	12372
NURSE	0.1	2474	0.1	1322	0.5	12372
COUNSELORS	2.0	61228	1.1	32718	1.5	45921
COUNSELOR SECY	1.0	11813	0.5	6312	1.0	11813
LD TEACHER	1.4	34642	0.7	18511	1.0	24744
LIBRARIAN	1.0	22580	0.5	12066	1.0	22580
AV AIDE	1.0	3912	0.5	2090	1.0	3912
LIBRARY AIDE	1.0	3912	0.5	2090	0.0	0
PRINCIPALS	2.0	62384	1.1	33336	1.5	46788
GEN SECRETARIES	3.0	35439	1.6	18938	2.0	23626
CUSTODIANS	2.0	37336	1.1	19951	2.0	37336
CLEANERS	8.0	16384	4.3	8755	7.0	14336
CAF WORKERS	6.0	21288	3.2	11376	3.0	10644
	64.0	1150140	34.2	614598	47.0	843380

4B. seventh to twelfth grade
4C. ninth to twelfth grade
5. Offer one foreign language
   5A. first to twelfth grade
   5B. seventh to twelfth grade
   5C. ninth to twelfth grade
6. Immersion program — a school or section of a school that functions entirely in a foreign language, therefore not requiring a separate staff.
7. Change class size policy
8. Require competency in a foreign language for graduation

The many alternatives that are possible can be examined using a computer without an undue expenditure of energy and time.

LIBRARY SERVICE AS A SERIES OF DECISION PACKAGES

The following materials are basically the cost estimates of several levels of providing library service in the Independence schools. Not all possibilities are shown. The likelihood is that a group examining the possibilities would come up with other alternatives to consider. The process of as-

signing appropriate costs to various items is important and, in a sense, is a cooperative effort between staff that would be affected and the consultant. The alternatives that are finally developed should be ranked in a process that would involve staff, community and board views.

The following levels are illustrated as these scenarios illustrate.

1. *Business as usual.* This level reduces the library book and supply costs in proportion to the decline in enrollment. The staffing remains the same.
2. *Business as usual with a reduction in AV expenditures.* The level proposed here would result in sharp reductions in AV supply costs. The shared costs are for a TV studio. This would be eliminated. The AV aide time would be reduced. There would be permanent improvements. Other costs, particularly in books for the primary school, were reduced.
3. *Reduce number of libraries.* This scenario assumes the consolida-

---

DECISION PACKAGE — LIBRARIES

Direct Costs of Library Services, 1989 Independence, OH, All Schools Scenario: Business as Usual

The Costs are expressed in 1979 dollars. Staffing and direct expenditures for libraries are included. The enrollment is expected to decline.

```
                    COST OF LIBRARY OPERATION
                    SCENARIO BUSINESS AS USUAL
                  COST EXPRESSED IN 1979 DOLLARS
```

POSITION	BASE YEAR 1979 849.5 STUDENTS NO.	COST	EST. YEAR 1989 567 STUDENTS NO.	COST	ADJUST YEAR 1989 567 STUDENTS NO.	COST
PRIM LIBRARY AIDE	1.0	12373	0.67	8258	0.5	6187
PRIM AV AIDE	0.2	2475	0.13	1652	0.1	1237
MIDDLE LIBRARIAN	1.0	22580	0.67	15071	0.5	11290
MIDDLE AV AIDE	0.3	3712	0.20	2478	0.2	2475
HS LIBRARIAN	1.0	22580	0.67	15071	1.0	22580
HS LIBRARY AIDE	1.0	12373	0.67	8258	0.5	6187
HS AV AIDE	0.5	6187	0.33	4129	0.3	3712
TOTALS	5.0	82279	3.34	54917	3.1	53667

```
            STANTON LEGGETT & ASSOCIATES
```

tion of the middle school into the high school with elimination of the middle school library. The primary school library is converted into superior classroom book collections. Money is retained in the primary school to add to the classroom book collections and to use films. A part-time library and AV aide continues at the pri-

mary school to manage materials.

4. *Use the public library.* This scenario eliminates all library services, uses classroom collections, retains one aide in the system to manage materials, and contributes half of the materials and supplies budget to the public library to use to augment the collection.

Scenario: Business as Usual Direct Library Costs (Excluding Salaries) Related to Numbers of Students

Code	Description	Primary	Costs 1979 Middle	High	Total	Est. Cost 1989 (in 1979 dollars) Primary	Middle	High	Total
						(.98)	(.69)	(.53)	(.67)
2222	Books	3,200	3,200	10,500	16,900	3,136	2,208	5,565	10,909
2222	Subscriptions	700	800	2,500	4,000	686	552	1,325	2,563
2223	Audio Suppl's	500	2,500	8,000	11,000	490	1,725	4,240	6,455
2223	Films	100	800	2,100	3,000	98	552	1,113	763
2223	Perm Improv's	2,000	4,000	3,500	9,500	1,960	2,760	1,855	6,575
2223	Share-Undist Costs	931	1,184	2,385	4,500	914	820	1,281	3,015
	TOTALS:	7,431	12,484	28,985	48,900	7,284	7,617	15,379	30,280

NOTES: Estimated cost is 1979 cost x ratio 1989 enrollment ÷ 1979 enrollment. Share undistributed costs distributed by percentage that estimated enrollment in each school is of total estimated 1989 enrollment.

SUMMARY

Scenario: Business as Usual, 1989

Staffing: Salaries and Fringe Benefits $53,667
Other Direct Library Costs 30,280

TOTAL $83,947

DECISION PACKAGE — LIBRARIES

Direct Costs of Library Services, 1989 Independence, OH, All Schools Scenario: Business as Usual with a Reduction in AV Services

Costs are expressed in 1979 dollars. Staffing and direct expenditures for libraries are included. The enrollment is expected to decline.

```
                        COST OF LIBRARY OPERATION
                SCENARIO BUSINESS AS USUAL WITH LIMITED AV
                        COST EXPRESSED IN 1979 DOLLARS
-----------------------------------------------------------------------------
                    BASE YEAR 1979      EST. YEAR 1989      ADJUST YEAR 1989
                    849.5  STUDENTS     567  STUDENTS       567  STUDENTS
POSITION            NO.       COST      NO.      COST       NO.       COST
-----------------------------------------------------------------------------
PRIM LIBRARY AIDE   1.0      12373      0.67     8258       0.5      6187
PRIM AV AIDE        0.2       2475      0.13     1652       0.0         0
MIDDLE LIBRARIAN    1.0      22580      0.67    15071       0.5     11290
MIDDLE AV AIDE      0.3       3712      0.20     2478       0.0         0
HS LIBRARIAN        1.0      22580      0.67    15071       1.0     22580
HS LIBRARY AIDE     1.0      12373      0.67     8258       0.5      6187
HS AV AIDE          0.5       6187      0.33     4129       0.0         0
-----------------------------------------------------------------------------
TOTALS              5.0      82279      3.34    54917       2.5     46243
                        STANTON LEGGETT & ASSOCIATES
```

Scenario: Business as Usual with Reduced AV Direct Library Costs, Excluding Salaries, Estimated for 1989

Code	Description	Est. Cost 1989 (in 1979 dollars)			
		Primary	Middle	High	Total
2222	Books	1,400	3,000	5,000	9,400
2222	Subscriptions	500	1,300	1,500	3,300
2223	Audio Supplies	500	700	1,000	2,200
2223	Films	100	600	1,000	1,700
2223	Permanent Improvements	200	200	400	800
2223	Share-Undistributed Costs	0	0	0	0
	TOTALS:	2,700	5,800	8,900	17,400

Notes on Reducing AV Cost Share: Reduce audio supplies.
Eliminate undistributed costs which are TV studio related.
Reduce permanent improvements.

SUMMARY

Scenario: Business as Usual with Reduced Expenditures for AV, 1989

Staffing: Salaries and Fringe Benefits $46,243
Other direct library costs 17,400

TOTAL: $63,643

DECISION PACKAGE — LIBRARIES

Direct Cost of Library Services, 1989 Independence, OH, All Schools Scenario: Reduce Number of Libraries

Costs are expressed in 1979 dollars. Staffing costs, including salaries and fringe benefits, and direct expenditures for libraries, are included. The enrollment is expected to decline.

```
                    COST OF LIBRARY OPERATION
               SCENARIO REDUCE NUMBER OF LIBRARIES
                   COST EXPRESSED IN 1979 DOLLARS
```

POSITION	BASE YEAR 1979 849.5 STUDENTS NO.	COST	EST. YEAR 1989 567 STUDENTS NO.	COST	ADJUST YEAR 1989 567 STUDENTS NO.	COST
PRIM LIBRARY AIDE	1.0	12373	0.67	8258	0.5	6187
PRIM AV AIDE	0.2	2475	0.13	1652	0.0	0
MIDDLE LIBRARIAN	1.0	22580	0.67	15071	0.0	0
MIDDLE AV AIDE	0.3	3712	0.20	2478	0.0	0
HS LIBRARIAN	1.0	22580	0.67	15071	1.0	22580
HS LIBRARY AIDE	1.0	12373	0.67	8258	1.0	12373
HS AV AIDE	0.5	6187	0.33	4129	0.5	6187
TOTALS	5.0	82279	3.34	54917	3.0	47326

```
               STANTON LEGGETT & ASSOCIATES
```

Scenario: Reduce Number of Libraries, Direct Library Costs, Excluding Salaries, Estimated for 1989

Code	Description	Est. Costs 1989 (in 1979 dollars)			
		Primary	Middle	High	Total
2222	Books	700	0	5,000	5,700
2222	Subscriptions	250	0	1,500	1,750
2223	Audio Supplies	200	0	1,000	1,200
2223	Films	100	0	1,000	1,100
2223	Permanent Improvements	200	0	400	600
2223	Share-Undistributed Costs	0	0	0	0
	TOTALS:	1,450	0	8,900	10,350

NOTES: Eliminate middle school library as middle school is merged with high school. Primary school uses classroom libraries.

SUMMARY

Scenario: Reduce Number of Libraries

Staffing: Salaries and Fringe Benefits $47,326
Other direct library costs 10,350
     TOTAL: $57,676

DECISION PACKAGE — LIBRARIES

Direct Cost of Library Services, 1989 Independence, OH, All Schools Scenario: Use Public Library

Costs are expressed in 1979 dollars. Staffing costs, including salaries and fringe benefits, and direct expenditures for libraries, are included. The enrollment is expected to decline.

```
                    COST OF LIBRARY OPERATION
                  SCENARIO USE THE PUBLIC LIBRARY
                   COST EXPRESSED IN 1979 DOLLARS
```

POSITION	BASE YEAR 1979 849.5 STUDENTS		EST. YEAR 1989 567 STUDENTS		ADJUST YEAR 1989 567 STUDENTS	
	NO.	COST	NO.	COST	NO.	COST
PRIM LIBRARY AIDE	1.0	12373	0.67	8258	0.2	2475
PRIM AV AIDE	0.2	2475	0.13	1652	0.0	0
MIDDLE LIBRARIAN	1.0	22580	0.67	15071	0.0	0
MIDDLE AV AIDE	0.3	3712	0.20	2478	0.3	3712
HS LIBRARIAN	1.0	22580	0.67	15071	0.0	0
HS LIBRARY AIDE	1.0	12373	0.67	8258	0.5	6187
HS AV AIDE	0.5	6187	0.33	4129	0.0	0
TOTALS	5.0	82279	3.34	54917	1.0	12373

```
                 STANTON LEGGETT & ASSOCIATES
```

Scenario: Use Public Library, Direct Library Costs, Excluding Salaries, Estimated for 1989

		Est. Costs 1989 (in 1979 dollars)			
Code	Description	Primary	Middle	High	Total
2222	Books, subscriptions				$ 5,000
2222	Purchase of materials for public library distribution				5,000
	TOTAL:				$10,000

NOTES: The school system does not provide library service. It uses classroom libraries and provides some funds to augment public library resources. An aide works in the schools to handle liaison with public library and to handle AV materials, ordering and the like.

SUMMARY

Scenario: Use Public Library

Staffing: Salaries and Fringe Benefits $12,373
Other direct library costs 10,000

TOTAL: $22,373

18

TRENDS IN SCHOOL PLANNING AND DESIGN

C. William Brubaker, F.A.I.A.

On the sketchbook pages that follow, Mr. Brubaker explores such trends as:

— *the career center, using old and new buildings*
— *a mall concept for vocational-technical education*
— *the high school as a village cluster*
— *in the city, a magnet high school*
— *design for energy conservation*
— *the community school concept*
— *recycling surplus school space, with imagination*
— *comparing and evaluating existing school buildings.*

Mr. Brubaker is executive vice president, Perkins & Will Architects, Two N. LaSalle St., Chicago, IL 60602. A former president of the Council of Educational Facilities Planners, he specializes in school design and planning and is a popular lecturer and writer on these topics.

OLD & NEW BUILDINGS CLUSTERED TO CREATE A CAREER CENTER

For the Columbus, Ohio, school system, new buildings are combined with old buildings on a downtown campus to serve students from all parts of the district.

CENTURY-OLD ARSENAL HAS BEEN RESTORED TO SERVE AS A NEW ART CENTER, FOR THE VISUAL ARTS.

NEW BUILDINGS INCLUDE PERFORMING ARTS, HEALTH OCCUPATIONS, AND "THE MALL" FOR BUSINESS ED.

sketch below ; plan on opposite page →

" THE MALL " FOR CAREER EDUCATION

Student Mall is the focal point for circulation & social interchange, with all labs on display.

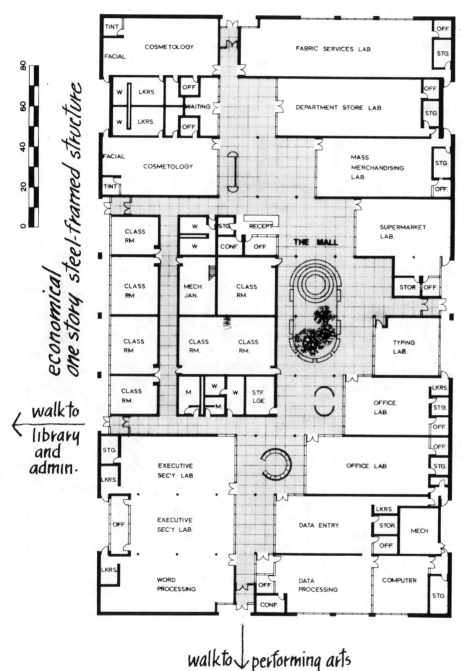

economical one story steel-framed structure

All labs are inward looking to The Mall ... and are on display.

walk to
library
and
admin.

walk to ↓ performing arts

FORT HAYES CAREER CENTER   COLUMBUS, OHIO
Dan A. Carmichael   and   Perkins & Will Architects

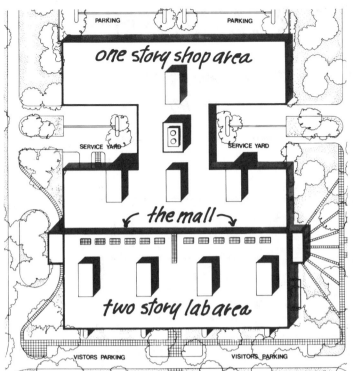

one story shop area

PARKING PARKING

SERVICE YARD SERVICE YARD

← the mall →

two story lab area

VISTORS PARKING VISITORS PARKING

Hedrich-Blessing photograph

MALL CONCEPT FOR A WARM CLIMATE

In Dade Co., Florida, the student mall is open air and not air conditioned, providing shelter while reducing energy costs.

THE ROBERT MORGAN VOCATIONAL-TECHNICAL INSTITUTE IS FRAMED WITH CONCRETE TWIN TEES.

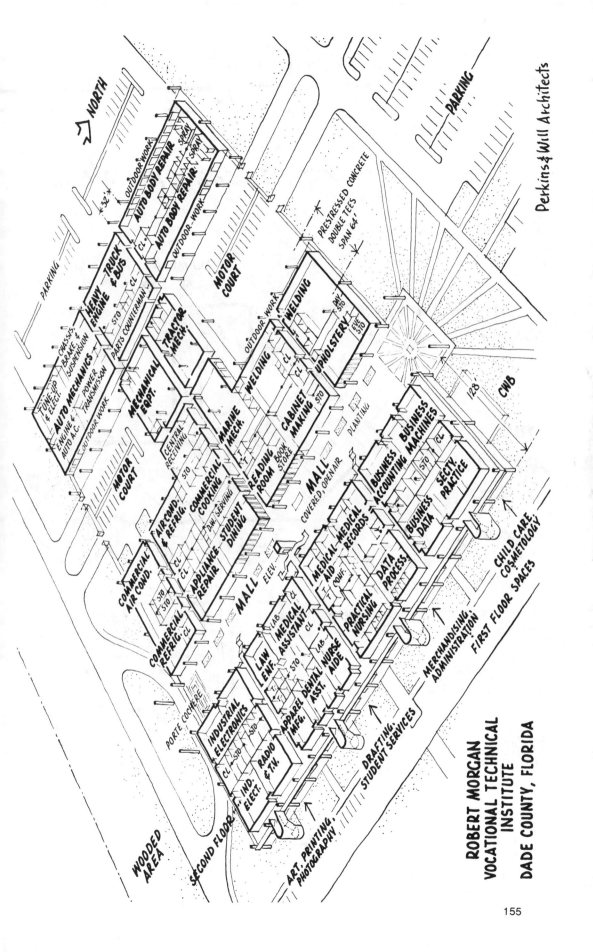

ROBERT MORGAN
VOCATIONAL TECHNICAL
INSTITUTE
DADE COUNTY, FLORIDA

Perkins & Will Architects

155

Design for a benign climate ....
VILLAGE·LIKE CLUSTER OF SMALL BUILDINGS
.... with outdoor circulation

In Irvine, California, the new high school is in the spirit of the informal architecture of the Village of Woodbridge.

THE OUTDOOR SPACES

ALAMEDA

"a public walk or promenade, especially one with trees"

ARBOR

"a sheltered place formed by a trellis covered with vines"

BOSQUE

"a dense growth of trees"

PLAZA

"a public square ... a broad paved open-air area"

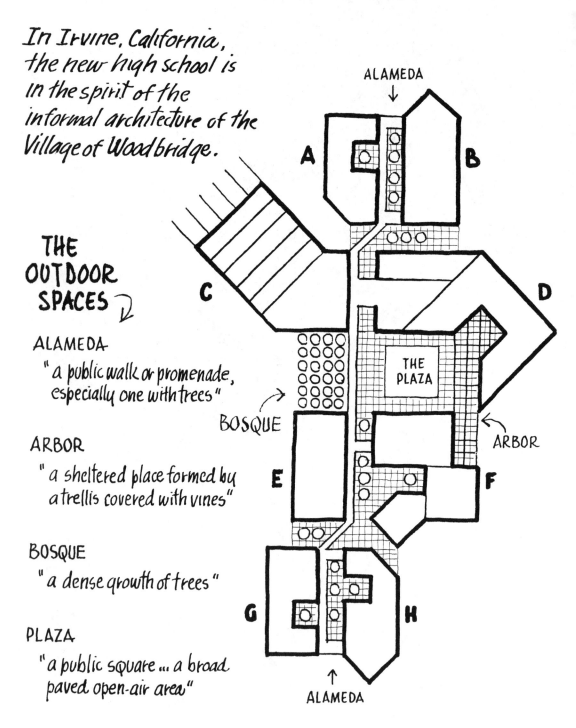

ALAMEDA

A   B

C   D

THE PLAZA

BOSQUE

ARBOR

E   F

G   H

ALAMEDA

Perkins & Will Architects

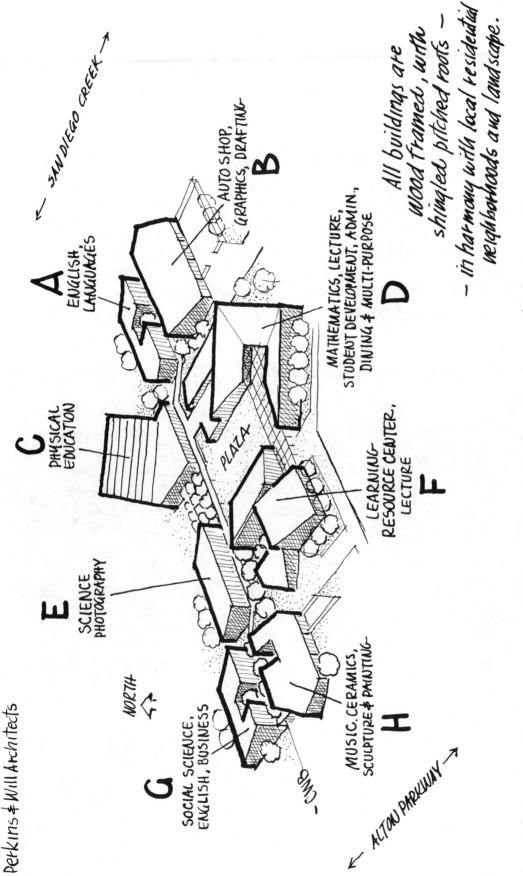

← — SAN DIEGO CREEK →

A
ENGLISH
LANGUAGES

B
AUTO SHOP,
GRAPHICS, DRAFTING

C
PHYSICAL
EDUCATION

D
MATHEMATICS, LECTURE,
STUDENT DEVELOPMENT, ADMIN,
DINING & MULTI-PURPOSE

E
SCIENCE
PHOTOGRAPHY

F
LEARNING-
RESOURCE CENTER,
LECTURE

G
SOCIAL SCIENCE,
ENGLISH, BUSINESS

H
MUSIC, CERAMICS,
SCULPTURE & PAINTING

PLAZA

NORTH

— CWD

← ALTON PARKWAY →

All buildings are
wood framed, with
shingled pitched roofs —

— in harmony with local residential
neighborhoods and landscape.

WOODBRIDGE HIGH SCHOOL   Irvine Unified School District   Irvine, California

MAGNET HIGH SCHOOL IN THE URBAN ENVIRONMENT

2650 students are drawn from many city neighborhoods to an efficient new education center. Four houses of 500 students each, plus a fifth house for 650 hearing-impaired students, occupy the center building. Bridges connect it to a physical education unit and to an arts unit.

Quality education is the key to keeping and attracting a broad range of citizens in the city.

WHITNEY M. YOUNG MAGNET HIGH SCHOOL   CHICAGO. IL

Hedrich-Blessing photograph   Perkins & Will Architects

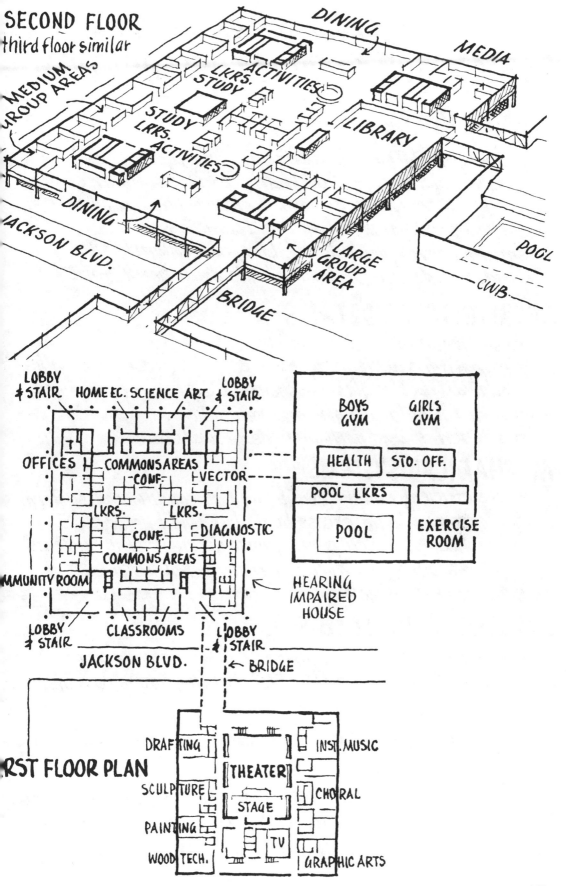

SECOND FLOOR
third floor similar

DINING

MEDIA

MEDIUM GROUP AREAS

LKRS. STUDY

ACTIVITIES

STUDY LKRS. ACTIVITIES

LIBRARY

JACKSON BLVD.

DINING

LARGE GROUP AREA

BRIDGE

POOL

CWB.

LOBBY & STAIR

HOME EC. SCIENCE ART

LOBBY & STAIR

BOYS GYM

GIRLS GYM

OFFICES

COMMONS AREAS

CONF.

VECTOR

HEALTH

STO. OFF.

LKRS.

LKRS.

CONF.

DIAGNOSTIC

POOL LKRS

COMMONS AREAS

POOL

EXERCISE ROOM

MMUNITY ROOM

HEARING IMPAIRED HOUSE

LOBBY & STAIR

CLASSROOMS

LOBBY & STAIR

JACKSON BLVD.

BRIDGE

RST FLOOR PLAN

DRAFTING

INST. MUSIC

THEATER

SCULPTURE

CHORAL

STAGE

PAINTING

TV

WOOD TECH.

GRAPHIC ARTS

A new planning consideration—
DESIGN FOR ENERGY CONSERVATION

PLANNING & DESIGN—

proper orientation (south-facing windows are best)
passive solar design (overhangs provide summer shade,
   but allow low winter sun to enter south windows)
compact buildings in hot and cold climates.
smaller, naturally ventilated buildings in benign climates.
landscape design for south shade and north protection.

ARCHITECTURAL DETAILS—

better roof and wall insulation.
thermal mass walls, using insulated brick or concrete walls.
insulated (double) glass;   sheltered entrances & vestibules.
design for natural light and ventilation.
earth berms and partially underground space.

MECHANICAL SYSTEMS—

more efficient heating, ventilating & air conditioning systems.
heat recovery, with excess heat stored until needed.
new concepts, as heat pumps, variable air volume systems.
insulated pipes and ducts;   better control systems.
solar energy collectors.

ELECTRICAL SYSTEMS—

lower lighting levels (lower watts per square foot)
more efficient lighting;   task lighting where possible.
timers on lights.

OPERATING HABITS—

adjust thermostats;   reduce fresh air intake.
improve maintenance of heating, ventilating and air conditioning.
turn off lights when spaces are not in use.

THE RESULT= YOUR SCHOOL MAY USE ONLY HALF AS MUCH ENERGY!

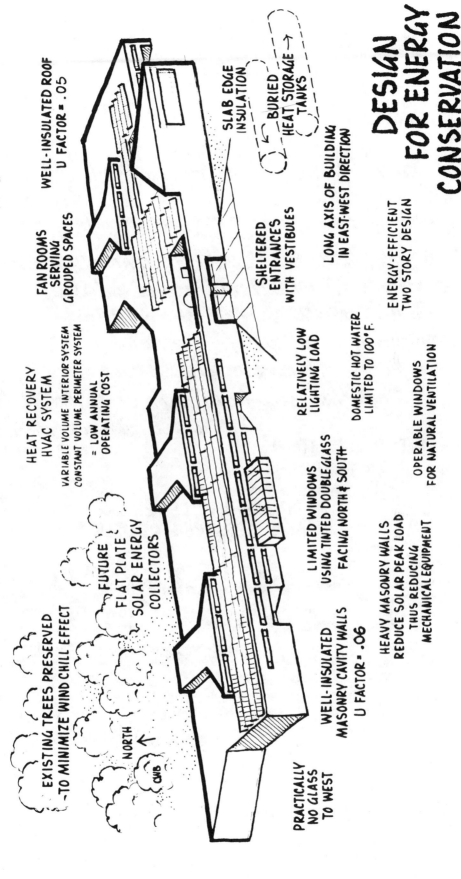

HEAT RECOVERY SYSTEM — During the day, excess heat is generated by lights & people. Warmed water is pumped into buried heat storage tanks. At night, the warm water is pumped out to heat the building.

WELL-INSULATED ROOF
U FACTOR = .05

SLAB EDGE
INSULATION

BURIED
HEAT STORAGE
TANKS

FAN ROOMS
SERVING
GROUPED SPACES

SHELTERED
ENTRANCES
WITH VESTIBULES

LONG AXIS OF BUILDING
IN EAST-WEST DIRECTION

HEAT RECOVERY
HVAC SYSTEM

VARIABLE VOLUME INTERIOR SYSTEM
CONSTANT VOLUME PERIMETER SYSTEM
= LOW ANNUAL
OPERATING COST

RELATIVELY LOW
LIGHTING LOAD

DOMESTIC HOT WATER
LIMITED TO 100°F.

ENERGY-EFFICIENT
TWO STORY DESIGN

FUTURE
FLAT PLATE
SOLAR ENERGY
COLLECTORS

LIMITED WINDOWS
USING TINTED DOUBLE GLASS
FACING NORTH & SOUTH

OPERABLE WINDOWS
FOR NATURAL VENTILATION

EXISTING TREES PRESERVED
—TO MINIMIZE WIND CHILL EFFECT

HEAVY MASONRY WALLS
REDUCE SOLAR PEAK LOAD
THUS REDUCING
MECHANICAL EQUIPMENT

NORTH

WELL-INSULATED
MASONRY CAVITY WALLS
U FACTOR = .06

PRACTICALLY
NO GLASS
TO WEST

DESIGN FOR ENERGY CONSERVATION

Perkins & Will Architects

OAKTON COMMUNITY COLLEGE, Des Plaines, Illinois

THE COMMUNITY SCHOOL —
SHARING THE FACILITIES
AND SHARING THE COSTS !

The community school — serving all citizens —
makes good sense.
  Adults, involved in the facility, are supportive.

In Springfield, Mass., the NewNorth Community School →
  tunnels under an expressway and railroad
  to link two neighborhoods and parks.

The community school concept is a natural
  for places with surplus school space.
    A typical high school can easily be converted to serve
      a wider range of functions.

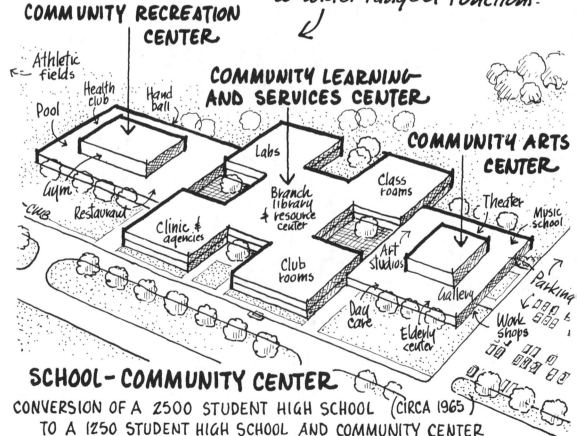

COMMUNITY RECREATION CENTER

COMMUNITY LEARNING AND SERVICES CENTER

COMMUNITY ARTS CENTER

Athletic fields
Pool
Health club
Hand ball
Gym
Club
Restaurant
Labs
Branch library & resource center
Clinic & agencies
Club rooms
Class rooms
Art studios
Day care
Elderly center
Gallery
Theater
Music school
Parking
Work shops

SCHOOL-COMMUNITY CENTER
CONVERSION OF A 2500 STUDENT HIGH SCHOOL (CIRCA 1965)
TO A 1250 STUDENT HIGH SCHOOL AND COMMUNITY CENTER

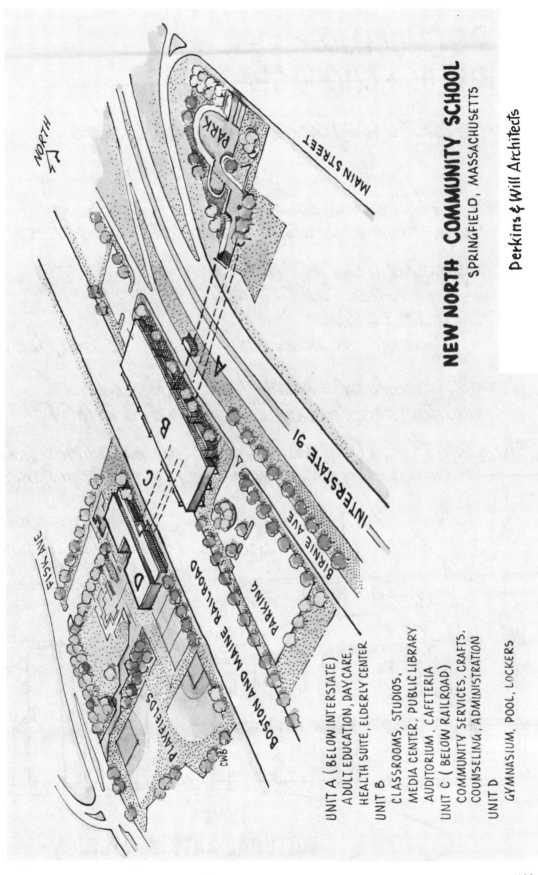

NORTH

PARK

MAIN STREET

INTERSTATE 91

BIRNIE AVE

PARKING

FISK AVE

BOSTON AND MAINE RAILROAD

PLAYFIELDS

CWB

A

B

C

D

UNIT A (BELOW INTERSTATE)
ADULT EDUCATION, DAY CARE,
HEALTH SUITE, ELDERLY CENTER

UNIT B
CLASSROOMS, STUDIOS,
MEDIA CENTER, PUBLIC LIBRARY
AUDITORIUM, CAFETERIA

UNIT C (BELOW RAILROAD)
COMMUNITY SERVICES, CRAFTS,
COUNSELING, ADMINISTRATION

UNIT D
GYMNASIUM, POOL, LOCKERS

NEW NORTH COMMUNITY SCHOOL
SPRINGFIELD, MASSACHUSETTS

Perkins & Will Architects

163

RECYCLING
SURPLUS SCHOOL SPACE

.... *new uses for good old buildings.*

Many surplus school buildings
   have been successfully converted to other uses.

A lively recent trend in America is
   the restoration and adaptive re-use
   of older buildings.
        Schools are being restored and re-used, too.

Thoughtful real estate marketing, along with
   sensitive architectural design, will be helpful.

Evanston, Illinois (population 75,000) closed seven schools
   but each is being used imaginatively for new purposes.

Noyes' classrooms are now artists' studios

CWB

NOYES
CULTURAL ARTS CENTER
CITY OF EVANSTON, ILLINOIS

RECYCLING SURPLUS SCHOOL SPACE ...

"GRISWOLD'S OLD SCHOOL HOUSE"
SHOPPING CENTER

RECYCLED 1920s HIGH SCHOOL - CLAREMONT, CALIFORNIA

SEDCO, INC.
CORPORATE HEADQUARTERS

DOWNTOWN DALLAS, TEXAS

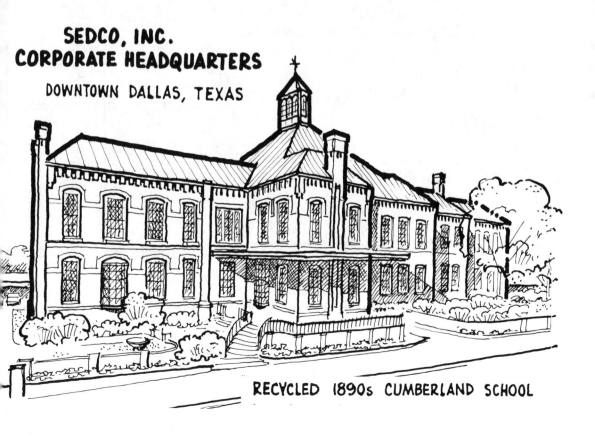

RECYCLED 1890s CUMBERLAND SCHOOL

COMPARING AND EVALUATING
EXISTING SCHOOL BUILDINGS –

Especially when some schools are to be closed
an easily understood system is needed
for comparison and evaluation
of existing facilities ....

EXCELLENT = 5
GOOD = 4
AVERAGE = 3
BELOW AVERAGE = 2
POOR = 1

SCHOOL *Jefferson Elementary*	POINTSCORE
INSTRUCTIONAL ADEQUACY –	
1 Regular classrooms	5
2 Special program spaces	4
3 Laboratories and studios	3
4 Gymnasium and cafeteria	4
5 Library – media center	4
6 Adaptability to future programs	4
7 Equipment and furnishings	4
8 Program offering capabilities sub-total	4
	32
BUILDING –	
9 Size, capacity and utilization	4
10 Interior quality and conditions	5
11 Exterior quality and conditions	4
→12 Energy costs for heating, power and lighting	3
13 Custodial and other operating costs	4
14 Handicapped accessibility sub-total	2
	22
SITE –	
15 Size of site related to size of building	3
16 Location	5
17 Environment of the area	4
18 Site development and landscaping	4
19 Community use of site and building	3
20 Vehicular traffic and access sub-total	4
	23
TOTAL EVALUATION SCORE	77

20 items for comparison and evaluation of existing buildings

A perfect score would be 100
A good school might be about 75
A poor school might be about 45

19

HOW TO CUT SCHOOL COSTS — WISELY

Oliver S. Brown

Let's put everything you have read together — and take it all apart with specific suggestions, more than 100 of them, that can lead your district to save money. And, please remember, if you must cut budget be sure you know what you're in for — the good and bad consequences — so that you are not caught unprepared.

Mr. Brown knows whereof he speaks. He is Assistant Superintendent for Planning and Management services for the Cambridge (MA) school department. He also teaches administrators at the Harvard Graduate School of Education and is former president of the Massachusetts School Business Officials. Formerly, Mr. Brown was a consultant and manager with the firm of Price Waterhouse and Company.

Much of this material originally appeared and is reprinted here, with permission, from the American School Board Journal, October 1978. Copyright 1978, the National School Boards Association. All rights reserved.

If you intend to reduce the school budget for the coming fiscal year, start working on it six months ago. At least get going on it now and even if you don't know how deep the cuts will have to be, have a contingency plan ready. And while you are about it, plan for reductions in the next three fiscal years.

The need to reduce expenditures drastically, perhaps too drastically, isn't going away. *Competent* school administrators and school board members will take the task to heart and will involve community leaders, take the flak, and try to make the best of a difficult situation. Unfortunately, other school officials will be controlled by events, make unimaginative and unnecessarily damaging cuts, and lose the confidence of their communities. What's worse, they will unnecessarily reduce services to students because they haven't found the most efficient and effective way to slash school district expenditures.

This special chapter is organized in three parts: a look at the budget cutting process; a discussion of some analytic tools; and an amended and augmented list of reduction ideas.

A school system's resources can be categorized (and cut) in five major ways: by organizational unit (school, office); by program (physical education, mathematics); by function (administration, instruction); by fund (general, Title I); and by line item or object (texts, printing, salaries of custodians). Looking at each of these resources is useful if you ask the right questions. Clearly, to cut costs in several dimensions requires special care to make sure that the same item is not cut twice, and a close look at what has been accomplished at the end of the process is essential.

Another caution: This five-dimensional matrix may intersect at 3,000 points in a medium-sized district. It is important not to waste time. Pick and choose those particular units, programs, and line items that are likely to pay off in significant savings.

It may seem a lot easier to let each organizational unit or program manager look at the functions and line items within his jurisdiction, make cuts and then stop there. That approach is not wrong — it's

insufficient. What's needed is a school board or superintendent to take an over-all view of the situation.

For example: Each unit administrator may be able to reduce costs for printing and copying by more careful planning. The savings probably will be minor. But if someone looks at the printing budget *across all* programs, organizations, and functions, a different order of cost reduction opportunity appears. One begins to look at alternatives: contracting some or all of the service; use of work-study students at a central site; coordination with the municipal printing operation; making printing a sheltered workshop operation (a nonprofit work experience program for handicapped youngsters); and cutting back on printing by making a *policy* decision.

The same process holds true when looking for opportunities to eliminate, consolidate, or reduce schools or operational offices.

So start with a comprehensive list of each category of school spending — name all the organizational units, all the programs and functions, all the income sources, and all the school system's goals. Then look at the resources allocated to each. Bring together business administrators, educational administrators *and* board members to discuss ways to save money in each category. Obviously, giving extended discussions to small items (in-city travel) and brief discussions to larger items (salaries of teachers) isn't going to produce much success. The time of the participants is limited and valuable, so concentrate on significant opportunities for savings. Reductions of small items often can be accomplished without formal study: administrators can just be told to "do it."

What are the key questions your cost-cutting group should ask? First: Is the program, organization, or service needed at all? Second: If it is needed, is it essential by the board's standards; mandated by law or regulation; needed but not essential; or simply nice to have? And if it is needed, must funding come from local taxes or can it be funded by user (parent/student) fees; federal or state grants; an economical combination of various different sources?

Once everyone knows what kinds of questions must be asked, it's time to examine the principles of realistic cost reduction. While these principles apply both to long and short-term cost reduction plans, the emphasis here is on examining ways to make reductions that must be implemented in one year — decisions of an acute nature with which school boards are all too familiar. The examination includes five — sometimes not so easy — steps:

First step: The process of cutting costs begins (and ends) with the school board, and the board should take three actions to get the unpleasant task off the ground. *Appoint a manager.* Most school boards appoint the superintendent or a person directly responsible to him. All members of the project should be briefed about the objectives and confidential nature of their work; sometimes legal assistance — and working space away from the district offices — must be arranged. *Set a goal and pad it.* The board should determine how much money must be cut from the budget, and then give the project team a dollar figure goal that is *higher,* thus allowing the board some leeway in choosing final budget cuts. This is your fudge factor and it will give you some room in which to operate. *Clarify educational priorities.* The board says, for example: "Improvement in the basic skills of reading and mathematics should receive highest priority because lack of these skills is our district's single most serious problem." This translates to the project manager as: "Don't make budget cuts that will create any adverse effects upon the existing reading and mathematics programs."

Second step: Identify alternatives. What are your options? To answer that properly, the project team must be able to see the school system from a number of vantage points. This doesn't mean that the entire effort must be "committed" to death with extensive teacher-parent-administrator participation, but the team should be able to get help from people who can bring expertise to the project.

One good way to organize the search for sensible cost reduction alternatives is to review school district expenditures from several different perspectives or levels, including *program categories.* Some questions to ask yourself: At what grade levels or with what subjects can class size or average teacher load be increased? What does research indicate will be the consequences of increasing class size? Can other groups in the community assume services now performed by the schools, or can some services be made self-supporting? Have circumstances changed so that some supportive programs (personnel, for example) can be reduced? Can costs of certain programs (driver education and physical education, as examples) be reduced by making these activities self-supporting* or by using volunteers and paraprofessionals or by eliminating some ancillary activities?

Now consider *object categories,* and look at some options open to you: Make across-the-board cuts in all categories — people, facilities, materials, supplies, services, and equipment; drastically cut expenditures in less essential categories, and don't touch the others; *increase* expenditures in categories most necessary for attaining your district's priorities, and make drastic cuts in the other categories. This last approach usually is the least harmful to the education of students.

When analyzing *fund levels,* you should: properly identify and report Title I administrative support costs (this can improve the general fund revenue picture); improve the reporting of special education costs (this action almost invariably results in an increase in state subsidies); tighten cafeteria operations by increasing staff productivity and by charging adult meals at cost (this usually can be done without affecting free or reduced-cost lunches); consider rentals, renovations, modular buildings, and lease-back arrangements when your schools need more space (these are alternatives to large capital outlays for buildings). In fact, take a hard look at all assets which could produce revenue (e.g.

---

*Two typical ways of making programs self-supporting: (1) charge tuition and fees; (2) seek outside sponsors — an automobile dealer, for example, may be willing to supply training vehicles and, in some cases, even underwrite the cost of the driver education program in exchange for, say, a courtesy sign on the vehicles.

the computer, busses, buildings, the pool, the stage, kitchens, and so on).

Third step: Determine opportunities for cost reductions. You may not believe it, but there *are* parts of your system's budget that offer opportunities for cutting costs. Generally, the greatest opportunities are found in large expenditure categories such as salaries, but there are other places to cut (see following pages for some typical examples). One big chunk of salary expenditures — instructional and administrative — is the heavy emphasis on (and cost of) credentials. Some systems pay employees extra for having educational credentials, when, in fact, the systems really need persons with business or financial training. Where necessary, school systems should seek waivers of state requirements in order to hire such persons. Also, many educational administrators and supervisors work an unbelievably short day and year. Take a good look at "full year equivalent" costs of employees. Example: Many school administrators work approximately 90 per cent of the time worked by a person in an equivalent position in private industry. A $25,000-a-year administrator who works one month less than his corporate counterpart is, in effect, getting an annual salary *rate* of $27,500.

Fourth step: Report to the school board. The school board launched the unpleasant cutting project with a goal and a guideline. Once the cost-cutting team completes its task, the project should go back to the board as a report that restates the objectives of the project, includes a one or two-page summary of possible reductions, and lists all the supportive details for each of those reduction possibilities. This report, of course, should be prepared only after the project team has reviewed expenditures from all levels and has discussed alternative cuts.

Fifth step: Select reductions and implement them. One bit of advice about the selection of final budget cuts: The school board should do it. Because of political implications, the school board should not and cannot delegate its authority in this area; in fact, the board should hold public hearings before making final decisions, but final decisions still belong to the school board.

Implementation is going to be a headache, but it doesn't have to be a migraine. Boards should understand the rights of school personnel, rely on legal advice when faced with the complexities of state tenure laws, and, when jobs are affected by budget cuts, be prepared to offer assistance in placing individuals in other positions.

HOW TO MAKE CUTS FOR THE LONG HAUL

The process just described is fine for short-range reductions, but school boards also must learn the skills needed for long-range planning. The annual budget process followed by virtually all governmental agencies — state, local and national — is an anachronism. Year after year, the real opportunities for major restructuring and for redirecting resources are missed. These opportunities are blocked by immediate concerns about factors such as the high school scheduling process and the "April date" by which teachers must be notified of dismissal. One often hears: A change cannot be made this year because it is too late. And in the relief everyone experiences once this year's budget is approved, the opportunity to work on next year's budget slips by.

The following process is suggested not as a cost reduction method as such, but as a general model for long-range planning. It was developed jointly by the author and Thomas Beyer of the Management Advisory Services of Price Waterhouse and Company. It grew out of a concern that while both program budgeting and zero-based budgeting are valuable tools in the long-range planning and budgeting process, these systems often are too cumbersome; they drown top administrators in too much unread (and sometimes unreadable) paper. To "zero base" a program, unit or service is helpful and productive. To "zero base" the whole budget every year — while theoretically sound — often is impossible from a practical standpoint. The same is true of program budgeting ("maximizing all resources toward the achievement of a set of goals and objectives") as a total process.

The model we suggest requires three steps.

Step one: *Project the base case or present level of services.* Develop a projection of current school system expenditures and revenues for the next three to five years. Include *all* assumptions about enrollments, salaries, inflation, and changes in revenues so that planning errors can be distinguished from projection errors. This projection should be based upon current policies, laws, regulations, and practices. It assumes no changes except those already decided upon.

Step two: *Make program and cost analyses.* Identify 10 to 20 programs, organizational units, line items, functions or funds that show significant promise of possible cost reduction (or of improving the relationship between cost and benefits). Analyze these items and report on the following elements: current situation; costs in detail; problems associated with the product or service definition of the quality level of product or service (a) required and (b) desired; alternatives to required or desired product or service, including the alternatives' three to five-year effects on expenditures and revenues. Make recommendations for the most cost-effective reductions.

Step three: *Develop the long-range plan.* The superintendent and school board should adopt a set of alternative program and financial plans (after checking for duplication of effects among alternatives), and then adjust the projection of the current level of services (or base case). In effect, the adjusted base case becomes a long-range plan. Annually, the base case projection is extended by one year and a new set of services, products, line items or policies is examined in the same way.

The point of this approach (which is an adaptation of practice used in industry) is to develop a way to accomplish orderly long-range program and cost planning (and cost reduction) so that school administrators — already pressed for precious time — can keep the district operating properly.

Can consultants or volunteers help in this process? Most assuredly they can. Time and effort, however, may be wasted by insiders who "sandbag" outsiders to avoid change. Be aware of this problem and take steps to see that it doesn't happen to you.

WHAT YOU'LL NEED TO MAKE LONG-RANGE CUTS

Now let's look at some of the analytic tools needed to make this planning work. Some cost reduction opportunities are obvious, simple to analyze, and easy to implement. Turning down the boilers to night heat at 1:00 p.m. and allowing a building to ride on retained heat until school closes is an example of this kind of reduction. Other opportunities are more complex and require more formal analysis. That's what this next section is all about.

A school system should adopt a formal budget structure to save time and ensure quality control. Superintendents and school board members have a great deal to do and should not have to waste time when examining budget studies and when looking for recommended courses of action. It is a great deal easier to separate good studies from poor ones if the structures of all recommendations or reports are comparable and logical.

We suggest the following structure for all reports going to the school board:

Start with an introduction: purpose, scope, problems.

Then include:

1. Summary and Recommendations
2. Current Problems, Policy, Practice and Costs
3. Alternative Policies, Practices and Costs
4. Comparative Analysis of Alternative Benefits, Effects, Costs
5. Rationale for Recommendations
6. Implementation Alternatives
7. Recommended Implementation Plan Including Tasks, Responsibilities, and a Timetable

Conclude with appendices.

The summary presented to the board should be brief — two to three pages or less — and cover the important points of the study including major recommended changes in policy and practice. It should be worded in such a way that it can be adopted as policy by the board.

There are a number of different types of analyses that may be useful in any report (depending upon the objective).

Cost-effectiveness analysis: This is a study of alternative programs' benefits, as expressed in nonmonetary terms. For example: A cost-effectiveness study might look at alternatives in reading programs and then list anticipated score changes for each alternative.

Cost-benefit analysis: The same as cost-effectiveness, except that the benefits are expressed in monetary terms.

Zero-based budgeting: This form of analysis arranges elements of the budget into "packages" that are listed in ascending order from zero. Levels of service (and other implications) that can be attained at each level of funding are defined in each package. The zero-based approach can be used for the budget as a whole (in which case all packages are set in priority order). or as a tool to be used in reducing expenditures in a particular program, organizational unit or line item.

Zero-based budgeting for all programs every year is not in my judgment a good use of time and resources.

Functional analysis: This is the author's term for a study that sets forth a comprehensive list of functions to be performed within a program and then relates each function to alternative agencies or organizations. The point: find the least costly and most effective combination of agencies to do the required work. Example: List on a vertical axis every single function to be performed in the pupil transportation program; on a horizontal axis, list every possible agency or organization that can perform the functions. See chart below.

The most cost-effective pattern will vary from system to system and state to state. The strength of this functional analysis is that it encourages school administrators to look outside the school department for the least costly way to achieve a given objective.

Cost-reduction study: Any of the forms of analysis just outlined also can be called a cost-reduction study, depending upon how the objective of the study is stated. A cost-reduction study is one that seeks (1) to retain the same level of service and reduce the costs; (2) to reduce services to some acceptable level and make significant cost cuts, or (3) to identify programs, organizations or items that can be eliminated.

There are other forms of analysis. What the good ones all have in common is an emphasis upon using a formal study to examine the relationship between required resources and obtained benefits so that sensible and sound budgeting alternatives can be explored.

WHO ELSE CAN PERFORM THE TASKS YOU'RE PERFORMING RIGHT NOW?

Function (examples)	School Committee	School Dept.	Organizations Public Works	City Procure.	Private Contract.
Policy setting	X				
Fuel procurement				X	
Fuel distribution			X		
Dispatching					X
Operations					X
Maintenance		X			

ONE HUNDRED WAYS TO CUT COSTS IN YOUR SCHOOL SYSTEM

The list on the following pages is neither comprehensive nor is it wholly applicable to any one school system. We hope that many of the suggestions may be useful in your system and may stimulate administrators to identify as many as a hundred more. Be careful to check the legality of an idea in your state. But even if you find that you cannot carry out some perfectly sound idea because of an existing state regulation or statute, don't give up. Many of the barriers to effective school management were quietly pushed into law by special interest groups when taxpayer interests were not well organized. Now is the time to seek reform. The public and its legislators are listening.

You may wish to annotate it as follows:

W — Worth investigating for our system.

P — Possibly worth investigating for our system.

N — Not useful or possible in our system.

I — Illegal in our state/city system.

HOW TO CUT COSTS IN YOUR INSTRUCTIONAL PROGRAM

What to do	**How it works**
1. Hold the line on salary schedule increases this year (but remind everyone that step increases will remain intact).	Lack of schedule increase encourages early retirement. Ms. Jones retires at $20,000 and is replaced by someone at $10,000. You keep most of it — $9,000 + per turnover.
2. Freeze salaries (no increases for anybody).	Same as No. 1, only more so.
3. Encourage early retirement of staff by providing a cash bonus or retroactive pay raise (and let retirees have first choice on substitute lists).	Ten teachers averaging $18,000 in annual wages retire early; each receives a $2,000 bonus. You hire ten replacements at $10,000, thus saving $60,000.
4. Reduce number of small classes in secondary schools.	Combine third, fourth and fifth level French students into one individualized class to save the cost of one teacher's salary.
5. Schedule staff in accordance with a carefully projected (probably lower) enrollment.	Births in 1972 were down 25 per cent over 1971, so you may need one fewer kindergarten teacher.
6. Reduce the tenured staff with a bonus plan for resignation within specific programs.	Coach Jones receives an offer to work somewhere else. Your bonus of $1,000 tips the scales.
7. Use paraprofessionals to replace staff that has study hall or corridor duty, to enable teachers to devote this time to instruction.	Five teachers teach four periods and each has one nonprofessional duty period. You substitute one teacher aide for these periods and save the difference between a $12,000 teacher and a $5,500 aide.
8. Replace credentialed educators in specific administrative positions with lower salaried, specialized, full-year/full-time personnel.	One of four vice-principalships opens up a large high school. Hire a young, MBA at lower salary *for 12 months,* full time, rather than adhering to the former ten-month, six-hour day pattern.
9. Hold off some teacher hiring until September if elementary class sizes are the least bit indefinite.	Your contract requires a limit of 30 in a class. Your projection shows 65 enrolled in Grade 6 for one school. But it's 50-50 that only 60 pupils will appear. So you take the chance and don't hire that third teacher unless you actually must.
10. Combine certain grades.	Six classes of 22 students each, with six teachers (Grades 1-6), become five classes of 27 each by combining pupils (such as a class comprising third and fourth graders).
11. Put all administrators on an eight-hour day, 12-month year (with four-week vacations, of course).	You put several administrators say, on refining bus routes, and they come up with a revision that eliminates the need to buy one bus that would have cost $10,000.
12. Adopt new textbooks less frequently (but that doesn't mean being lax about adoption standards).	You increase from three to five years the mandated period of adoption.

How you'll save	The consequences (not all of them are bad)
Turnover of staff (exchange of higher-step for lower-step personnel) saves money.	Stiff opposition from teacher union; and little turnover.
Same as No. 1, only more so.	Same as No. 1, only more so.
Increased turnover of staff saves difference between topstep and entry-step salary level.	Possible ill-feeling from older, dedicated staff; opening of some positions for younger, unemployed teachers; high retirement income in case of retroactive salary raise.
By offering certain courses every other semester or year, and/or by increasing class sizes, you'll need fewer teachers on the payroll.	Opposition from teacher union and from parents of children in such advanced courses: also, greater individualization of instruction because of greater diversity of instructional levels in a class; some investment in staff development may be required.
Staffing for next year's projected enrollment can mean fewer unintended small classes, lower payroll costs.	Opposition from teachers and parents; need for some reshuffling of classes in September (and a contingency plan if you guessed wrong).
You eliminate unnecessary staff and you reduce salary costs.	Possible opposition from parent, student, and teacher groups — especially if popular personalities are involved.
Fewer teachers required to staff schools if actual teaching periods are recovered; lower salary costs.	Opposition from teacher unions; some investment in paraprofessional staff training supervision required if plan is to work.
Administrative costs should decrease (and effectiveness should increase).	Opposition from teacher union: more hours and days of job coverage for less money: more specific training and experience for job.
You'll save on staff salaries.	A less smooth start for a few classes.
You'll reduce numbers of small classes that occur when classes are organized strictly by grade level.	Opposition from teachers and parents; investment in staff training for more individualization of instruction required.
More time for long-range planning will produce lower future costs.	Opposition from those individuals directly involved.
Outlays for textbooks will go down.	Some embarrassing instances of out-of-date material in hands of students if not carefully monitored.

What to do	**How it works**

What to do

13. Collect on lost, damaged, or stolen books — or require student who is responsible to perform work to earn cost of books.

14. Charge fees for adult education equal to district's direct costs (with exceptions for low-income and elderly).

15. Place curriculum development projects on a competitive contracted basis (encourage groups of teachers to bid).

16. Eliminate foreign language program in those elementary schools that cannot demonstrate that youngsters are learning the language sufficiently to write and speak it. Make junior high foreign language program strictly voluntary within the curriculum.

17. Reduce number of specialist teachers, eliminate their formal teaching load, and have them help the regular teachers.

18. Use paraprofessionals instead of teachers for on-the-road segments of driver training instruction.

19. Replace your all-teacher physical education staff with a team of professionals and trained paraprofessionals.

20. As vacancies occur, subject each to thorough reassessment before filling (but be sure this is based on a long-range staffing plan).

21. Review your labor contracts paragraph by paragraph with an eye to negotiating more service, productivity, and other conditions that should result in lower costs — in exchange for benefits, reasonable job security.

22. Perform a cost comparative study of your schools. Identify high-cost schools and develop plans to remedy differences not justified.

23. Perform a cost comparative study of programs. Identify high-cost programs and develop plans to remedy differences not justified.

How it works

Replacement costs of, say, $20,000 are reduced to $15,000. Collections increase from $1,000 to $2,000.

You charge $35 rather than $20 per course, thereby cutting your subsidy costs $1,500 per 100 adult students.

Six teachers work on a curriculum project for six weeks during the summer. You agree to pay $6,000 for the contract, but to make no payment until the product is finished and approved. You could save $4,000 and get a better product, but be sure to develop specs carefully.

A number of teaching positions can be eliminated through elimination of say, a Grade 4-6 foreign language program.

You eliminate, say, two of four specialist teaching positions in science, and you assign the remaining specialist teachers the new role of helping regular teachers teach science more effectively.

Jones, a teacher, earns $15,000 a year. He works five hours a day, 180 days, and gets extra pay for summers and afternoons. Smith, a trained paraprofessional, is paid $4 an hour ($7,000 a year for an 8-hour day, 11 months a year).

Three teachers cost $45,000. One teacher and three trained aides cost $30,000.

The position of director of physical education becomes vacant. You combine it with the job of a department head.

You specify (in the contract) opening and closing times for all schools, rendering second and third runs on buses no longer possible.

You discover a school that continues to run a higher cost experimental program with no significant improvement in results. Program is eliminated.

You discover that music and mathematics programs have high costs per pupil hour. Investigation reveals teachers are performing other duties not authorized, so you eliminate those duties and consequently reduce need for staff.

How you'll save	The consequences (not all of them are bad)
Textbook losses and replacement costs will go down.	Some unpleasant situations with parents, students; requires flexibility in enforcement where situation is beyond control of students.
Subsidies to these adult programs out of tax revenues will go down.	Opposition from those currently benefiting; some drop in enrollments, elimination of some programs.
Curriculum development costs may go down.	Possible opposition from teacher union.
Salary and material costs will go down.	Opposition from some teachers and parents; some students could miss experience because course is made noncompulsory (perhaps some investment required in aptitude testing to minimize this).
Salary costs will go down.	Opposition from teacher union, some parents; fewer interruptions of classes and less fragmentation of programs.
You'll save as much as $12 an hour in rate difference between a teacher and a paraprofessional.	Opposition from teacher union and state department of education middle management group; careful training, supervision required; result could be more effective program.
Salary costs will go down.	Stiff opposition from teacher union; if well-planned and organized, a more effective program could result.
Salary and benefit costs will go down.	Fewer promotional opportunities for staff; some effect on morale of those who are ambitious for management roles.
Salary and other costs will go down.	Protracted negotiations and possible job action; some short-lived increase in staff ill-feeling.
Salary and other costs will go down.	Opposition and ill-feeling, especially from parents of children involved in program.
Salary and other costs will go down.	Opposition from individuals involved and, possibly, from teacher union.

177

What to do

24. Study your pattern of teacher absentees and crack down on the teachers whose excuses are suspect.

25. For printing utilize vocational education resources after school and during summer rather than have printing done outside.

26. Negotiate a new, lower beginning step in employee contracts, not affecting any present employees.

27. Develop a long-term strategy in negotiating all labor contracts to improve productivity and output.

28. Establish "average teaching load" factors for secondary level subject areas and reassign or transfer excess staff to other vacancies.

29. Reduce number of small half-day kindergarten classes by consolidating and assigning teachers to more than one school.

30. Define job duties of department heads and educational leaders to include curriculum development during the course of the regular school year to eliminate need for some summer curriculum workshops.

31. When vacancies occur in school psychologist and adjustment counselor staff (or other high paperwork functions), hire clerical staff to assume paperwork functions.

32. Eliminate supervised study halls *except* for students who require supervision.

33. Hold all vacancies open for at least two months in all but the most essential positions to find out whether you *really* need a position.

34. Analyze supporting staff to see the extent to which hourly tutors retained on an "as needed" basis can be hired to take the place of regularly paid teachers.

35. Review each federal aid grant proposal for frill expenditures.

How it works

Several teachers have a suspicious Monday and every-other-Friday absentee record. Your principals call a halt to the practice.

Schedule teacher and student workers for printing jobs on inhouse equipment, using an authorized job ticket approach to controlling work.

Each new employee comes in at a step $500 per year below current first step.

Make list of such objectives as straight time pay for regular overtime work, a wider definition of allowable work by each employee classification and so on.

ATL is calculated based on number of teaching periods per day and desired number of students per period, which will vary based on subject area demands (e.g. higher ATL for social studies than for English).

Combine small a.m. and p.m. classes into one larger class in a.m. and assign teacher to cover similar p.m. class in another school.

Establish a time-line plan with administrators for curriculum development with specific dates for producing output.

Redefine function of professional staff to assign much of paperwork to clerical function and use staff for more direct student services.

Allow study in cafeteria, library, and in back of small classes.

A statistical clerk in the food service office retires. Three other personnel combine to do his work if they can be housed next to one another.

You have teachers working "one on one" with students performing tutorial work. You reassign the teachers to regular classrooms and hire tutors at $10.00 per hour for specific students.

Eliminate some of the food, travel, and convention expense in grant proposals. Reallocate funds to benefit children more directly. Obtain implied training in other ways.

How you'll save	The consequences (not all of them are bad)
Costs for substitutes will go down.	Some understandable ill-feeling if individual circumstances of each case are not carefully reviewed.
Save on higher cost of outside vendor work with those jobs able to be done in-house.	Tight control to make sure unauthorized work not being run. Additional lead time needed.
You save $500 per year per employee for five years on a five step schedule. Over the next ten years, you might save $60,000 in a 100-employee group.	Be prepared for hard bargaining, although this one is easier to achieve because no current employee is affected.
Save on personnel expenses, including overtime.	Tough bargaining may produce temporary ill-feelings.
Excess staff in some subject areas can fill other vacancies in system thus saving cost of new hires.	Short-term opposition from teachers union and some department heads. Long-range — more equitable allocation of staff.
Save teacher salary depending on number of classes consolidates ($10-$12,000 per teacher).	Opposition from teachers and some parents.
Reduce cost of summer workshop stipends for curriculum work.	Results-oriented curriculum development and vehicle for further evaluation of educators' performance.
Difference between teacher and clerical salaries: $5,000.	Opposition from teachers' union. More direct and more efficient student services.
If teachers now supervise a study hall in place of teaching a class, part of a teacher's salary is saved each time a study hall is eliminated.	Opposition from teachers' union.
An $11,000 senior clerk position is eliminated.	Opposition from those looking for a promotional opportunity.
A $16,000 teacher with $1,500 of benefits costs over $19 per hour. You save $10 per hour or more.	Flak from teachers and parents during implementation.
More results from limited grant funds.	Complaints from staff that "Washington" encourages (or mandates) such expenditures.

What to do	**How it works**

36. Take a hard look at sabbatical leaves and develop plan to use such leaves as a means to achieve district goals. Cut appropriations in half.

You need to develop a capability in computer science. You reserve two sabbatical slots for that type of training.

37. Analyze sabbatical leave participants and determine benefits, length of stay after return to district. Consider lengthening number of years person must commit to the district. Change of laws may be necessary before you can take action.

You find out that half your returning teachers leave after one year; some don't come back at all.

HOW TO CUT COSTS IN YOUR FACILITIES AND OPERATIONS

What to do	**How it works**

38. Consolidate evening educational and community programs into fewer schools, on fewer nights.

By consolidation of programs, you reduce the number of evening administrators and support personnel from, say, six to two.

39. Where possible, use fewer, larger school buildings.

You close a small elementary school and transfer children to other schools.

40. Reduce fuel consumption by turning off fresh air intake fans after school.

Ten to fifteen per cent or more of the fuel costs in most newer schools goes for heating outside air. Much of this is not necessary (new, relaxed standards are being set by states and cities).

41. Reduce fuel consumption by reducing fresh air intake during the school day to required level during heating season.

Same as No. 40.

42. Turn off lights when rooms are not in use; cut down on unnecessary lighting.

Your electric bill could be reduced by 5 to 10 per cent with careful management.

43. Use C.E.T.A. (Comprehensive Employment Training Act) or work-study employees to do some renovation and repair.

C.E.T.A. employees renovate a vandalized washroom for, say, $5,000 less than what regular labor would cost.

44. Sweet talk city hall into letting you use municipal employees (rather than contracting) for repairs to buildings.

City painters paint school classrooms. City electricians string wires for vandalism alarm system, and you save $2,000.

45. Reduce heat loss and vandalism by designing buildings with smaller, "rockproof" windows.

By halving the amount of window openings, you may be able to save 5 to 10 per cent or more of the cost of fuel.

46. Cut overtime by starting a second shift.

Hourly cost of custodians on night duty drops by 50 per cent or more.

47. Collect *all* direct costs when outside non-profit groups use school buildings.

The local Rotary Club pays full direct costs rather than just custodian wages.

48. Implement training program for custodial personnel on small repairs.

Your custodian replaces corroded leaking trap; saves you $100.

How you'll save

Fifty percent reduction in investment; increase in benefits to district.

After changing regulations and laws, fewer people skip out or stay only minimum time because they understand that the school district expects a fair return in time and commitment.

The consequences (not all of them are bad)

Opposition from teachers.

Opposition from teachers' union.

How you'll save

Administrative, instructional, and plant operations costs will go down.

Numbers of administrators, custodians and secretaries will go down, as will fuel and maintenance costs. Consider returning property to tax rolls (add back cost of transportation, if needed).

Fuel costs will go down; small saving in electricity also will result.

Fuel costs will go down.

Electricity costs will go down.

Contracted maintenance bills will be lower.

Repair and maintenance costs will be lower.

Fuel and repair costs will go down.

Custodial salary costs will go down.

Custodial, fuel and electricity costs will go down.

Contracted repair costs will go down.

The consequences (not all of them are bad)

Some opposition from neighborhood groups and possibly a drop in enrollment.

Increase costs of transportation; strong opposition from neighborhood school groups; specialized programs are less expensive because of larger student body; real estate can be returned to tax rolls.

Investment in modification of new control system may be required.

Same as No. 40.

Investment of time and attention of school administrators, teachers, custodians required.

Possible opposition of organized employees; lower quality, slower work; opposition from contractors.

Opposition from contractors.

General opposition if structure is in any way aesthetically displeasing.

Stiff opposition voiced by labor organization(s).

Opposition from special groups no longer subsidized; less use of school buildings.

Opposition from some custodians and the custodian organization because of extra work; lower quality work results in some instances, *better* work in other instances.

What to do	**How it works**
49. Don't build a new school; schedule students on a 45-15 (or similar) plan instead.	You save cost of new elementary school, plus part of cost of operation.
50. Increase protection against vandalism and theft.	You install listening systems. Net cost reduction of vandalism in one school: $10,000.
51. Develop and implement, in cooperation with police, a policy of apprehending and prosecuting those who vandalize schools.	Example of getting tough helps to diminish incident rate.
52. Utilize lower paid personnel to perform simple tasks.	Use a part-time security aide at $3 an hour to replace one of two custodians handling a building for evening functions. Aide watches the door, empties ashtrays, etc.
53. Utilize state bids where quality warrants.	You pay 10 per cent less for bus tires.
54. Implement an energy use audit of each school building.	A team of specialists from state energy office or professional consulting engineering group develops plan for energy conservation for each building.
55. Evaluate the use of contracted maintenance vs. in-house mechanics to service transportation equipment.	Depending on size of fleet, savings could be realized on labor cost, especially with older fleet. Be sure to analyze *all* costs including vacations, retirement costs, etc.
56. Review transportation program and reimbursement aid formula to see if different approach will reduce net costs.	By owning buses and contracting driver services, one district reduced its net cost to taxpayers. In other circumstances, reverse might be true.
57. Examine your transportation system to see if more students could walk to school.	Children in special classes and/or living on borderline of busing distance walk or use parent-provided transportation.
58. Develop and implement a computerized vandalism and theft information system.	You pinpoint a pattern of thefts, alert the police ahead of vandal's "schedule."
59. Mark all equipment with an electric engraving pen.	Thieves can't fence your typewriters and will go elsewhere to ply their trade. Personnel won't be so likely to "forget" to return what belongs to the schools.
60. Develop and implement a computerized perpetual inventory system for all equipment.	When principals change, you know what equipment belongs in a school. A principal will know exactly what he or she should have and be more concerned about not being caught short.
61. Review school opening and closing times to develop a new pattern of staggered openings that requires use of fewer buses.	Staggering times could result in three rather than two routes per bus, and could cut costs 25 per cent.

How you'll save	The consequences (not all of them are bad)
Capital operating costs will be reduced.	A lot of citizen, parent, student and staff preparation required; data on this option varies greatly as to whether savings result.
Costs of repair will be reduced significantly.	Time and attention drawn from other, more affirmative programs.
Plant maintenance costs will be reduced.	Same as No. 50.
Salary costs will go down.	Stiff opposition from custodian group.
Net costs of materials purchased will be reduced.	Poor quality on some low bid items (watch out for the floor wax).
Fuel and utility costs go down.	Some savings now — more later when capital energy saving investments are paid off.
Less cost for maintenance per bus.	Workload and costs may not justify adding a position. Decreased equipment downtime.
Subsidies go up, net local contribution goes down.	Some personnel problems possible during implementation.
Costs of buses, drivers, gasoline will go down.	Opposition from those adversely affected, especially on basis of safety.
Costs of replacing vandalized and stolen property will go down.	Irritation of staff at one more form to fill out; but you'll have better information for planning a rational response.
Chances of vandalism and theft will be reduced.	One-time massive effort to mark equipment; better control of inventory.
Same as No. 59.	One-time systems development and implementation cost.
Transportation costs will go down.	Implementation may inhibit staff development programs in the afternoon because teachers will not all be free at the same time.

HOW TO CUT COSTS IN YOUR CENTRAL OFFICE

What to do	**How it works**
62. Tighten up on money management techniques.	All receipts are deposited in interest bearing accounts on the date received.
63. Eliminate costly and unnecessary paper processing of small items.	You establish a quick order system by which purchase orders are handled at school building level for all items under $25.
64. Develop an effective, integrated budgetary and payroll control and statistical reporting system.	No longer will an extra teacher be put on the payroll (in excess of the budget) because someone forgot that the vacancy has been eliminated. Saving: $12,000.
65. Use work sampling and work measurement techniques to establish standards for planning, measuring, and controlling clerical performance.	A study of work production shows that you don't need an extra clerk in purchasing; you need greater typing speed on purchase orders.
66. Update organizational structure, and clarify responsibility and authority.	A poorly planned, worthless workshop is avoided because an administrator now knows he will be held accountable for its lack of results.
67. Give each sub-unit in the school system a budget and hold respective administrators responsible for it.	You avoid buying equipment and materials you don't need.
68. Make it clear that one key to the future of administrators is their ability to come up with specific suggestions for reducing costs, improving efficiency and productivity on a quarterly basis — in writing.	An administrator of the night school devises an evening building use schedule that saves you $5,000 a year.
69. Substitute mechanized activities for those manual processes that are costing you money and efficiency.	You eliminate the need for a $7,000 clerk in the payroll department because the bank gives you all the records you need.
70. Review and standardize salary and fringe benefit programs for all employees; eliminate costly exceptions.	You save $10,000 by reducing aide salary schedule, which exceeds regular salary schedule.
71. Consolidate advertising for staff to reduce scattershot approach to filling vacancies as they occur.	Determine vacancies to be filled well in advance and place consolidated ads on a scheduled basis; also evaluate results from high cost media and eliminate if results are not justified.
72. Develop a long-range revenue plan.	Isolate each current and potential source of revenue. Analyze each to find administrative, legislative and judicial avenues to increased revenues.

How you'll save	The consequences (not all of them are bad)
Interest income will go up.	Procedures for quickly identifying correct account for deposit must be developed — especially for some state and federal grants that have poor check identification notations.
Fewer clerks will be needed; more time can be spent on purchasing larger items; costs of clerical help will go down; better cost quality relationship will result.	You may have to defend a few foolish decisions that may be made at the local school level.
Expenditures resulting from "gaps" in the control of budgetary units will go down.	A lot of development work and some costs required.
Productivity will go up, and perhaps you can avoid an increase or not fill a vacancy.	Opposition from clerical staff to standards.
Manpower efficiency and control of costs will improve. Fewer costly bad decisions will result because "no one" was responsible.	Noses will go out of joint — especially those belonging to persons who had been directly responsible to the superintendent or other top administrator in the system.
Requisitions will be challenged more effectively at lower levels and stopped at a point where details are better known. You'll get more for your money.	More time spent in this area — especially at first; better use of resources if budget decisions are related to goals and objectives.
Your administrators often know where to save, but you offer them no motivation for offering appropriate suggestions. Once you do so, you'll save.	Some administrators may be exceedingly uncomfortable in the new environment.
Fewer people will be needed to perform a given level of work; salary costs will go down.	Opposition from organized employee groups; bunkish charges that you are dehumanizing the schools.
Salary and benefit costs will go down. If you're making a general fund contribution to a federal program, you'll decrease need for the contribution (often policies set in federal funds projects become a part of the general operation, and increase costs to your local taxpayers).	Opposition from those employees adversely affected.
Several specific job ads will be replaced with a consolidated ad on a less frequent basis. Also: maintenance of application files will eliminate need for some advertising.	More efficient use of media.
As revenues increase, local tax support is reduced.	All positive.

What to do	How it works
73. Use after-school secondary student workers to help with peak-load clerical work rather than hire additional regular staff.	Work with the high school business ed. department to recruit students to perform various part-time clerical functions, under supervision of regular clerical staff. Hire at lower student rate.
74. Microfilm old records rather than retain paper storage.	Verify record retention legal requirement as well as local requirements and implement a program of departmental microfilming with verification of output before destroying paper records.
75. Allow students to run the printing and copying machines.	Work-study, occupational students or a sheltered workshop can run the copy center.
76. Decentralize materials procurement systems to provide direct delivery to schools for most materials rather than using central supply.	Organize purchasing for direct delivery with schools participating in decisions on set-up of system. Each school will need to assign responsibility internally for receiving.
77. Analyze most cost-effective method of repairing and servicing audio-visual equipment — in-house or contractor.	You determine if it is less costly to contract repairs rather than have full-time teaching staff performing work.
78. Examine each federal fund project budget carefully and determine: (1) whether direct overhead can be charged to help support central office costs resulting from the project, and (2) whether cost reduction techniques outlined on these pages can get you more for your project dollar.	You save the cost of a $7,000 clerk, which now can be charged to federal project work load in central office.
79. Establish effective policies for record control and management-procedures.	No more filing cabinets needed next year; you save $100 each.
80. Reduce clerical help and use temporary help and/or high school students for peak periods; plan your staffing needs for *average* loads only.	You net a savings of $10,000 by eliminating two clerks and adding back $4,000 for temporary help.
81. Devise better control of office copiers.	Clerical personnel are using a copier when they should be using a duplicator. By putting a stop to this, you could save 2.5 cents per copy.
82. Schedule buying in large lots.	Equipment cost can be reduced 5 to 10 per cent in larger lots.
83. Retain a public accounting firm to review your state return like a corporate tax return (do this with eye to maximizing income.)	By using staff rather than pupils as basis for allocating overhead, you may be able to gain 10 per cent more aid in, say, special education.

How you'll save

Savings based on lower pay rate, plus flexibility to employ on short-term basis rather than add additional regular staff.

Reduction in storage space requirements, less time spent researching old records, less file storage equipment needed.

Eliminate a position and/or improve copy control.

Savings of staff cost of handling materials twice (central supply and school) and extra transportation between central supply and schools, partially offset by some increased delivery charges.

Cost of teacher less contract cost: $10,000.

You'll decrease salary and other direct contribution costs to federal project, and you'll increase reimbursement to the general fund to support central office expenses.

You'll waste less space and time on obsolete, unneeded information storage, and on duplication of information on different forms.

Full-time clerical staff salary costs will go down.

Costs of unauthorized and wasteful copier use will go down.

Competitive bidding on larger numbers of items will reduce unit cost.

More state aid means less burden on local taxes.

The consequences (not all of them are bad)

Additional training time required, but frequently pays off with more enthusiastic and productive workers.

More accessible record retention system, with side effect of identifying some documents that need not be retained. Increased cost for equipment and film processing.

Reduced copy bills and/or one less position to pay for.

Generally faster delivery of materials to schools with some delays in central office receipt of necessary reports. Some increased in delivery charges.

Some time delays in response on small repairs. More time spent monitoring vendor work.

Opposition from granting agency, parent advisory groups, and staff; they will accuse you of diverting funds from students.

Be careful to record on a central record exactly where everything is stored — especially in cases where there is offsite storage.

Opposition from organized clerical staff group.

Irritation on part of those who want to use copier for any and every purpose.

More long-range planning is to be expected.

One-time cost for service.

HOW TO CUT COSTS IN YOUR FOOD SERVICE PROGRAM

What do to	How it works
84. Encourage all those who qualify to apply for free or reduced-price lunches *at any time during the year* that they become eligible.	You charge 30 cents per meal; your subsidy is 67 cents per meal. Unemployment goes up during the year. One hundred more students qualify, which saves you 37 cents per day per student (or $5,000 a year).
85. Increase fees to faculty to cover full direct costs of lunch.	You have 300 teachers eating lunch. You no longer subsidize them at 15 cents per meal. You save $4,500.
86. Utilize more intensive competitive bidding for food items, including those used in home economics courses.	You use more vendors to obtain competitive prices. Your costs go down, say 5 per cent.
87. Use a central kitchen and satellite meals, including sales to others (or purchase satellite meals from other public facilities).	Productivity rises from nine meals per man-hour to 20. Cost of meals is cut by a full 50 per cent.
88. Deliver money from the schools directly to the bank, rather than recounting it in the central office.	Your district eliminates $1,400 in the budget, and decreases risk of theft.
89. Reduce supply inventory of items.	You have a $25,000 inventory. You reduce purchases by $5,000 and let the inventory sink to $10,000. You save $15,000.
90. Cut the teacher cafeterias completely loose from the school system. Let the faculties operate them (or eat regular fare at full cost).	All school department personnel and services are pulled out. Faculty organizes to operate the teacher cafeteria.
91. Maximize use of federal surplus foods in menu preparation.	Have cooks and nutrition staff prepare menus maximizing surplus food items consistent with local, state, and federal standards, thereby decreasing cost of purchased food.
92. Contract out the teacher cafeterias in larger schools.	Put out to bid the operation of the teacher cafeterias, thus eliminating the local taxpayer subsidy. Some indirect cost, such as space and utilities, may remain. Reassign staff.

HOW TO CUT COSTS IN YOUR COMPUTER OPERATION

What to do	How it works
93. Establish an effective equipment scheduling and control system.	No longer does a low priority item displace an important report because somebody forgot that the school board needs a report of its own tonight. Overtime no longer is required to meet the board's preemptive deadline.
94. Use the same computer for educational and business functions.	Perform your cost data (comparing unit costs of instruction, schools) on a second shift when computer is not being used by students.

How you'll save

Federal subsidies are greater than charge to student. You save 20 to 30 cents per meal.

You'll reduce your food service subsidy.

You'll decrease your food subsidy or cost to student.

You'll reduce cost of meals to district and/or students.

You'll eliminate extra part-time help to count money.

A lowering of supply inventory will result in a one-time saving equal to the amount of supplies and material not purchased by your district.

One teacher cafeteria in one large city high school was costing $30,000 per year to local taxpayers.

Savings on purchased food.

You'll reduce your food services subsidy.

The consequences (not all of them are bad)

Appreciation from those affected; be sure careful documentation is prepared for exceptions to income guidelines.

Opposition from staff organizations and support of state department lunch agency.

You must keep control over quality and reliability of delivery.

Opposition from school parent groups affected by change.

More problems when cash count differs (between school and bank).

Increased chances of stock-out situations and irritation of staff unless carefully managed from all angles.

Opposition from school personnel.

Be careful to maintain nutrition and quality standards.

Staff opposition to increased prices.

How you'll save

You'll get more production, and need less overtime to get reports out on time.

Shared-basis usually means shared costs (between you and somebody else).

The consequences (not all of them are bad)

Staff training and consulting assistance may be necessary to plan and implement the system.

Unless the computer is of recent vintage, you'll encounter inconvenience of off-peak use only (late afternoon, evening use when adult education groups are not in session).

What to do

95. Carefully review assignment of budget category of cost of EDP equipment and service in an effort to qualify for more state aid.

96. Let outside organizations rent available time on your EDP equipment.

97. Establish effective security for EDP equipment, discs and tapes.

98. Contract your EDP staffing from a facilities management firm.

99. Reexamine your EDP hardware costs through a feasibility study based upon current and future equipment requirements.

100. You have developed ten excellent computer applications useful to others.

How it works

By using best applicable accounting convention, you might be able to charge 25 per cent of the EDP cost to vocational education and receive 50 per cent of this back in state aid.

You share your computer with, say, the park district, which picks up part of the costs.

You avoid cost of "blowing" a disc because shutdown procedures are clearly and thoroughly detailed.

You contract for an equipment inventory and control system. You pay when it works.

You're spending hours handling cards and sorting on your XYZ computer. Costs would be excessive if you were to program this computer for new applications needed. You save money over a five-year period with more efficient equipment.

You sell to, lease to, or trade with other school districts or commercial enterprises based upon the value of computer software you have developed.

How you'll save

Your state pays more; your local taxpayers, less.

Your own EDP costs will go down.

You'll save from reduced vandalism and unintentional damage and consequent costly rebuilding of a data base.

Higher performance at lower cost often results from limited time contracts.

Newer, more efficient equipment may save you money in personnel and other costs in the long run.

One school district will "make" in excess of $25,000 on sales of software applications to a commercial enterprise. Another will completely support its operation by sales of software.

The consequences (not all of them are bad)

Be careful to document rationale and accounting conventions used.

Watch out for your own growth requirements and problems of security.

Irritation on part of personnel because the EDP shop is not open and accessible at all times.

Less direct control over staff; more planning, priority-setting required.

Short-term costs actually may go up.

Legal department will be nervous about the implications with respect to liability.

INDEX